In Fielding's Wake

Other Books of Interest from St. Augustine's Press

Jeremy Black, *Smollett's Britain*

Jeremy Black, *The Importance of Being Poirot*

Jeremy Black, *The Age of Nightmare*

Jeremy Black, *Defoe's Britain*

Joseph Bottum, *The Decline of the Novel*

David Ramsay Steele, *The Mystery of Fascism*

Rémi Brague, *The Anchors in the Heavens*

Rémi Brague, *Moderately Modern*

Marvin R. O'Connell, *Telling Stories that Matter: Memoirs and Essays*

Josef Picper, *Traditional Truth, Poetry, Sacrament:
For My Mother, on Her 70th Birthday*

Peter Kreeft, *Socrates' Children: The 100 Greatest Philosophers*

John von Heyking, *Comprehensive Judgment and Absolute Selflessness:
Winston Churchill on Politics as Friendship*

David Lowenthal, *Slave State: Rereading Orwell's 1984*

Gene Fendt, *Camus' Plague: Myth for Our World*

Jean-Luc Marion, *Descartes's Grey Ontology:
Cartesian Science and Aristotelian Thought in the Regulae*

Nathan Lefler, *Tale of a Criminal Mind Gone Good*

Will Morrisey, *Herman Melville's Ship of State*

Roger Scruton, *The Politics of Culture and Other Essays*

Roger Scruton, *The Meaning of Conservatism: Revised 3rd Edition*

Roger Scruton, *On Hunting*

Gabriel Marcel, *The Invisible Threshold: Two Plays by Gabriel Marcel*

Stanley Rosen, *The Language of Love: An Interpretation of Plato's Phaedrus*

Winston Churchill, *Savrola*

Winston Churchill, *The River War*

In Fielding's Wake

Jeremy Black

THE WEIGHT OF WORDS SERIES

ST. AUGUSTINE'S PRESS

South Bend, Indiana

Manufactured in the United States of America.

1 2 3 4 5 6 29 28 27 26 25 24

Library of Congress Control Number: 2022951335

Paperback ISBN: 978-1-58731-428-5
Hardback ISBN: 978-1-58731-429-2
Ebook ISBN: 978-1-58731-430-8

∞ The paper used in this publication meets the minimum
requirements of the American National Standard for Information Sciences –
Permanence of Paper for Printed Materials, ANSI Z39.48-1984.

St. Augustine's Press
www.staugustine.net

For
Alan Downie

Table of Contents

PREFACE

"Upon the whole, the man of candour and of true understanding is never hasty to condemn. He can censure an imperfection, or even a vice, without rage against the guilty party ... the same folly, the same childlessness, the same ill-breeding, and the same ill-nature ... raise all the clamours and uproars both in life and on the stage."

Life and art, the two commenting on each other, ensure that Henry Fielding, the master of the authorial voice and the deployer of Tom Jones and a host of others we can readily imagine, will be our guide to England during his lifetime. We will discover that there was so much more to Fielding as writer and as individual, but this is a guide to his writings, and not a biography. His novels, plays and journalism will be center-stage, but, in large part, so as to throw light on a crucial part of England's development to become the country that took the world into the modern age.

I love the energy, the variety, and the authorial voice of Fielding's novels. Confident and exciting, it is young man's work, as Fielding (1707-54) died in Lisbon while on an unsuccessful health cure, leaving his *Journal of a Voyage to Lisbon* (1755) to be published posthumously. Fielding's work still excites, and I have tried to convey the enjoyment here. There is also much thought and meaning. As Fielding pointed out in *Amelia*, "it is our business to discharge the part of a faithful historian, and to describe human nature as it is, not as we would wish it to be" (X,iv).

I am most grateful to colleagues and friends, Grayson Ditchfield, Alan Downie, and Bill Gibson for commenting on an earlier draft. They are not responsible for any remaining errors. Kate Godfrey has proved a most supportive editor. This book is dedicated to Alan Downie, a distinguished Fielding expert, skilful navigator of the History/Literature divide, fellow Athenaeum member and friend.

ABBREVIATIONS

Add   Additional Manuscripts

AE   Paris, Ministère des Affaires Etrangères Angleterre

BL   London, British Library, Department of Manuscripts

Bod   Oxford, Bodleian Library

CP   Correspondance Politique

CRO   Country Record Office

NA   London, National Archives

SP   State Papers

1. A SUMMARY BIOGRAPHY

The dramas of his life matched those of his creations. Henry Fielding was not born into obscurity, but certainly into turmoil, both familial and national. Honorable antecedents could not prevent the hard throws of demographic chance and family discord.

His father, Edmund Fielding (1676–1741), an army officer, came from an aristocratic and clerical background and was to be steadily promoted in the army, becoming a Lieutenant-General in 1739. Whereas other officers, both senior and junior, notably William Pitt the Elder in 1736, fell foul of the Walpole government of 1721–42, Edmund Fielding enjoyed steady patronage, which was just as well, as his finances were precarious.

Edmund's wife, Sarah, was the daughter of Sir Henry Gould of Sharpham Park near Glastonbury in Somerset; and it was there that Fielding was born on 22 April 1707. Gould was a successful lawyer who had become a Judge of King's Bench. After he died in 1710, the Fieldings moved to East Stour in Dorset. In addition to the three children born at Sharpham, another four were born in Dorset. Bar Henry, all were girls (including the novelist Sarah) apart from his younger brother Edmund who entered the navy. Educated first by a rural curate, Henry was sent to Eton where he was part of a distinguished group including Pitt, George Lyttelton, and Charles Hanbury-Williams, a group that was to help place him politically later in his life. Lyttelton, the dedicatee of *Tom Jones*, was a writer as well as a prominent politician.

The harshness of demography hit Fielding hard: Sarah Gould died when Henry was eleven, while one of his sisters, Anne, died young, although all his other siblings survived to adulthood. Family tensions saw Henry and his siblings, as a result of a Chancery suit, placed in his maternal grandmother's care in order to lessen the influence of his father, who had scandalously remarried an Italian Catholic widow. After Eton, in 1725,

Henry sought the hand of Sarah Andrews, a wealthy 15 year old cousin by marriage, resident in Lyme Regis. He unsuccessfully tried to elope with her, failing in an attempt that nearly brought him prosecution. He subsequently described himself as "an injured lover."

The episode could not but have influenced his first work, *Love in Several Masques*, which was staged at London's Theatre Royal in Drury Lane in February 1728. That year, Fielding also produced *The Masquerade*, a satirical poem that reflected both his interest in disguise and the controversial nature of the fashionable masquerades, which were attacked not only by clerics but by others as well.

Fielding soon after travelled to study law and classics in Leiden in the Netherlands (Pitt went to Utrecht), but he gave this up, possibly due to a lack of money, although completing degree courses was far less the norm in his period. His father's marriage to a widow, Eleanor, by whom he had six sons did not help family finances; although, like much else, the paucity of Fielding correspondence does not assist in the assessment of his actions, let alone drives and feelings. While in Leiden, he began *Don Quixote in England* (1733).

Henry returned to London in 1729, and became a regular and successful playwright, which produced a precarious income as well as much stimulus. In 1734, he eloped with Charlotte Craddock, marrying her at St Mary Charlcombe near Bath, a practice that was possible prior to the Marriage Act of 1753. They had a close marriage and five children. His theatrical career, however, was ended by Walpole's 1737 legislation introducing censorship of the stage, a measure that very much hit his finances. To support his family, Fielding became a law student, entering the Middle Temple in London in November 1737, being called to the bar in June 1740, and joining the Western Circuit where he became a good friend of James Harris who subsequently wrote *An Essay on the Life and Genius of Henry Fielding Esq* (1758). In this and other cases, for example with Lyttelton, talent attracted talent.

Fielding's legal career was not a great success. Nevertheless, this career helped ensure the use of legal references in his work and looked toward both his later role as a magistrate and the place of the law in his fiction and other writing. The law was both a means for order, whether contractual settlement or restricting disorder, and a guide to a rational organization of social relations.[1] That lawyers had serious failings did not mean that the law was foolish, an attitude also true of Fielding's approach to clerics.

Fielding also continued his writing, notably co-editing the anti-ministerial (but also anti-Jacobite) London newspaper the *Champion* (1739–41). In a fashion, his attack on Samuel Richardson's successful novel *Pamela: or, Virtue Rewarded* followed and widened this anti-establishment theme, in this case taking aim at self-interested morality and what he saw as misplaced fame. Fielding began with a parody, *Shamela* (1741), and followed with the well-purposed *Joseph Andrews* (1742). As with his 1740 translation of a history of Charles XII of Sweden, for which he received a part-payment of £45,[2] a need for money would have been an important factor in his high rate of activity.

Other novels followed, notably *The Life and Death of Jonathan Wild, the Great* (1743); *A Journey from this World to the Next* (1743); *The Female Husband* (1746), a fictionalized report; *The History of Tom Jones* (1749), his classic; and *Amelia* (1751). As Fielding emphasized, these novels drew on experience. In the preface to *Joseph Andrews*, he observed "though everything is copied from the book of nature, and scarce a character or action produced which I have not taken from my own observations and experience."

Meanwhile, his life had taken very different directions. Charlotte died in his arms in 1744, soon after a daughter had died. He was left responsible for the surviving children, as well as under the financial pressure that was a recurrent feature of his life and that proved repeatedly acute in the 1740s. In 1745, Fielding resumed journalism, with the *True Patriot*, a pro-government weekly directed against the Jacobite threat. This theme continued in his next newspaper, the *Jacobite's Journal*.

This journalism was an aspect of Fielding's engagement with problems. Indeed, whether against Jacobitism or criminality, hypocrisy or corruption, Fielding very much responded actively against what he saw as wrong. In

1   John Zomchick, *Family and the Law in Eighteenth-Century Fiction: The Public Conscience in the Private Sphere* (Cambridge: Cambridge University Press, 1993).

2   John Edwin Wells, "Henry Fielding and the History of Charles XII," *Journal of English and Germanic Philology*, 11 (1912): 603–13.

doing so, he was aware both of the continual morality of good and evil, and the more trivial impact of fashion. The latter was seen by Fielding and others as a repeated field for grandstanding, conceit and hypocrisy. In practice, however there was not solely a moral dimension. Thus, an interplay of custom and fashion was seen across a range of activities including essential ones such as food preparation, with the publication of cookery books reflecting need and entrepreneurial activity.[3] In the case of morality, Fielding referred back to traditional texts, in the shape of the Bible and the classics. For politics, he drew on John Locke, notably the *Two Treatises of Government*. This was establishment Whig ideology, not least the idea of social contract and limited government.

In November 1747, Fielding married anew, the pregnant Mary Daniel who had been Charlotte's maid. She looked after him and bore him five children, three of whom died young. This was very much the demographics of the time. At the time of the marriage, he was living in Twickenham.

A new direction was taken in December 1748, when Fielding, thanks to the support of his schoolfriend George Lyttelton, was appointed a Justice of the Peace (JP) for Westminster, being helped financially by John, 4th Duke of Bedford, who helped establish him in Bow Street. Lyttelton had introduced him to the wealthy Bedford, one of the two Secretaries of State in 1748–51, who became a protector. Ralph Allen was another supporter, while Fielding made £600 from *Tom Jones* which was published in February 1749. An assiduous JP who was committed to justice and social reform, Fielding took on these cases with his new journal, the *Covent Garden Journal* (1752), and with his *Proposal for Making an Effectual Provision for the Poor* (1753).

By then, his health, already in difficulties by late 1749, was deteriorating seriously. "Gout," which may well have been liver disease or something associated with Fielding's heavy drinking, was a major problem among many, and, in 1754, Fielding set off for Lisbon only to die there on 8 October, being buried in the English cemetery. He left not only his wife and children, but the good regards of many for his diligence and integrity as a magistrate, and the delight that his works have since caused. Death, indeed,

3   Gilly Lehmann, *The British Housewife. Cookery Books, Cooking and Society in Eighteenth-Century Britain* (London: Prospect Books, 2003).

was a frequent theme in Fielding's novels, as it was in life.[4] In *Joseph Andrews*, Parson Adams has lost three of his eleven children, and in *Tom Jones*, Squire Allworthy's three children all perished in infancy, while his wife had also died. These are good characters who have faced this fate. Smallpox underlined the apparently arbitrary nature of life, one that helped ensure that morality amidst mortality pressed hard in the thought of the period.

4   For example Benjamin Keene to Abraham Castres, 15 November 1740, BL. Add. 43441 fol. 9.

2. DRAMAS

Sensing opportunity from the outset, Fielding very much wrote for a London audience, one that was well-experienced in drama and used not only to the conventional theater, but also to other forms, including the sometimes intoxicating theatrical illusion of pleasure gardens, the lively daily theater of the streets, and the theater of the pulpit in which the preacher was a performer. This audience benefited from the vibrant and expanding theatrical world of the late 1720s and early 1730s, a world that included the change from one-play programs to evening entertainments including afterpieces that were generally lighter in tone. There were more stages than hitherto, with Goodman's Fields theater opened in 1729, and enough audience interest to support several theaters. There was a new company of young actors at the Little Haymarket theater, and Fielding, a new author, in 1730–1 provided them with his plays. He also provided plays for other companies at Lincoln's Inn Fields and Goodman's Fields.

As a result of his energy, range and popularity, Fielding became the leading comic playwright in England. He had his audience strongly in mind in writing readily-accessible pieces, and using comedy to provide moral and instructive points made more benign by the eventual happy outcome. In doing so, Fielding, who took Molière as a model, indeed translating his *Le Medecin malgré lui* as *The Mock Doctor* (1732), attacked affectation and deception, while praising what he saw as true about the middling orders. In this, he followed earlier writers such as Nicholas Rowe in *The Tragedy of Jane Shore* (1714).

Although making fun of Politic and Dabble in *Rape upon Rape* (1730), Fielding's magnanimous, indeed positive, gaze also encompassed the public as a whole, following George Lillo's *The London Merchant* (1731). As he noted in the prologue to Lillo's tragedy *Fatal Curiosity* (1736):

"No fustian hero rages here tonight
No armies fall, to fix a tyrant's right:

6

From lower life we draw our scene's distress:
Let not your equals move your pity less."

In *Rape upon Rape*, a well-constructed play set in London, Fielding knows that the audience would share the joke when he satirizes Politic being so concerned by reports of international developments that he neglects threats to his daughter Hilaret's virtue from Squeezum, the corrupt JP, and Ramble, a sinister rogue who was probably modelled on Colonel Francis Charteris, a notorious rapist. Politic's first soliloquy is devoted to the Turks:

> "I cannot rest for these preparations of the Turks: what can be their design? –It must be against the Emperor. –Aye, ay, we shall have another campaign in Hungary. I wish we may feel no other effect from them. –Should the Turkish galleys once find a passage through the Straits [of Gibraltar], who can tell the consequence? I hope I shall not live to see that day." (I,iii)

A Turkish threat reappears in the next scene and then, at greater length, in the following act:

> "I dread and abhor the Turks. I wish we do not feel them before we are aware ... what can be the reason of all this warlike preparation, which all our newspapers have informed us of.... Suppose we should see Turkish galleys in the Channel? We may feel them, yes, we may feel them in the midst of our security. Troy was taken in its sleep, and so may we ... the justest apprehensions may be styled dreams.... Should the Turks come among us, what would become of our daughters then? and our sons, and our wives, and our estates, and our houses, and our religion, and our liberty? When a Turkish aga should command our nobility, and janissaries make grandfathers of Lords, where should we look for Britain then?... Give us leave to show you how it is possible for the Grand Signior [Sultan] to find an ingress into Europe. Suppose the spot I stand on to be Turkey—then here is Hungary—very well—here is France, and here is England

granted—then we will suppose he had possession of Hungary—
what then remains but to conquer France, before we find him
at our own coast."

There is no doubt that Fielding was satirising unwarranted newspaper-
driven fears in Politic. The prospect of the Turks, who had been heavily defeated by Austria in the wars of 1682–99 and 1716–18, advancing to the
English Channel was slight. Indeed, Politic's demonstration of the ease with
which the Turks could advance through Europe, clearly betrays an absence
of geographical knowledge. Politic's speech was a fairly accurate representation of the confusion affecting the press in discussing the Turks,[1] but an
exaggeration of their potential, even though the Turks were to defeat the
Austrians in their next war, that of 1737–39. Moreover, in May 1730, there
were reports of Algerine corsairs in the Channel for the first time in many
years; although these certainly did not equate with the idea of an Islamic
fleet there, such as was to be facetiously discussed by Edward Gibbon in
his *The Decline and Fall of the Roman Empire*, let alone the "new enemies
and unknown dangers" that "may *possibly* arise."[2]

It is probable that Fielding was mocking, or understood to be mocking,
those who feared a Jacobite invasion, as his comments upon the threat from
the Turks to the liberty, religion, property and daughters of the British is
reminiscent of the fears expressed of similar dangers from the Jacobites.
Opposition politicians and newspapers frequently argued that the ministry
was deliberately exaggerating this threat for political ends. If so, the satire
was indirect.

Politic is also repeating ministerial propaganda in being concerned by
"the monstrous power which the Emperor may be possessed of." After the
Treaty of Seville with Spain of November 1729, the ministerial press in
preparing public opinion for British action against Austria, stressed the au-
tocratic policies of the Emperor, Charles VI, the ruler of Austria, the threat
his power presented to the balance of power, and the argument that he

---

1   *London Evening Post*, 21, 26 March, *Daily Post Boy*, 31 March, 6, 13 April,
    Evening Post, 4 April, *Weekly News and Daily Register*, 22 May 1730.
2   Edward Gibbon, *The History of the Decline and Fall of the Roman Empire*, ed-
    ited by J.B. Bury (7 volumes, London, 1897–1901), IV, 164–5.

could be weakened in Italy without threat to the balance. These arguments had marked ministerial propaganda since 1725 when Anglo-Austrian relations collapsed. They are satirized by Fielding in his portrayal of Politic as a man who fears the Emperor, but lacks geographical knowledge, and exaggerates grossly the power of the Turks. Dabble takes a contrary view, being sceptical of the Turkish threat and concerned about the dangers represented by the British agreement to establish Don Carlos, a son of Philip V of Spain, with an Italian territory.

In his characteristic helter-skelter fashion, Fielding introduces an element that would have disconcerted a ministerial apologist: Dabble rushes in to declare "We are all undone … all blown up! all ruined…. An express is arrived with an account of the Dauphin's death" (I,iv). Only born the previous September, the Dauphin, the son of the king of France, was apparently a guarantee that Philip V would not succeed his nephew, Louis XV (who had nearly died in 1728), and thus create the danger of a Franco-Spanish union. Dabble hopes that the news, which is denied two scenes later, will lead to an end to the schemes for the Anglo-French-supported introduction of Don Carlos (elder son of Philip V's second marriage) into Italy, which was regarded by critics as threatening Austria and the true British interests of opposing France. The report of the death of the Dauphin therefore is politically charged. Dabble could easily have rushed in to announce the death of Peter II of Russia, who died early in 1730, or of the ailing Gian Gastone, Grand Duke of Tuscany, a key figure in the Italian question, or that of Augustus II of Saxony-Poland. Instead, Fielding makes an important political point: the Anglo-French alliance is precarious and prone to the vagaries of dynastic chance.

As with so much else in this rich play, a play which would have meant much, in detail as well as generalities, to newspaper readers of the period, there are several levels of satire. There is the fun frequently poked at coffee-house politicians and those obsessed with the news,[3] who, with a reference often to be used by Fielding, are described by Worthy as "Quixotes." The tendency to speculate mocked by Fielding was seen by others and helped ensure that, as so often, Fielding was able to draw on a predisposition in his audience or, at least, an established response. Thus, the *Whitehall Journal*

3   *St James's Journal*, 12 July 1722; *Universal Journal*, 13 June 1724.

of 2 April 1723 referred to the *Quid Nuncs?* or What Nows?, those eager
for news, who, in this case, also were anxious about a possible invasion:

> "The great armaments of the Porte [Turks] and Muscovite
> awaken all the princes within their reach…. O'ye Quid Nuncs!
> this is a rare season for ye to lay schemes, to settle Empires and
> levy wars etc…. Great joy, yesterday, was expressed by a body
> of Quid Nuncs, in the Park that the Turkish and Russian armies
> are not to invade the Empire [Germany], or England, but that
> their fleets and armies were to be employed in reducing Persia
> and dividing the [that] Empire between the Czar and Sultan."

In his newspaper the *Hyp-Doctor* of 27 January 1736, "Orator" Henley
criticized the tendency, including in coffee houses, to draw misleading links
between foreign and domestic affairs. On 1741, George Harbin reported
from London on both a general confidence that Cartagena had been captured and that "all our connoisseurs in politics tell us, that if Cartagena is
ours, we are in effect, masters of the Spanish West Indies."[4] It did not fall.
With an instructive comparison, the *London Journal* in 1720 put the greater
game of politics alongside that at any "common play" to suggest that by-
standers could see more than grandees.

In *Rape upon Rape*, there were also more elusive and suggestive political
overtones, allusions that were too frequent not to be noted. In particular,
Squeezum, the corrupt JP, is interested in packing juries (II,i), which reflects
contentious legislation in 1730 enabling the government to select the jurors
in London and Westminster. As a result, the government, in 1731, succeeded in a second prosecution of Richard Francklin, the publisher of the
Craftsman newspaper, who had been acquitted in November 1729.

As he experimented with his own writing and probed commercial opportunity, Fielding's range was impressive, and notably so in topic and format,
including ballad operas, farces and more restrained comedies. The economics
of drama were clearly of great concern. Thus, encouraged by the weakness of
the Copyright Act for the Encouragement of Learning (passed in 1709; came

---

4   Harbin to Miss Bampfyld, 18 June 1741, Taunton, Somerset CRO, DD/SAS
     FA41 C/795.

into operation in 1710), some publishers produced pirate editions. This was part of the Grub Street free-for-all Fielding satirized in *The Author's Farce and the Pleasures of the Town* (1730). Very differently, plays could make reference to each other. In *The Universal Gallant*, Captain Spark remarks: "I am very fond of the entertainments at the New-house.... Pray which is your ladyship's favourite? Most ladies are fond of Perseus and Andromeda."

Not all of Fielding's plays succeeded. Thus *The Wedding Day* was rejected by the impresario John Rich in about 1730, only to be staged in 1743 when Fielding needed a new play for his friend David Garrick, whom he also praised in his fiction. With its inconsistent plot and limited characterization, this was not the best of comedies, not least because it was neither engaging nor skilfully comic. Moreover, Fielding was disappointed by the response.

Although *The Modern Husband* (1731) was dedicated to Walpole, Fielding's satire more generally was not free of anti-governmental political point, and may have earned him some lack of ministerial favor, although evidence is usually suggestive at best. A variety of observations, some more pointed than others, could be drawn from particular plays. Individuals were frequently depicted by Fielding in the plays as the worst enemies of their own humanity, with the lesson accordingly being that of needing to take steps to secure society. Thus, the introduction of *The Grub-Street Opera* (1731) claimed to teach men how to regulate their lives, that clerics should be heeded, and that virtue was "the maid's best store." The satire in this play, however, was more obvious. It clearly included Queen Caroline, wife of George II, as both she and the wife in the play bossed their husbands around, were interested in religion, and had had another very good offer of marriage. In this play, a lack of true charity provided a model for the hypocrisy satirized later in the novels. At the same time, Fielding's criticism in the play was widely distributed. Robin, the butler, who was intended to represent Walpole (for whom Robin was a frequent use), "cheats" his master, who stands for George II; but, in turn, those who cry "all is corruption and cheating" are held to take their anger from their loss of favor. There is commonplace xenophobia in the praise of "old English hospitality," with Susan, the cook, wishing she had been born "before we had learnt this French politeness, and been taught to dress our meat by nations that had no meat to dress." The use of a household in order to make comments about the royal family and politics was commonplace, as for example in the *Craftsman* of 7 April 1733 and, in the case of international relations, *The Late Gallant Exploits of a Famous Balancing Captain*, a ballad of 1741.[5] Moreover, the role of the royal court as a form of political and social theater,[6] contributed to this tendency. Borrowing foreign styles was a butt of opposition criticism, as in Lyttelton's *Letters from a Persian in England* where the favor for Italian cultural ideas is presented as a "kind of epidemical madness."[7] King Arthur's court offers Fielding a setting for burlesque drama in *The Tragedy of Tragedies, or The Life and Death of Tom Thumb the Great* (1731).

In 1731, possibly in response to the proposed staging of *The Grub-Street Opera*, following on the already critical *The Tragedy of Tragedies*, *The Welsh Opera* and *The Fall of Mortimer*, the theater at the Little Haymarket was closed. However, management changes and politics, not national politics, were principally responsible for Fielding's changes of theater, this closure helping lead Fielding to transfer to Drury Lane.

Most of his works of that period were relatively uncontentious, with the emphasis being on wit not ideology. These plays included *The Modern Husband*, a sentimental comedy; *The Lottery* and *The Mock Doctor*, both of which were ballad operas; *The Old Debauchees*, an anti-Catholic farce based on real events; and *The Covent-Garden Tragedy*. Fielding's energy was devoted in part to caricature, and notably to the exposure of hypocrisy which proved to be a *leitmotif* in his work, both fictional and factual, one that turned satire to moral purpose and vice versa. Moral strictures were made easier as a consequence of the use of archetypes, as with Lord Pride, Lord Puff, Colonel Bluff, and Rakeit, who were among the characters in *The Intriguing Chambermaid* (1733), or Lord Place, Colonel Promise, Sir Harry Fox-Chace, and Squire Tankard in *Pasquin* (1736).

The Modern Husband focused on the classic topics of marital relations, seduction and the subterfuges of life and some of the discussion of marriage was blunt in the extreme, "Mr Modern" telling his wife:

5   Jeremy Black, "Lord Bolingbroke's Operatic Allegory," *Scriblerian*, 16 (1984): 97–99.
6   Hannah Smith, "The Court in England, 1714–1760: A Declining Political Institution?," *History*, 90 (2005): 23–41, especially 36–38.
7   *Letters from a Persian in England* (London: J. Millan, 1735): 120.

"You shall not drive a separate trade at my expense. Your person is mine: I bought it lawfully in the church; and unless I am to profit by the disposal, I shall keep it all for my own use…. Have I not winked at all your intrigues? Have I not pretended business, to leave you and your gallants together … it is surely reasonable I should share the profit."

This theme of co-operation between husbands and wives in affairs was one later to be seen in the novels, notably *Amelia*.

The plays were clearly written at quite a rate, but that did not mean that the plotting and language were weak. Thus, *The Covent-Garden Tragedy* (1732) has an arresting image of the power of sexual desire, when Lovegirls tells Kissinda:

"I'll mortgage all my lands to deck thee fine.
Thou shalt wear farms and houses in each ear,
Ten thousand load of timber shall embrace
Thy necklac'd neck. I'll make thy glitt'ring form
Shine thro' th'admiring Mall a blazing star.
Neglected virtue shall with envy die." (II,vi)

The Mall was a fashionable parade-ground for the *beau monde*. *The Old Debauchees*, a comedy set in Toulon and first performed at Drury Lane in 1732, presented the lascivious French cleric, Martin, not only as a figure of fun but also as a disturbingly malevolent force, with lines such as "Superstition, I adore thee" (I,x), "Burning four or five hundred such fellows in a morning, would be the best way of deterring others," and "Religion loves to warm itself at the fire of a heretic" (II,ix). The play was revived in 1745, a time of acute sensitivity about Jacobitism. Originally, like *Rape upon Rape*, *The Old Debauchees* was very much a response to current news and what audiences accordingly would be interested in and able to understand, being a product of the 1730–1 Cadière case.[8] The bitter and lengthy

8   Jason Kuznicki, "Sorcery and Publicity: the Cadière-Girard scandal of 1730–1731," *French History*, 21 (2007): 289–312; Mita Choudhury, *The Wanton Jesuit and the Wayward Saint* (College Park, Penn State, 2015).

trial in 1731 of Jean-Baptiste Girard, a Jesuit confessor, at Aix-en-Provence, for the seduction of Marie-Catherine Cadière, lent pornographic interest to British national prejudice about both the French and Catholics, and led to an exuberant literature of broadsheets, prints, pamphlets and newspaper reports, the anonymous pamphlet *The Case of Mary Katherine Cadiere* (1731) running through at least nine editions. In 1732, Millan brought out in one volume, three works: *A Complete Translation of the Memorial of the Jesuit Father John Baptist Girard*; *A Complete Translation of the whole case of Mary Catherine Cadiere*, and *A Complete Translation of the Sequel of the Proceedings of Mary Catherine Cadiere*. The theme of Catholic priestly lascivious was a frequent one, as in a 1727 publication upon *The late Trial of the Reverend Abbé Des Rues at Paris for committing rapes upon one hundred and thirty three virgins*.

The opportunity was also taken in *The Old Debauchees* to criticize what Fielding did not like in England. Jourdain, a Toulon merchant, confesses to being a cheat, a rogue and a liar, whose career included taking refuge in London, renouncing his Catholicism, and being made a JP:

"With the whores of Babylon did I unite: I protected them from justice: gaming-houses and bawdy-houses did I license, nay, and frequent too; I never punished any vice but poverty: for Oh! I dread to name it, I once committed a priest to Newgate for picking pockets." (I,x)

Poverty means an inability to pay off the JP, a theme that looks toward corrupt justice in *Amelia*. Setting the story in France, allowed the plot and language to be free from restraint. When Jourdain is falsely told that his daughter is pregnant, Old Laroon, a figure of comic bluntness, tells him that it would be wrong to send her to a nunnery: "it would be very hard indeed, when a girl has once had her belly full, that she must fast all her life afterwards" (II,iii).

Dedicated to Philip, 4th Earl of Chesterfield, a Whig who joined the opposition that year, Fielding's *Don Quixote in England* (1733) referred to "the calamities brought on a country by general corruption." The play included sentiments of English confidence, the innkeeper, Guzzle, telling Sancho: "I am an Englishman, where no one is above the law." In a reflection found throughout Fielding's work, notably in *Jonathan Wild*, Quixote soon after remarks: "If a poor fellow robs a man of fashion of five shillings, to gaol with him; but the man of fashion may plunder a thousand poor." The play shows a great fertility of imagination on Fielding's part, with the translation of Quixote to England used to expose the character of the country, not least as he is pressed by the Mayor to stand for Parliament so as to ensure an electoral contest that will force rival candidates to spend money on the constituency. Based on cupidity, not political principle, this attitude by the Mayor is a resistance to the habit of local interests, usually landed interests, arranging elections so that there is no contest.

Don Quixote was frequently referred to. A Spanish name, Don Gulimo, was used in a non-Fielding pro-government piece, *The State Juggler: or, Sir Politick Ribband. A new Excise Opera* (1733), with Gulimo clearly William Pulteney, the leader of the opposition Whigs, who is presented as self-seeking in his opposition to Walpole (III,i). That year, a government supporter writing of the election campaign argued that the populace, whipped up by the opposition press, was "become Don Quixots that whosoever is but suspected of favouring the Excise Scheme is to be pulled to pieces."[9]

Fielding's dedication of *The Intriguing Chambermaid* (1733) to the young actress Mrs Clive made a strong placing of drama in cultural politics:

> "It is your misfortune to bring the greatest genius for acting on
> the stage, at a time when the factions and divisions among the
> players have conspired with the folly, injustice, and barbarity of
> the town, to finish the ruin of the stage, and sacrifice our own
> native entertainments, to a wanton affected fondness for foreign
> music; and when our nobility seem eagerly to rival each other,
> in distinguishing themselves in favour of Italian theatres, and
> in neglect of our own."

Born Catherine Raftor, Kitty Clive (1711–85) was Drury Lane's leading comedy actress, and was also a noted soprano.[10]

9   A. Duncombe to Henry Ellison, 28 October 1733, Gateshead, Public Library, Ellison papers A53 no. 18.
10 Berta Joncus, *Kitty Clive, or the Fair Songster* (Woodbridge: Boydell, 2019).

Fielding's own farces were pretty boisterous, and the double-entendres shine through such speeches as that of Lucy, the rural heiress, in *An Old Man taught Wisdom: or, The Virgin Unmasked* (1734) when she responds to approaches by Coupee, a dancing-master who has lived all his life in London:

> "O la! now I think on it, he pull'd out his fiddling thing, and I did not ask him to play a tune upon't.—But when we are married, I'll make him play upon't; I'cod, he shall teach me to dance too."

Lucy is also attracted to the looks of Thomas, "my lord Bounce's footman." His competitors all prove flawed, and Thomas is presented as worthy and wise:

> "As for my having worn a livery, let not that grieve you; as I have lived in a great family, I have seen that no one is respected for what he is, but for what he has; the world pays no regard at present to anything but money; and if my own industry should add to your fortune, so as to entitle any of my posterity to grandeur, it will be no reason against making my son, or grandson, a lord, than his father, or grandfather, was a footman."

This last was true of the highly-influential Fox family: Stephen Fox (1627–1716) started off as a servant.

The moral tone was repeated in *The Universal Gallant: or, The Different Husbands* (1734), a comedy that received a poor reception, one that was blamed on hostile critics who damned it unseen. The prologue argued for Fielding's satire being general, not personal, and for a national response in cultural affairs:

> "… if our strokes be general and nice,
> If tenderly we laugh you out of vice,
> Do not your native entertainments leave;
> Let us at least our share of smiles received:
> Nor while you censure us, keep all your boons,
> For soft Italian airs, and French buffoons."

Appearances are a key theme in the play, notably that of virtue, a topic much debated by Lady Raffler and her sister, Mrs Raffler, the latter arguing: "Art goes beyond nature; and a woman who has only virtue in her face, will pass much better through the world, than she who has it only in her heart." Subsequently Gaylove discusses whether a painting is an original by Hannibal Carraccio (Annibale Caracci, 1560–1609) or a copy: "there is so much difference between a copy and an original"—a discussion that is really about an extramarital relationship.

The epilogue to *The Universal Gallant* very much advanced the nationalist or xenophobic theme of true value that was important to opposition arguments. Italian singers and French plays are accordingly criticized, before Fielding turns to the need for a national revival, one that was both commonplace and a particular theme of the opposition:

> "Happy old England, in those glorious days,
> When good plain English food and sense could please:
> When men were dressed like men, nor curl'd their hair
> Instead of charming; to outcharm the fair.
> They knew by manly means soft hearts to move.
> Nor asked an eunuch's voice to melt their nymphs to love.
> Ladies, 'tis yours to reinstate that age:
> Do you assist the satire of the stage;
> · Teach foreign mimics by a generous scorn
> You're not ashamed of being Britons born.
> Make it to your eternal honour know
> that men must bear your frowns, wherever shewn,
> That they prefer all countries to their own."

Fielding's critiques continued, and some remain impressive, notably *Pasquin*, and *The Historical Register*, both of which also made very good narrative and satirical use of the idea of a play-within-a-play. *Pasquin, A Dramatick Satire on the Times: Being the Rehearsal of Two Plays, viz. A Comedy called "The Election"; and a tragedy called "The Life and Death of Common-Sense,"* first staged in April 1736, began with a reference to state control:

"1ˢᵗ Player: When does the rehearsal begin?
2ⁿᵈ Player: I suppose we shall hardly rehearse the comedy this
morning; for the author was arrested as he was going home from
King's coffeehouse; and, as I heard, it was for upwards of four
pound: I suppose he will hardly get bail."

The comedy shows the Court parliamentary candidates, Lord Place
and Colonel Promise, bribing the Corporation, with the author noting,
"this play is an exact representation of nature." Sir Henry (Harry) Fox-
Chace and Squire Tankard are the Country candidates, both local gentry.
Sir Harry proposes the health "Liberty and property, and no excise," the
latter a reference to unpopular government proposals of 1733, and, finding
the Corporation unwilling, asks:

"Where do you think these courtiers get the money they bribe
you with, but from you yourselves? Do you think a man who
will give a bribe won't take one? If you would be served faithfully, you must choose faithfully."

Sir Harry, however, also bribes the Corporation, thus vindicating the prologue's claim to show:

"you here at once both Whig and Tory;
Or court and country party you may call 'em."

The Corporation is depicted as without conscience, while the Mayoress
seeks an election and the resulting entertainment, saying to Lord Place:

"mention not those dear ridottoes to me, who have been confined these twelve long months in the country; where we have
no entertainment, but a set of hideous, strolling players; nor
have I seen any one human creature, till your Lordship came to
town; heaven send us a controverted election...."

The assault on the Court candidates is brutal. Lord Place declaring:

"I hope we shall have no such people as tradesmen shortly.... I'll bring in a bill to extirpate all trade out of the nation.... When I mention trade, I only mean low, dull, mechanic trade; such as the Canaille practice; there are several trades reputable enough, which people of fashion may practise; such as gaming, intriguing, voting, and running in debt."

The Corporation are presented as greedy, although this greed combines with family strife, as the rival candidates contest and win support accordingly:

"Mayor. Liberty and Property, and no excise, Wife.

Mrs Mayoress. Ah! filthy beast, come not near me.

Mayor. But I will though; I am for liberty and property; I'll vote for no courtiers. Wife.

Mrs. Indeed but you shall, Sir.

Miss Mayoress. I hope you won't vote for a nasty stinking tory, Papa.

Mayor. What a pox! Are you for the courtiers too?

Miss. Yes, I hope I am a friend to my country; I am not for bringing in the Pope.

Mayor. No, nor I an't for a standing army.

Mrs. But I am for a standing army, Sir; a standing army is a good thing: you pretend to be afraid of your liberties and your properties. You are afraid of your wives and daughters: I love to see soldiers in the town;"

Subsequently, the "Country" (Opposition) mob is shouting out "Down with the Rump,[11] No Courtiers! ... no Excise,"[12] while their opponents'

---

11 The Rump Parliament responsible for the execution of Charles I in 1649.

12 For pro-government claims that the opposition relied on mobs at elections, *Norwich Mercury*, 1, 22 June 1734. For claim Mayor of Durham at head of a mob armed with clubs and other weapons, memorandum by Henry Lambton, 1730, Dean and Chapter Library, Durham, Sharp papers, volume 82. For pe-

mob proclaim "No Jacobites! Down with the Pope." This activity captured the theatrical nature of elections. Indeed, a pro-ministerial demonstration at Camelford in Cornwall in December 1733 used the cries "No Pretender, No Popery, No Craftsman, No Disturbances," the *Craftsman* being an opposition newspaper. Sir Harry Fox-Chace brings forth the theme of national culture:

> "Those were glorious days when honest English hospitality flourished; when a country gentleman could afford to make his neighbours drunk, before your damn'd French fashions were brought over.... All the money is spent ... in houses, pictures, lace, embroidery, nicknacks, Italian singers, and French tumblers."

Deceit in every respect is to the fore in the presentation of politicians and electors, Mrs Mayoress reflecting:

> "What signifies what he is in his heart; have not a hundred, whom every body knows to be as great Jacobites as he, acted like very good whigs? What has a man's heart to do with his lips? I don't trouble my head with what he thinks, I only desire him to vote." (II,i)

Electoral bribery, often in the form of "treating" to generous meals, was a frequent theme of political correspondence, patronage, discussions, and newspaper comment.[13] "Treating" was an aspect of elections in which the social hierarchy was both strained, notably by "rude work,"[14] and reaffirmed. Corruption was more significant in borough elections, with their smaller electorates than in county elections, and, as in Bedford in 1731,

---

titions over Newcastle 1741 and Northumberland 1747 and 1748 election returns, Northumberland, CRO, Ridley of Blagdon papers, ZRI 25, number 1, Allgood of Nunwick papers, ZAL 83, numbers 3,4.

13 For example, *York Courant*, 20 October 1741.

14 George Liddell to Henry Ellison, 15 January 1734, Gateshead Public Library, Ellison papers, A34, number 13.

these elections were characterized by strong and ambitious expectations of expenditure on them by the electors.[15] Some candidates, such as George Liddell for Berwick in 1734, found the process so exhausting and costly that they regretted involvement.[16]

A frequent device, Pasquin was differently used in an able anonymous opposition pamphlet published in 1736, *Political Dialogues between the Celebrated Statues of Pasquin and Marsorio at Rome in which the Origin and Views of the late War, the secret Mediation of the present Peace and the genuine conditions of it are brought to light.*

The Historical Register for the Year 1736, which was first staged in May 1737, included a strong attack on corruption. However, in the dedication, Fielding sought to protect himself from the charge of partisanship by claiming that he was drawing attention to faults that were more widespread, a view that is self-serving but not necessarily inaccurate, as there can be too strong a tendency to label him an opposition writer and/or to explain his career and writings accordingly:

> "I hope it will be remarked that the politicians are represented as a set of cunning self-interested fellows, who for a little paltry bribe would give up the liberties and properties of their country. Here is the danger, here is the rock on which our constitution must, if ever it does, split. The liberties of a people have been subdued by the conquest of valour and force, and have been betrayed by the subtle and dexterous arts of refined policy … a general corruption."

As in *Pasquin*, the play was set in the playhouse, which was an aspect of using a longstanding practice of a rehearsal of a play as a means to provide satire on the theater[17] and to offer multiple viewpoints which prefigured

15 J. Collett-White, *How Bedfordshire Voted, 1685–1735: The Evidence of Local Poll Books, Volume 2 1716–1735* (Bedford: Bedfordshire Historical Record Society, 2008).

16 Liddell to Henry Ellison, 29 December 1733, 1 January 1734, Gateshead Public Library, Ellison papers, A34, numbers 5,7.

17 Samuel Macey, "Fielding's Tom Thumb as the Heir to Buckingham's Rehearsal," *Texas Studies in Literature and Language*, 10 (1968): 405–14.

Fielding's later use of *Hamlet* in *Tom Jones*. The Critic plays a role in *Tom Thumb*. There are attacks in *Pasquin* on hypocrisy, political and sexual, and on pretensions to courage, wit, conscience, common-sense and virtue. The wise playwright, Medley, observes:

> "that there was a strict resemblance between the states political and theatrical; there is a ministry in the latter as well as the former … parts are given in the latter to actors with much the same regard to capacity, as places in the former have sometimes been." (III,i)

The play ends with satire directed at the Patriots. In turn, *Eurydice* (1737) suggests that Hell is highly appropriate for those who were prominent on Earth, notably politicians. Linking Italian opera, London society and marital dynamics, it, however, was a failure that was only staged once.

Honor was a particular butt of Fielding's satire, and wordplay allowed bringing this to the fore, as in his play *Miss Lucy in Town*, which was a satire of mistaken identities as Miss Lucy and her husband go to London. The brothel-keeper, Mrs Midnight, offers to sell a virgin ward to the rake, Lord Bawble; but says she "shall not betray my trust" unless for ready money:

> "Lord Bawble. If I like her—upon my honour-
> Mrs Midnight. I have too much value for your lordship's honour, to have it left in pawn. Besides, I have more right honourable honour in my hands unredeemed already, than I know what to do with. However, I think you may depend on my honour! deposit a cool hundred, and you shall see her; and then take either the lady or the money.
> Lord Bawble. I know thee to be inexorable. I'll step home and fetch the money. I gave that sum to my wife this morning to buy her cloaths. I'll take it from her again, and let her tick with the tradesmen. Look'e, if this be stale goods, I'll break every window in the house.
> Mrs Midnight. I'll give you leave. He'll be tired of her in a week, and then I may dispose of her again. I am afraid I did wrong in putting her off for a virgin, for he'll certainly discover she is married. However, I can forswear the knowing it."

The play is a high-speed comedy of manners and deception, a satire in burlesque form. It includes a patriotic passage in which Thomas rejects Bawble's attempt to take over his wife:

> "Fortune which made me poor, made me a servant; but nature, which made me an Englishman, preserved me from being a slave. I have as good right to the little I claim, as the proudest peer hath to his great possessions; and whilst I am able, I will defend it ... the country, where there is still something of Old England remaining."

The conclusion is clear, Goodwill, Thomas' aptly-named father-in-law, declaring:

> "Henceforth, I will know no degree, no difference between men, but what the standards of honour and virtue create: the noblest birth without these is but splendid infamy; and a footman with these qualities, is a man of honour,"

which is very much the theme of *Joseph Andrews*. In turn, Lucy, rejecting London, sings:

> "Welcome again, ye rural plains,
> Innocent nymphs and virtuous swains:
> Farewell town, and all its sights;
> Beaus and lords, and gay delights:
> All is idle pomp and noise;
> Virtuous love gives greater joys."

The play was widely-circulated, the printed version being advertised in the *Cirencester Flying-Post* of 20 December 1742 as one of those that could be purchased or rented at the printing office in Cirencester.

For *The Wedding Day*, there is praise of country: "Mine is a true English heart; it is an equal stranger to the heat of the equator and the frost of the pole. Love still nourishes it with a temperate heat" (I,vi). There is also concern about developments in Britain: "Our dull forefathers were either rough soldiers, pedantic scholars, or clownish farmers. And it was as difficult to find a true gentleman among us then, as it is a true Briton among us now" (II,v).

On the whole, the style of the plays puts realism of plot and context aside in order to focus on entertainment and commentary, the two in counterpoint around the shared topic of hypocrisy, with character accordingly largely a matter of archetypes. That approach provided both moral reflection and comic action, not least in the concealment of people and action in closets, as in *The Letter Writers*. The knock-about pace and frequent comic reversals are arresting, but there is also a serious moral purpose in showing how the young need to avoid the vices of rogues and yet also their own potential for entering into vice through greed, not least a greed for fashionability. There is an emphasis on husbands and wives putting aside suspicion and acting as equals.[18]

The energy of the writing is readily apparent and helps explain why Fielding was a highly-successful playwright. Mary Pendarves observed to Swift: "When I went out of town last autumn [1735] the reigning madness was Faranelli.[19] I find it now turned on Pasquin." George Bernard Shaw called Fielding, who was a major influence alongside Henrik Ibsen, the most successful practicing dramatist between the Middle Ages and his own day with the sole exception of Shakespeare.

Indeed, far from Fielding being rescued from an unsuccessful career by the Licensing Act of 1737, and thus able to turn to fiction, the Act cut short a well-paid and impressive career in comic drama, one that could have gained greater depth with time. However, it has also been argued that Fielding accepted the new situation because he wanted to turn to other fields.[20] His career had certainly led Fielding in 1737 to consider building his own theater which, as in his struggle with his actors in 1733–34, reflected his determination to take control of his circumstances, which was very different to the plight of the playwright represented in *Joseph Andrews*:

18 Earle Wilputte, "'A Friendly Conspiracy': Sexual Power-Plays In Fielding's Early Comedies," *Wascana Review*, 24 (1989): 17–32.
19 Sic. The leading operatic castrato.
20 Thomas Lockwood, "Fielding and the Licensing Act," *Huntington Library Quarterly*, 51 (1988): 379–93.

"... upon applying to the prompter to know when it came into rehearsal, he informed me he had received orders from the managers to return me the play again, for that they could not possibly act it that season, but, if I would take it and revise it against the next, they would be glad to see it again." (III,iii)

After legislation failed in Parliament in 1735, the Theatrical Licensing Act of 1737 gave the Lord Chamberlain the power to censor plays (a power that lasted, much to Shaw's fury, until 1968) and made unlicensed theaters illegal.[21] This legislation, passed in part due to reaction against the obscenity of the farce *The Golden Rump* (1737), a farce that was later attributed by some, notably the *Grub Street Journal* and Robert Walpole's son, Horace, to Fielding, although there is no conclusive evidence to that effect. However, whether or not the popularity of Fielding's anti-establishment satire led to the Act, it certainly annoyed Walpole. The Act confirmed the position of the two London theaters with royal patents to stage spoken drama: Drury Lane and the new Covent Garden theater, opened in 1732. By this stage, Fielding was writing more pointed political satire, notably *The Political Register* and *Eurydice Hiss'd*, or at least plays that were understood in those terms, which may well have reflected his alignment with a political group, that of Lyttelton and his friends.

The legislation was less severe in practice than might be suggested, and its severity was principally in the short term, but it contributed to a slackening of theatrical energy, with relatively few new plays staged each season; indeed an average of only three in the decade after the Act. Furthermore, the range of plays that had been on offer in the early 1730s was curtailed, especially with Fielding's abandonment of satirical plays for novels, and with the loss of tragedies that were politically pointed. Hit by less money, Fielding was forced both into the legal career he did not want, and to write in other forms.[22]

---

21 L.W. Conolly, *The Censorship of English Drama, 1737–1824* (San Marino, California, 1976); V.J. Leisenfeld, *The Licensing Act of 1737* (Madison, Wisconsin, 1984).

22 R.D. Hume, *Henry Fielding and the London Theatre, 1728–1737* (Oxford: Oxford University Press, 1988); Albert Rivero, *The Plays of Henry Fielding: A Critical Study of His Dramatic Career* (Charlottesville, Virginia, 1989).

Fielding's subsequent remarks indicate dissatisfaction with the theater. In *Joseph Andrews*, there is discussion of why there are "no good new plays," the hostile response of the audience being cited as one factor (III,x). In the following chapter, the more dour Adams adds, "There is nothing but heathenism to be learned from plays," but that is a criticism of Adams and not of the theater. An ironic attack on censorship was offered in *Jonathan Wild* (III,v).

Separately, in the *Champion* of 9 September 1740, Fielding complained about "miserable farces, below the dignity of the theatre," and congratulated the management of Drury Lane for raising its sights so that audiences did not have to put up with "tumbling, farce and puppet-show." The following decade saw legal action against popular drama outside the licensed theaters, notably in 1744, 1749 and 1750. The Middlesex Quarter Sessions were involved. In practice, theater of a different type had seen Fielding operate a puppet show from March to June 1748 in Panton Street, London, while also writing for *The Jacobite's Journal*. In the exuberant *Tumble-down Dick: or, Phaeton in the Suds* (1744), he complained about the preference for pantomime over *Othello*.

Meanwhile, Fielding continued his earlier disagreements from the heavily personalized theatrical world, being sardonic, for example, in *Joseph Andrews* about Colley Cibber, Poet Laureate from 1730 to 1757; just as in *Pasquin* (1736) he mocked Cibber when a voter who loved the drink sack, the reward for the post, is offered it:

> "Poet! no, my lord, I am no poet, I can't make verses.
> Lord Place. No matter for that—you'll be able to make odes.
> 2nd Voter. Odes, my lord! what are those?
> Lord Place. Faith, Sir, I can't tell well what they are; but I know
> you may be qualified for the place without being a poet." (II,i)[23]

The popularity of the novels, both then and subsequently, has led to a general tendency (although not by specialists) to overlook the plays. They are often regarded as ephemeral, or as, in effect, apprentice work, whether or not that is seen as leading toward Fielding's becoming a novelist. Most

---

23 On Cibber, Leonard Ashley, *Colley Cibber* (Boston: Twayne, 1989).

are never staged. Moreover, interest in the "rise of the novel" as an issue has helped direct attention to that aspect of Fielding's work. This process has been encouraged by the overall weakness of mid-eighteenth century British drama. It is as if Fielding's work did not lead anywhere, which is a misleading approach. While writing within established genres, Fielding is also inventive and interesting in his ability both to take them further and to borrow between them.[24] This ability was linked to the defense of comedy that Fielding is subsequently strongly to offer in his novels.

The plays worked as texts, but even more as dramatic occasions. In turn, the novels show a theatricality that reflects Fielding's skill in drama. A very different impression is produced by the ponderous and worthy character of *Agrippina*, an unpublished tragedy written in about 1736 by John, Lord Hervey, the basis for the corrupt and menacing Beau Didapper in *Joseph Andrews*.[25]

The content of both Fielding's drama and his novels was that of plays of character in which performance is a key aspect of a world in which everything is unfixed, including categories, appearance, personality and time.[26] Indeed, there is a degree to which the contrast, yet also overlap, between appearance, in action and sentiment, and reality, apparently lead in this direction of a lack of clarity. However, to argue thus would be to underplay the clear moral code that is presented, notably in the novels and particularly with the significant role for Christianity. Thus, Wilson in *Joseph Andrews* provides a warning about relativism (II,iii). The attacks on hypocrisy indeed come from a clear Christian moral stance and, in *Tom Jones*, from notions of appropriate masculinity and femininity. Joseph Andrews lacks Tom Jones' sexuality, but is ready to fight hard when necessary in defense of wronged women, and this provides another instance of masculinity.

As a reminder that Fielding's comic plots are not necessarily particularly ridiculous, the Haymarket, on 16 January 1749, saw a large crowd arrive to watch a magician conjure himself into a quart bottle, only for the crowd

24 Elena Penskaya, "Fielding's Farces: Travestying the Historiosophical Discourse," https://doi.org/10.1515/9783110604276–010:106–111.

25 BL. Egerton Mss 3787.

26 Jill Campbell, *Natural Masques: Gender and Identity in Fielding's Plays and Novels* (Stanford, Calif: Stanford University Press, 1995).

to wreak destruction when there was no show for their payments which indeed disappeared that evening. John, 2nd Duke of Montagu, a keen practical joker, was one suspect, while Dudley Bradstreet, an adventurer and confidence man, claimed responsibility, and allegedly wrote a play on the incident which he included in his memoirs. Bradstreet also claimed to have misled Bonnie Prince Charlie with false information in December 1745 and to have managed the numerous mistresses of the elderly doctor Richard Mead. In one incident, an ex-mistress allegedly assembled a mob on Mead's doorstep by making the sort of noisy scene[27] that might have been seen in a Fielding play.

Fielding used one of his section-opening disquisitions in *Tom Jones*, which were both reflective and scene-setting or shifting, to compare the world and the stage. He took this beyond the idea of the theater as representation to argue that people put on character, notably as hypocrites, before focusing on the readers of novels as the theatrical audience. Fielding also emphasized complexity:

> "it is often the same person who represents the villain and the hero; and he who engages your admiration today, will probably attract your contempt tomorrow.... A single bad act no more constitutes a villain in life, than a single bad part on the stage. The passions, like the managers of a playhouse, often force men upon parts, without consulting their judgment." (VII,i)

27   A.C. Elias, "The Bottle Conjuror," *Factotum*, 39 (February 1995): 4–6.

3. POLITICS AND THE PRESS

> "There now ensured between the squire and the parson a most excellent political discourse, framed out of newspapers, and political pamphlets; in which they made a libation of four bottles of wine to the good of their country."
> *Tom Jones*, IV,x

Writing for any "side of a question" was a standard description of those who took part in the writing characterized as Grub Street, which was a description of writers willing to offer a wide-ranging coverage of genres, generally in a highly opportunistic fashion.[1] A broadside of about 1720 advertised an author of that area:

> "Who writeth all manner of books and pamphlets, in verse or prose, at reasonable rates: And furnisheth, at a minute's warning, any customer with elegies, pastorals, epithalamiums, and congratulatory verses adapted to all manner of persons and professions, ready written, with blanks to insert the names of the parties addressed to…. He taketh any side of a question, and writeth for or against, or both, if required."[2]

This, however, was not really Fielding's trajectory. He wrote for newspapers on both sides politically, but in response to particular circumstances and not at the same times. The broadside captured the requirement for journalists to be adaptable, but there is also a need for scholars to be cautious in ascribing lots to political direction, noting for example a comment by Robert's brother, Horatio, in 1740:

1 Pat Rogers, *Grub Street: Studies in a subculture* (London: Methuen, 1972).
2 Bridget Ikin, "The Re-Talesman of Grub Street," *Factotum*, 5 (April 1979): 27.

"what the printed papers will say I cannot tell, nor are we masters of the authors: some of them at present although they may write in favour of the administration are not under our direction or control."[3]

The press had already played a role in Fielding's writing. This was notably so in *Rape Upon Rape* (1730), in which a major government newspaper, the *Flying Post or Post Master* is singled out for attack as the "Lying Post" (V,iii), a frequent opposition description of the newspaper. It is also likely that Politic's ridiculous speech about the Turkish threat to Britain was a parody of anti-Jacobite ministerial propaganda which was frequent in this newspaper. The style of Fielding's supposed *Flying Post* captured brilliantly a tendency in press reporting:

"It is observable that Cardinal Fleury [first minister of France, 1726–43] hath, for several days last past, been in close conference with the minister of a certain state, which causes various speculations…. We hear daily murmurs here concerning certain measures taken by a certain northern potentate; but cannot certainly learn either who that potentate is, or what are the measures which he hath taken."[4]

Yet not only in that play. Indeed, in *Tom Jones*, where Mrs Western is "found reading and expounding the *Gazette* to Parson Supple," thus adding a feminine equivalent to exposition by a male cleric, she tells her Tory brother: "Things look so well in the north that I was never in a better humour" (VI,iv). Although dealing with the chronology of composition of the novel and the intrusion of the Forty-Five into the narrative is tricky, that is probably a reference to Jacobite moves in Scotland and northern England, rather than the far less interesting Baltic power-politics of 1745 as frequently assumed. In *The Letter-Writers* (1731), Mr Softly "will divert the time with one of these newspapers: ay, here's the Grub-Street Journal—An exceeding good paper this; and hath commonly a great deal of wit in it." In *Pasquin*, one of the mercenary

---

3   Horatio Walpole to Robert Trevor, 4 January 1740, Aylesbury, Buckinghamshire CRO, D/MH, Trevor papers, volume 20.

4   For satire of this type of article, *Craftsman*, 13 February 1731.

voters says to Colonel Promise, a Court candidate: "I have read in a book called Fog's Journal, that your honour's men are to be made of wax; now, Sir, I have served my time as a waxwork-maker, and desire to make your honour's regiment" (II,i), a critique of the corrupt padding of muster rolls.

Fog's Weekly Journal was one of the leading opposition newspapers. Subsequently, Miss Stitch reveals that she reads the *Craftsman* (for which Fielding *may* have written), whereas Miss Mayoress, who hates that paper, reads the pro-ministerial "*Daily Gazetteer*. My father has six of them sent him every week, for nothing" (II,i), a reference to the government's use of public money in order to skew the public debate by distributing material for free. In the event, the gift of a fan buys Miss Stitch's vote for Colonel Promise. The majority of the electors vote for the opposition candidates, only for the Mayor to be persuaded by his wife to return the government ones. Sex provides a frisson not seen in most of the writing about corruption. Mrs Mayoress goes into her closet to "equip" Lord Place and urges her daughter to go "into keeping" so as to benefit her family.

It is possible that Fielding wrote specific pieces for the *Craftsman* in 1728 and 1730, for *Mist's Weekly Journal* in 1728, and for *Fog's Weekly Journal* in 1730, notably "The Norfolk Lanthom," an attack on Walpole in the *Craftsman* on 20 July 1728[5]; and the fact that he was also trying to win Walpole's patronage may simply have contributed as he displayed both skill and irritation by this method, thus raising his value. Nevertheless, the circumstantial evidence in support of attribution is at best suggestive and weak. In turn, the dedication to "the Public" for the *Historical Register for the Year 1736* (1737), criticized the *Daily Gazetteer* for claiming that the play aimed at the overthrow of the ministry.

As a journalist, Fielding developed his ironic authorial distancing that was so important to his distinctive voice as a novelist. Yet alongside the voice of a moral reflector on habits and mores,[6] his journalism was in part

---

5   Martin Battestin, "Four New Fielding Attributions: His Earliest Satires of Walpole," *Studies in Bibliography*, 36 (1983): 69–109, and (ed.), *New Essays by Henry Fielding: His Contributions to the Craftsman (1734–1739) and Other Early Journalism* (Charlottesville, Virginia, 1989).

6   For *possible* pieces, Martin Battestin, "Fielding's Contributions to the *Universal Spectator* (1736–7)," *Studies in Philology*, 83 (1986): 88–116.

highly specific in its politics, albeit changing in response to major shifts in the context and circumstances of politics. In both moral reflections and politics, there was a fecund use of imaginative journalistic methods.

Under the title Captain Hercules Vinegar, Fielding was the editor of the *Champion; or, The British Mercury*, which began publication in November 1739. He also owned two of the sixteen shares and was one of the major contributors. In the issue of 22 December 1739, Fielding declared: "Whatever is wicked, hateful, absurd and ridiculous must be exposed and punished." The paper criticized much of the culture of print as partisan or otherwise flawed,[7] which was a means to develop the particular authority of the *Champion* and thus differentiate it from other opposition newspapers, in some respects its crucial competition, as well as the ministerial press, which was the ostensible competition.

The launch of the paper, Fielding's first significant role in journalism, was part of the revived energy of the opposition seen in the late 1730s. In part, as with politics as a whole, this energy entailed competition within the opposition, for example between the *Champion* and the established *Craftsman*. Walpole was not alone in feeling that opposition writings were less impressive (and certainly less original) than those in 1726–33,[8] but these opposition newspapers were able to draw on the theme that national honor and interests had been compromised in relations with Spain, a theme that was to be supported by Samuel Johnson. There was no countervailing popular support for ministerial policy, a feature reflected in the manner in which government papers, such as the *Daily Gazetteer*, and ministerial politicians, attacked the role being claimed for public opinion, rather than offering views of their own.

While aware of the frictions of the implementation of policy and military operations, such as the weather,[9] the *Champion* increasingly directed major attacks at Walpole, as in the issue of 13 May 1740, an issue introduced as a vision having seen "the body of a late criminal anatomised." At the same time, the need to respond to readers was a theme, as in the issue

7   For example, *Champion*, 16 February, 8, 10 May 1740.
8   William Cobbett, *Parliamentary History of England* (36 vols, London, 1806–20), XI, 881–82.
9   *Champion*, 3 January 1740.

on 16 September, in which the paper noted the criticism it received from its readers who disliked its comments or contents, for example writing on the theater rather than on the war with Spain.

The tone in the *Champion* was accessible, indeed more so than many of the essay newspapers of the period. Thus, on 19 April 1740, the Jülich-Berg dispute, a German dynastic inheritance quarrel of labyrinthine complexity and great international significance, was described:

> "To be cudgell'd for The Duchies of Bergue and Juliers, situated, as may be seen in the map, very conveniently for an appendage to the dominions of many great princes. The kings of Poland and Prussia ... are already on the list of champions ... the Emperor will be called upon to see fair play."

Modelled on John Dunton's *The Athenian Mercury* (1691–97), which introduced correspondence columns, the idea of the paper as a joint enterprise of author and audience, one that drew on Fielding's approach to drama and was to be taken forward with his novels, was shown in the issue of 10 January 1740:

> "I consider my paper as a sort of stage coach, a vehicle in which every one hath a right to a place. If any letter therefore should hereafter appear in it, which may give offence to particular persons, they can have no more anger to me on that account, than they would show to the master of a stage, who had brought their enemy to town."

The stage coach comparison was also employed in *Tom Jones*. Benefiting from Opposition sponsorship, issues of the *Champion* cost 1½d whereas most papers charged 2d. The paper was very hostile to the government, which provided a predictability that lessened the inventive possibility of Fielding's writing. The issue of 8 July 1740 used a London report in an Utrecht paper to support its unwarranted claim that the exploits against Spain in the Caribbean by Admiral Vernon, an opposition hero after his success at Porto Bello the previous year, were being hindered by a ministerial failure to send troops. This was part of a consistent argument that the ministry was not only inactive but also seeking peace.[10] From the summer of 1740, however, when he was called to the bar (20 June), Fielding began to lessen his active participation in the *Champion*, which continued to be critical of the government.[11] He claimed to have stopped writing for it in June 1741, and, in March 1742, he was to be voted out of the partnership.

Meanwhile, however, Fielding had used his fiction in order to attack the government press. In *Joseph Andrews*, the innkeeper explains "Gazetteers" to Adams: "It is a dirty newspaper which hath been given away all over for these many years to abuse trade and honest men, which I would not suffer to lie on my table, though it hath been offered me nothing" (II,xvii). The *Daily Gazetteer*, which had attacked the *Champion*,[12] was well-known to be written by "un homme payé par la cour."[13]

The criticism of Walpole was continued by Fielding in his contributions to a 1741 magazine *The History of Our Own Times*, which both reprinted material and produced fresh copy. Other proficient writers, notably James Ralph and, probably, John Banks, were involved in this work. The paper that the magazine most frequently resorted to for news, the *London Evening Post*, was a longstanding stalwart of the opposition press and one also used as a source for other newspapers.[14] *The History of Our Own Times* indicated Fielding's ambitions as a journalistic commentator.[15]

While inherently creative in this (and other) writing, Fielding's journalism very much has to be considered in terms of the complex and rapidly-changing politics of the late 1730s to early 1750s, more particularly the transition from Walpolean stability, via successive serious political crises, to Pelhamite stability. In Fielding's case, there was an accompanying change from opposition polemicist to government supporter, but he was far from

10 *Champion*, 17, 19, 24 July 1740.
11 For example, issue of 27 October 1741.
12 For example, *Daily Gazetteer*, 24, 30 July, 9 October, 12 November 1740.
13 François de Bussy, French envoy in London, to Jean-Jacques Amelot, French Foreign Minister, 11 March 1743, AE. CP. Ang. 416 folio 347, enclosing issue of 28 February.
14 For example, *York Courant*, 13, 20 October 1741.
15 Thomas Lockwood (ed.), *The History of Our Own Times* attributed to Henry Fielding (Delmar, New York: Scholars' Facsimiles, 1985), plus Lockwood's article in *Review of English Studies*, new series 35 (1984): 463–93.

alone in this. The same transition, for example, was made by William Pitt the Elder and John, 4th Duke of Bedford, and Fielding indeed can readily be seen as linked to the relevant opposition Whig group,[16] although there was scant cohesion or consistency in it.

The Walpolean system had its defeats and failures, some serious, but it lasted until 1742, the longest period of stable one-party rule in a system of regular parliamentary scrutiny in Britain. By keeping Britain at peace for most of the period, Walpole denied the Jacobites foreign support. He was certainly corrupt and his ministry was a Whig monopoly of power. Yet, Walpole probably caused offence principally to those who took a close interest in politics, rather than to the wider political nation, whose position was eased by his generally successful determination to reduce taxation. Indeed, Walpole actively promoted the relaxation of tension, and his ministry did witness a gradual lessening of political and religious tension that is readily apparent in comparison with the situation over the previous century.

The Walpolean system broke down in his last years as minister. Anglo-Spanish relations collapsed over vigorous Spanish policing of what they claimed was illegal British trade with their Caribbean possessions. This was symbolized by the display to a committee of the House of Commons of the allegedly severed ear of a merchant captain, Robert Jenkins. Such activity strongly challenged ideas of the defence of national interests, ideas that drew on a vibrant patriotism. Already, in Fielding's *Don Quixote in England* (1733), Sancho's fondness for "English roast beef and strong beer" had led to an air, "The king's old courtier":

> "When mighty roast beef was the Englishman's food,
> It ennobled our hearts, and enriched our blood;
> Our soldiers were brave, and our courtiers were good.
> Oh the roast beef of old England,
> And old England's roast beef.
> Then, Britons, from all nice dainties refrain,
> Which effeminate Italy, France, and Spain;

16 Thomas Cleary, *Henry Fielding: Political Writer* (Waterloo, Ontario: Wilfrid Laurier University Press, 1995).

And mighty roast beef shall command on the Main.
Oh the roast beef, etc."

The Main, meaning the Spanish Main, was a reference to competition with Spain in the Caribbean, while looking back to honest old courtiers was a theme of many writers, including Shakespeare. In *Joseph Andrews*, an innkeeper recounts that he had been:

"a master of a ship myself, and was in a fair way of making a fortune, when I was attacked by one of those cursed guarda-costas who took our ships before the beginning of the war, and after a fight ... I was forced to strike. The villains carried off my ship ... and put me, a man, and a boy into a little bad pink, in which, with much ado, we at last made Falmouth, though I believe the Spaniards did not imagine she could possibly live a day at sea." (II,xvii)

Sadism was popularly associated with Spain.

A peace deal, the Convention of the Pardo, was with difficulty negotiated in 1738, but it unravelled the following year, causing a war that Walpole had sought to avoid, one that lasted until 1748 and that came, from 1743, also to include hostilities with France as part of the War of the Austrian Succession. Initially, the war with Spain united the country, although also creating anxiety, as in March 1740 when Sir Arthur Owen wrote supporting the petition from the coastal town of Tenby for cannon as it was "very much exposed to the insults of the enemies."[17] However, amidst great and challenging public interest,[18] a lack of success gravely weakened Walpole politically. This lack of success included in 1740 arguments that the government was doing too little,[19] and in 1741 "that affair of Carthagena," the unsuccessful attack mentioned in *Joseph Andrews* (II,vii). Fielding's anti-ministerial writing of the period included *The Veroniad* (1741), in which Walpole's splendid new country seat at Houghton was criticized as the palace of Mammon.

17   Owen to Newcastle, 28 March 1740, BL. Add. 32693 fol. 119.
18   Lord Abergavenny to Newcastle, 13 July 1740, BL. Add. 32693 folio 485.
19   *Champion*, 12, 14 February 1740.

The vulnerability of Britain is hinted at in Fielding's work with his emphasis on the failure to reward merit in a system dominated by patronage. In *Jonathan Wild*, Mrs Heartfree, rescued from a French privateer, is taken onboard a British warship only to discover the captain is a lecherous tyrant. He injures himself in trying to rape her, and is succeeded by the eldest Lieutenant: "This was a virtuous and a brave fellow, who had been twenty five years in that post without being able to obtain a ship, and had seen several boys, the bastards of noblemen, put over his head" (IV,vii). This was an indictment of the Walpolean system as well as of British values.

Political chaos came to the fore in 1741, Henry, 3rd Duke of Beaufort observing: "It would be as much to the purpose for me to attempt to send you a definition of a phenomenon in the air as to endeavour to describe the present crisis of affairs."[20] As a reminder that individuals were not disembodied political commentators, Beaufort (1707–45), who succeeded his father as Duke in 1714, married an heiress, Frances Scudamore (1711–1740), in 1729; only in 1742 to file for divorce due to her adulterous relationship with William, Lord Talbot (1710–82), whose wife Mary left him as a result. Frances countersued on the grounds of Henry's impotence which he was able to disprove before court-appointed examiners in 1743. After the divorce, Beaufort sued Talbot for damages while, in 1743, Frances remarried Colonel Charles FitzRoy, an illegitimate son of Charles, 2nd Duke of Grafton (1683–1757), who had been married to Henry's aunt Lady Henrietta Somerset (1690–1726). Their daughter made a ducal marriage, but went insane. Beaufort, in turn, had an illegitimate daughter, Margaret Burr (*c.* 1728–*c.*1798) who married Thomas Gainsborough, the painter in 1746. Part of the élite world Fielding castigated, the Duke was also one of the founding governors of the Foundling Hospital. Such a carousel of infidelity made Fielding's plays highly plausible.

The ministry was divided, and, alongside his very strong showing in the parliamentary session in early 1741,[21] there was a sense that Walpole was losing his grip. Unwelcome military and international developments combined with poor relations between George II and his eldest son,

20 Beaufort to Reverend Parry, 18 February 1741, Bod., MS Ballard 29 folio 75.
21 Newcastle to Henry, 9th Earl of Lincoln, 16 March 1741, BL. Add. 33065 folio 397; Bussy to Amelot, 17 May 1741, AE. CP. Ang., 412 folio 28.

Frederick, Prince of Wales, to create a political crisis. He did very badly in the general election of late 1741 and his inability to continue to command majorities in the Commons led to his fall in February 1742.[22]

Fielding meanwhile had attacked the political system in *Joseph Andrews*, in the person of Beau Didapper who was modelled on John, Lord Hervey, the Lord Privy Seal:

> "though he was born to an immense fortune, he chose, for the pitiful and dirty consideration of a place of little consequence, to depend entirely on the will of a fellow whom they call a great man, who treated him with the utmost disrespect and exacted of him a plenary obedience to his commands, which he implicitly submitted to at the expense of his conscience, his honour, and of his country, in which he had himself so very large a share." (IV,ix)

The "great man" was Walpole who had brought Hervey forward politically.

At the same time, Walpole appears to have eased relations with Fielding in late 1741, possibly by buying him off,[23] which might have been an aspect of Fielding's "typical unsteadiness in political affairs"[24] if sufficient allowance is made for the degree to which these affairs were inherently highly changeable in the 1740s. It was not only a question of Fielding needing money. He also had to adapt to continual uncertainty as to the stance and identity of government and opposition alike. In 1743, Walpole was to help Fielding by buying ten sets of his *Miscellanies*, although *Jonathan Wild* that year inevitably suggested the comparison of Walpole with criminality. Thus, George Harbin noted in February 1742: "A Great Criminal (as he is called) will in due time be called to a strict account."[25]

Instead of Walpole being replaced in February 1742 by a united opposition ministry, most of the opposition Whig leaders abandoned their Tory

---

22 Jeremy Black, *Walpole in Power* (Stroud: Alan Sutton, 2001).
23 Frederick Ribble, "Fielding's Rapprochement with Walpole in Late 1741," *Philological Quarterly*, 80 (2001): 71–81.
24 Battestin, "Fielding's Contributions": 88.
25 Harbin to Mrs Bampfyld, 25 February 1742, Taunton, Somerset CRO, DD/SAS FA41 C/795.

allies, with whom co-operation had earlier been precarious,[26] and, instead, joined the bulk of the Walpolean Whigs in a new government. Although Walpole was out, ministries remained Whig, and the Tories continued in opposition. Disillusionment among Whigs still in opposition was in part expressed in terms of a repugnance at what was in their view simply a reshuffle, a form of abandonment of principles and therefore corruption that contributed to the moral critique of political culture that writers also advanced. Thus, remaining in opposition, Philip, 4th Earl of Chesterfield observed in March 1742:

> "I have opposed measures not men, and the change of two or three men only, is not a sufficient pledge to me that measures will be changed, nay rather an indication that they will not; and I am sure no employment whatsoever shall prevail with me to support measures I have so justly opposed. A good conscience is in my mind a better thing, than the best employment."[27]

This was the sort of dichotomous remark frequently made by Fielding, both through his characters and directly.

Under the dynamic leadership of John, Lord Carteret, the most prominent minister from 1742 to 1744 and a favorite of George II, the ministry abandoned Walpole's policy of peace with France and British troops were sent to the Continent in 1742, fighting the French from 1743. This led to French support for Jacobitism, but their invasion attempt of southern England in 1744 was blocked by a storm in the Channel.

The following year, "James III and VIII's" eldest son, Charles Edward (Bonnie Prince Charlie), evaded British warships and landed in the Western Isles of Scotland. He quickly overran most of Scotland, despite the reluctance of some Jacobite clans to rise for a prince who had brought no soldiers, and

26   Edward Southwell MP to Mr Brickdale, 21 February 1741, Bristol, City Library, Southwell papers, volume 7; John, 2nd Earl of Stair to Daniel, 3rd Earl of Nottingham, 27 June 1741, Leicester, Leicestershire CRO, Finch papers, DG/7/4952.
27   Chesterfield to Richard Chevenix, Bishop of Waterford, 6 March 1742, Bloomington, Indiana, University of Indiana, Lilly Library, Chesterfield papers, volume 3.

the hostility of many Scots who were not Jacobites. The British force in Scotland was outmanoeuvered and then fell victim to a Highland charge at Prestonpans outside Edinburgh on 21 September. The Jacobites, however, did not only want a Stuart Scotland, not least because a Hanoverian England would not allow its existence, and invaded England on 8 November 1745.

This threat prompted Fielding into print.[28] In the first issue of the *True Patriot*, that of 5 November 1745, he noted being told by his bookseller "that nobody at present reads anything but newspapers." In this issue, as he had in the first of *The History of Our Own Times*, he reviewed the press, commenting on the number of papers but also on the extent to which they lacked accuracy, sense or significance. Providing clues to his identity and goal, Fielding wrote: "I am of no party; a word which I hope, by these my labours, to eradicate out of our constitution; this being indeed the true source of all these evils which we have reason to complain of."

Charles Edward took Carlisle on 15 November after a brief siege and then, without any resistance, Lancaster, Preston (26 November), Manchester (28 November) and Derby, the last of which was entered on 4 December. In other cities where there was little support for Jacobitism, for example Leeds, there was nevertheless a caution about resisting a Jacobite advance.[29]

On 19 November, Fielding, in the *True Patriot*, focused on "the rebellion." He offered a dream-vision of its success, beginning with his arrest in London on the warrant of "several men, who were in Highland dresses, with broad swords by their side." Being dragged through the streets he saw: "Houses burnt down, dead bodies of men, women and children strewed everywhere as we passed, and great numbers of Highlanders, and Popish priests." Newgate was full, so he was taken "to a large booth in Smithfield ... where I was shut in with a great number of prisoners, amongst whom were many of the most considerable persons in this kingdom," including Archbishop Herring of York and Bishop Hoadly of Winchester. Taken to court, Fielding found land being restored to monasteries in a reversal of the Reformation, and was tried for high treason for having written the *True Patriot*. There was no jury, the Chief Justice,

28 For the press of the period, Robert Harris, *A Patriot Press: National Politics and the London Press in the 1740s* (Oxford: Oxford University Press, 1993).
29 Jonathan Oates, "Leeds and the Jacobite Rebellions of 1715 and 1745," *Publications of the Thoresby Society*, 2nd series, 14 (2004): 1–17, especially 15–16.

as a foreigner, spoke broken English, and Fielding was sentenced to execution. Fearful for the fate of his children, he witnesses a rape by two Highlanders, fires in which Protestants were roasting, and Catholic hatred. Dream-visions had already been used in the *Champion*. In the following issue of the *True Patriot*, that of 26 November, Fielding returned to the charge:

> "utter misery and desolation … the insecurity of our estates, properties, lives and families, under the government of an absolute Popish Prince (for absolute he would plainly be), introduced by the conquering arms of France, Spain and the Highlands."

He explained how all were threatened, including free-thinkers on religious matters. Fielding also shows a shift in his views as a writer from that seen when he was a playwright:

> "… there are many worthy persons who, though very little concerned for the true liberty of their country, have, however, the utmost respect for what is by several mistaken for it; I mean licentiousness, or a free power of abusing the king, ministry, and every thing great, noble, and solemn.
>
> The impunity with which this liberty hath been of late years practised, must be acknowledged by every man of the least candour. Indeed, to such a degree, that power and government, instead of being objects of reverence and terror, have been set up as the butts of ridicule and buffoonery, as if they were only intended to be laughed at by the people…. This is a liberty which hath only flourished under their royal family,"

a reference to the Hanoverian dynasty. Aside from the 33 issues of the *True Patriot*, which finished in June 1746, Fielding also produced three anonymous pamphlets as attacks on the Jacobite rebellion: *A Serious Address to the People of Great Britain*, *The History of the Present Rebellion in Scotland*, and *A Dialogue between the Devil, the Pope, and the Pretender*.[30]

30 W.B. Coley (ed.), *The True Patriot and Related Writings* (Middletown, Connecticut: Wesleyan, 1987).

In late 1745, George II's armies were outmaneuvered, and, although this was an invasion and few English Jacobites had risen to help Charles Edward, his opponents were hit by panic. Thomas Harris wrote from London to his brother, Fielding's friend, James: "if the two armies were to run a race, there seemed too good reason to fear that they would travel fastest."[31] Fielding mixed his genres in deploying one of his favorite fictional characters accordingly in the *True Patriot*. On 17 December, Abraham Adams from *Joseph Andrews* presented the rapid Jacobite advance as an instance of "the just judgment of God against an offending people." In order to rescue "our Sodom," Adams urges fasting, prayer and charity, and a turning away from lying and luxury. On the 31st, Fielding satirically added the need to part from Italian opera, a longstanding theme of his and notably in his plays.

The crisis of early December 1745 was recalled in *Tom Jones* when news arrived that Charles Edward had passed Cumberland's defending army:

> "and soon after arrived a famous Jacobite squire, who, with great joy in his countenance, shook the landlord by the hand, saying 'All's our own, boy, ten thousand honest Frenchmen are landed in Suffolk. Old England for ever!'" (XI,ii)

This was not a tarring of the Jacobites as they indeed sought French support, which, furthermore, appeared imminent at the time. Mrs Honour magnifies the news: "the French; several hundred thousands of them are landed, and we shall all be murdered and ravished" (XI,vi). There was indeed a report that the French had landed on the coast of Sussex, one that ministers briefly credited, and that looked to a broader pattern of a belief in false reports as from Salisbury in 1744:

> "You know how easy a matter it is to alarm such a country place as this, with a false report. A day or two ago, a vagabond seaman that was brought before our Mayor affirmed positively … and

31 Thomas to James Harris, 10 December 1745, Winchester, Hampshire CRO, 9M73/G309/16.

however incredible … it gained credit with the Mayor and some of the justices [JPs]."[32]

The Jacobite council, however, decided on 5 December 1745 to retreat, despite Charles's wish to press on to London. The lack of English support (as well as the absence of the French landing in southern England promised by Charles Edward) weighed most heavily with the Highland chiefs. There had been a crucial breakdown of confidence in the prince among his supporters, arising from the failure of his promises over support, and the Scots considered themselves as having been tricked into a risky situation.

Had the Jacobites pressed on, they might have won, capturing weakly-defended London, and, thereby, destroying the logistical and financial infrastructure of their opponents.[33] Indeed, in the *True Patriot* of 7 January 1746, Fielding offered a variation on his arresting *Journey from This World to the Next* in which the transmigration of souls enabled him readily to scour history in order to make present-points. As a further instance of his range as a writer, he returns to the theme in the issue of 19 November and, in this case, has a journal of the future predicting developments under Jacobite rule. These included "The cash, transfer-books, etc removed to the Tower, from the Bank, South-Sea and India houses." French garrisons were installed in Portsmouth, Berwick and Plymouth. *Habeas Corpus* was abolished, heretics burned at Smithfield, monastic lands restored, and so on at a frenetic pace. This device was also used by other writers, as with the Jewish Naturalization Act in 1753.

In *Tom Jones*, the protagonist, "a hearty well-wisher to the glorious cause of liberty, and of the Protestant religion," which very much demonstrates his virtue, volunteers to join troops moving north against the Jacobite "banditti" (Vii,xi). Debating the Jacobite cause with Partridge, a Jacobite who has taken advice from a Catholic priest that Charles Edward was a good Protestant, and who cites a prophecy, Jones robustly replies:

32 George to James Harris, 26 February 1744, Winchester, Hampshire CRO, 9M73/G308/10.
33 Jeremy Black, *Culloden and the '45* (Stroud: Alan Sutton, 1990); Murray Pittock, *Culloden* (Oxford: Oxford University Press, 2016).

"Monsters and prodigies are the proper arguments to support
monstrous and absurd doctrines. The cause of King George is
the cause of liberty and true rebellion. In other words, it is the
cause of common sense, my boy, and I warrant you will succeed." (8, VIII)

The contrast between the two men during the book very much establishes
Jones as forward-looking and Jacobitism as a dangerous absurdity, indeed
the product of a warped imagination.

Subsequently in the novel, the Man of the Hill provides an account of
the plight of Protestantism under James II (r. 1685–88), which offers Fielding an opportunity to deploy Jones to say that the Jacobite cause is now
"carried on by Protestants, against a king who hath never, in *one single instance*, made the least invasion of our liberties" (VIII,xiv). To a degree, this
example of the long shadow of 1688 was a continuance of arguments made
in the *Champion*, the issue of which for 22 May 1740 had condemned "big-
ots to the Restoration." There was no equivalent political placing or gloss
in *Jonathan Wild* or *Amelia*.

By retreating on December 1745, the Jacobites made defeat almost
certain, not least because, in combination with bad weather and the
British navy, the retreat led the French to abandon a planned supporting
invasion of southern England. Charles evaded pursuit, retreated to Scot-
land successfully, and, on 17 January 1746, beat a British army at Falkirk.
However, soon after Charles, under mounting pressure, abandoned the
Central Lowlands for the Highlands. The dynamic of Jacobite success
had been lost. George II's inexorable younger son, William, Duke of
Cumberland, brought up a formidable force and, on Culloden Moor near
Inverness on 16 April 1746, his superior numbers and firepower totally
smashed the outnumbered, underfed, and poorly-led, Jacobite army.
Cumberland had secured the Protestant Succession established by
William III in 1689 and 1701, ending the challenge feared by Fielding
and many others.

In the *True Patriot* of 7 January 1746, Fielding had predicted that Jacobite success would be followed by legislation against the freedom of the
press. In contrast, as he noted in the *Jacobite's Journal* (1747–48), his less
troubled successor newspaper, the ministry was unwilling to use its available

legal powers: "Is not treason written in our newspapers and talked and sung and toasted in our taverns every day with impunity? And yet if you consult our law books, you will find there are very severe laws for the punishment of all these offences." Fielding refuted opposition claims that the ministry wished to restrict press freedom.[34]

After Culloden, Jacobite conspiracies continued, and contemporaries were still concerned about the situation. Nevertheless, the strategic situation had altered greatly as a result of the crushing of Scottish Jacobitism, and support for "James III" in England appeared increasingly marginal and inconsequential. Charles Edward successfully fled into exile in France in 1746, but his idiosyncratic and undisciplined behavior in the following years greatly reduced foreign support, as did peace in 1748. Charles Edward's conversion to the Church of England on a secret visit to London in 1750 did not lead to any rallying to the Jacobite cause, and the Elibank Plot of 1751–53, a scheme for a *coup d'etat* in London involving the kidnapping of George II, was betrayed. It was part of the background to the policing of London in which Fielding was involved.

The combination in 1745–46 of the Jacobite threat and of French success in the War of the Austrian Succession had constituted what was truly a mid-eighteenth-century crisis for Britain, and underlines the extent to which issues were important in the politics of the period, a point very clear from both Fielding's journalism and *Tom Jones*. In the *True Patriot* of 15 April 1746, Fielding admitted that he had earlier underplayed the threat from Jacobitism. At the same time, issues of competence and of policy took a major role in the maneuvers of politicians for office. The crisis led in 1744–46 to the consolidation of a ministry, led by Henry Pelham, the talented First Lord of the Treasury from 1743 to 1754, that was based on widespread Whig support. Followed by the defeat of the Jacobites, the government's sweeping success in the 1747 general election, and the negotiation of generally acceptable (though far from triumphant) peace terms with France and Spain in 1748 after a less than successful war with both, all helped to lower the political temperature.

34 *Jacobite's Journal*, 13 February, 2 April 1748, refuting anonymous, *A Critical, Expatiatory, and Interesting Address to a Certain Right Honourable Apostate* (London, 1748): 11–12, 22–23.

Already, in the *True Patriot* of 8 April 1746, Fielding had referred to "the Opposition (if a handful of men, and those for the most part totally insignificant, as well in fortune as abilities, are worthy that name)." On 25 March 1746, he offered a hopeful look to the future, one that paralleled his general hope for incremental improvement through benign individuals:

"... let the situation of public affairs be what they will, if through the bounty of Providence it so happens that honest and worthy men are entrusted with the management of them, and the people themselves, from a due and a just concern for their own interest, heartily and unanimously espouse them, things must go right at last; and though many difficulties may be met with, and the happy change be brought about only by degrees, yet in the end it must absolutely be brought about, and all things settled to the wish of those who govern, and those who are governed."

This emphasis on personal integrity, rather than any particular system of government, was more generally seen. In his play *The Independent Patriot* (1737), Francis Lynch has "Medium" declare, "I shall never be persuaded that a covetous man can be a virtuous, steady Patriot, however loudly he may be heard to complain of the corruption of the age, or the measures of authority."[35]

A protégé of Walpole (who had died in 1745), Pelham was in a position to pursue Walpolean policies: fiscal restraint, unenterprising legislation, preserving both a Whig monopoly of power and the status quo in the Church, and trying to preserve peace. All of these presumably proved welcome to Fielding who was now, with his patrons included in it, a supporter of the Pelham ministry. To that end, he turned again to the press. Launched on 5 December 1747, the *Jacobite's Journal* was allegedly the work of John Trott-Plaid, a Jacobite. This pose provided an opportunity to satirize Jacobitism and use it to taint all opposition, Tory or otherwise, as well as the opposition press, notably *Old England* and the *London Evening Post*, as well as High Churchmen. The *Jacobite's Journal* of 13 February 1748 satirized

35 Francis Lynch, *The Independent Patriot* (London, 1737): 39.

the Tories in the form of a xenophobic letter from a "Humphry Gubbins" that displayed a comprehensive distrust of foreigners, their mores and policies. The previous week, opposition "incendiaries" had been addressed by the paper:

> "But I will admit that it was in their power to do all the mischief their rancorous hearts desire; that two or three of the lowest inhabitants of Grub-Street, abetted and encouraged by some who ought to be shut up in Bedlam, and by others who deserve a more ignominious confinement, should be able to raise a storm, which should become dangerous to a minister, nay, which should overwhelm him, while he is pursuing the good, nay the preservation of his country."

In the issue of 12 March 1748, Fielding presented the *London Evening Post* and *Old England* as under Jacobite influence. Indeed, the woodcut in the early issues of the *Jacobite's Journal* depicted Tories atop an ass being urged forward by a Jesuit with a copy of the *London Evening Post*. In turn, the opposition press attacked Fielding's politics and personality, presenting him as dishonorable in both respects. The *London Evening Post* of 15 March 1748 called him "the known pensioned scribbler" for the government, *Old England* of 26 March described him as "Lyttelton's informing jackal." In December 1744, Lyttelton had become one of the five Lord Commissioners of the Treasury, a position he held until April 1754. On 11 June 1748, *Old England* attacked "the hireling-pen of a dirty Drawcansir, set up for the coalition, as a weekly allowance, to form new distinctions among us." There were also ridiculous claims that Fielding was really a Jacobite.

In *Tom Jones*, Squire Western, who has stood twice as a Tory parliamentary candidate, who is described as "a man of no great observation," and whose name suggests provincialism, is pleased to be able to read the *London Evening Post* (VI,ii). His Tory sentiments are clearly demonstrated, as when he refers to the Sinking Fund being "sent to Hanover to corrupt our nation with" (VI,x), a confusion that reflects Western's anger but also lack of understanding. Subsequently, he refers to "a parcel of Roundheads and Hanover rats," twice adding "every man should enjoy his own," which was a Jacobite song. Providing a criticism of those who Viscount Bolingbroke had described in 1740 as "the obstinate Tories,"[36] Fielding was depicting the Tories as a whole, who are presented by Western as "the country interest," as Jacobites. Indeed, Western's first toast is "the King over the Water" (VII,iv). Western's sister is an unsympathetic individual, but perceptive when she refers to him as "one of those wise men whose nonsensical principles have undone the nation; by weakening the hands of our Government at home, and by discouraging our friends, and encouraging our enemies abroad" (VII,iii).

It is more appropriate to write of a duumvirate than a prime minister in these years. Pelham was the manager of the Commons and a crucial minister, but his elder brother, Thomas, Duke of Newcastle, as effective Foreign Minister, most influential politician in the Lords, and wielder of much government and church patronage, was definitely not subordinate. Fielding dealt with Newcastle in considering London's law and order crisis in 1753: this, indeed, was a responsibility of the two Secretaries of State, of whom Newcastle was one from 1724 to 1754, and, as such, had been one of the prime agents of the Walpolean system.

The '45 had both revealed the vulnerability of, and led to the firmer establishment of, the Hanoverian regime. It thus closed a long period of instability and, instead, provided the basis for a fundamental recasting of British politics in which Toryism lost its Jacobite aspect. This facilitated the dissolution of the Whig-Tory divide in the two decades after Culloden. Attempts to conciliate and comprehend opponents within ministerial ranks, and expectations concerning the future behavior of the heir to the throne, Frederick, Prince of Wales and, after his death in 1751, the future George III, compromised the cohesion and identity of both the Tories and the remaining opposition Whigs.

Parliamentary attendance slackened as the political situation eased in the late 1740s. There was a strong sense that existing policies and personnel would last until the ministerial revolution that was expected to follow the eventual accession of Frederick, Prince of Wales, a supporter of those Whigs who continued in opposition. The attention of foreign diplomats, an

36 Henry, St John, Viscount Bolingbroke to Hugh, Viscount Polwarth, 1 January 1740, George Rose (ed.), *Marchmont Papers* (3 volumes, London: John Murray, 1831): 205.

important gauge of the perception of the location of political power, was concentrated on Court and ministry, and not Parliament. Fielding moved from journalism.

The anticipated discontinuity did not occur for, far from the elderly George II dying, Frederick predeceased him in 1751. Indeed, George II, born in 1683, was to live to 1760, longer than any previous British monarch. Instead, it was the unexpected death of Pelham in 1754, like Fielding's before his time, that produced a serious discontinuity. Pelham's death touched off a lengthy struggle for power within the government, and the coming of war with France, the early stages of which were very unsuccessful.

Serious political problems were exacerbated by Newcastle's insecure, frenetic and over-anxious personality, for Newcastle lacked both the personality and the position to sustain the political structure that his paranoia dictated: a concentration of decision-making and power on his own person. He could not be a second Walpole, while his personality was not strong enough to take and, more crucially, bear responsibility for decisions, and his anxiety led to indecisiveness. Aside from lacking the character for the successful retention of high office, Newcastle did not hold an office that would free him from, or at least lessen, his anxieties. For all his frenetic activity, and the time and personal wealth he devoted to patronage, Newcastle was only the most important member of the government. Instead, George II, who was not close to Newcastle, played a crucial role in the complex political negotiations of 1754–57.

Newcastle was similarly unsure of Parliament. Despite devoting so much of his time to electoral patronage and parliamentary management, Newcastle knew that it was difficult to maintain the impression of governmental control of the Commons. This, as well as his difficulty in accepting criticism, led Newcastle to devote so much time to patronage and management. His was a personal example of a more general weakness. The "Old Corps" Whig political system could not cope with failure. The absence of a reliable party unity on which government could rest left politicians feeling vulnerable to attack. Thus, Pitt in opposition was an obvious threat, for, although also enjoying a measure of Tory support, he was a Whig able from 1755 to exploit adverse developments in the war, and it was difficult to feel confident of political success against such a figure. This exacerbated

Newcastle's anxiety. Controlling neither Crown nor Commons, Newcastle sought to be a crucial intermediary, but this was an unstable basis for political control.

When Pelham died in 1754, Newcastle sought to entrust the management of the Commons to Henry Fox, but he refused to accept the task when he discovered that the Duke intended to retain full control of all government patronage and to manage the forthcoming general election: that would have left him without the power to give substance to his management. Newcastle turned to Sir Thomas Robinson, a pliable ex-diplomat with no independent political base. Robinson was not strong enough to deal with the political problems of 1754–55 as Britain, moving closer to full-scale war with France, found her allies unwilling to support her. Newcastle tried to deal with the crisis by winning over opposition, neutering hostility by accommodating it in terms of government position. The different positions in which Newcastle found himself during the wartime political crises of 1741, 1744–46 and 1756–57 throw much light on the politics of the period, and offer a parallel to Fielding's need in his journalism to respond to circumstances.

Such a response to circumstances in others could be benign, although Fielding frequently presented it as hypocritical, as with Bellarmine in *Joseph Andrews*:

> "… one must encourage our own people what one can, especially as, before I had a place, I was in the country interest, hee, hee, hee! But for myself, I would see the dirty island at the bottom of the sea rather than wear a single rag of English work about me…." (II,iv)

Returning to journalism, Fielding's papers included some interestingly distinctive features. Thus, the *True Patriot* introduced his "Foreign History" section with a short essay describing principal developments before printing the items of foreign news. However, as he claimed, Fielding found that the existing newspaper proprietors sought to prevent the development of new papers. Groups of shareholding booksellers controlled much of the press and, as Arthur Murphy of the *Gray's Inn Journal* pointed out in 1754, tried to maintain the *status quo*.[37] This led to a sameness in the press.[38]

The relationship between the press and advertising was intimate. The subtitle of the *Champion* was the *Evening Advertiser*. Fielding founded his last paper, the *Covent-Garden Journal*, in 1752 in large part because of the difficulty of publishing advertisements for the Universal Register Office he and his brother John had helped found in 1750, as an agency for employment, insurance and commerce, in the face of a rival Register Office and the hostility of the *Daily Advertiser*. The first issue of the *Covent-Garden Journal*, that of 4 January, launched an attack on "hack writers." Moreover, the paper's criticism of "People of Fashion" reflected not a clear political stance, as earlier for example with *Mist's Weekly Journal*, a major Tory newspaper, but, instead, a politically unspecific sense of socio-moral tension.[39] In his new paper, Fielding defended *Amelia* from the bitter attacks of critics, notably John Hill in the *Daily Advertiser* of 8 January 1752 and Bonnell Thornton in the *Drury Lane Journal* on 16 January and 13 February. This was a key issue in the "Paper War" of 1752–53 between leading writers,[40] including Christopher Smart and Arthur Murphy.

Fielding also provided in *Amelia* an account of the difficult life of being "a very great writer or author" who was held in debt by a bookseller. Bondum, the bailiff, comments on how the author is writing for over 16 hours daily, for five or six booksellers, for only fifteen shillings a day. He writes history books, verses, and news for the newspapers, and parliamentary speeches for the magazines, all of which he makes up (X,ii). This is very much a picture of the author as hack.

In *Tom Jones*, Fielding had drawn on his knowledge of newspapers in his commentary on how his "history" of Jones differed from:

> "the painful and voluminous historian who, to preserve the regularity of his series, thinks himself obliged to fill up as much

---

37   *Gray's Inn Journal*, 4 May, 21 September 1754.
38   *London Advertiser*, 4 March 1751.
39   Fielding, *The Covent-Garden Journal and A Plan of the Universal Register Office*, ed. Bertrand Goldgar, Middletown (Connecticut: Wesleyan, 1988).
40   Betty Rizzo, "Notes on the War between Henry Fielding and John Hill, 1752–53," *The Library*, 6 (1985): 338–53.

paper with the detail of months and years in which nothing re-markable happened, as he employs upon those notable aeras when the greatest scenes have been transacted on the human stage. Such historians as these do, in reality, very much resemble a newspaper, which consists of just the same number of words, whether there be any news in it or not." (II,i)

Already, with the *True Patriot*, Fielding appears to have resented a lack of enthusiasm from Pelham in supporting ministerial newspapers. Even more, the postwar years were a difficult period for the press, the number of English provincial papers for example falling from 43 in 1748 to 32 in 1753. As the *Protestor* of 10 November 1753, explaining why it was ceasing publication, pointed out, years of peace and ministerial sta-bility were not great for newspapers which were best placed to provide political news. Instead, the more infrequently-appearing magazines pro-vided effective competition to the conventionally-priced papers. The reading public's interest in magazine-type material was shown by the foundation of essay papers, or essay series in conventional papers devoted to this material, such as the *Connoisseur, Adventurer, World, Gray's Inn Journal, Rambler,* and Fielding's *Covent Garden Journal.* Fielding's writ-ing matched those of the others, and it is instructive to see Fielding in this role alongside other *literati* such as Johnson. There was a combative element in Fielding's role, as with his attacks in the *Covent-Garden Jour-nal* on John Hill who wrote a similar column in the *London Daily Ad-vertiser.*

The *Covent-Garden Journal* took up some of the non-political themes of Fielding's earlier papers, such as the unchristian, selfish beau who Parson Adams dislikes and criticizes in the *True Patriot* of 28 January 1746. Field-ing has Adams observe:

"… we both lamented the peculiar hardiness of this country, which seems bent on its own destruction, nor will take warning by any visitation, till the utmost wrath of divine vengeance over-takes it.

In discoursing upon this subject, we imputed much of the present profligacy to the notorious want of care in parents in the education of youth, who ... with very little school learning, and not at all instructed in any principles of religion, virtue, and morality, are brought to the great city, or sent to travel to other great cities abroad, before they are twenty years of age, where they become their own masters, and enervate both their bodies and minds with all sorts of diseases and vices, before they are adult."

These themes were seen throughout Fielding's writing. In the *Covent-Garden Journal*, many of the essays were devoted to the cause of good behavior, both against specific abuses, such as gambling, adultery and an interest in pornography, and against the general problem of selfish and improper conduct; while much of the satire was directed at the abuses of the polite world, "People of Fashion" were criticized for their behavior and their attitudes, and were presented as dangerous role models for tradesmen, a longstanding theme, and one in which the Puritan-related criticism of the seventeenth century was reformulated.

Fielding was keen on the persona he took in this journal, that of "Knight Censor of Great Britain," and revised some of the pieces possibly for inclusion in a collected *Works*. He did not do so for his other periodicals, which may reflect the degree to which some were more focused on particular political issues, while his more recent essays appeared of more lasting value because of their clearer moral focus.

In 1753–54, the situation changed with the extraordinary furore over the Jewish Naturalization Act of 1753 placing the ministry in a difficult position on the eve of the general election of 1754, the first since that of 1747.[41] When Parliament debated the repeal of the Act in November 1753, several Whigs criticized the opposition press, a criticism springing directly from the success of the *London Evening Post* in stirring up a controversy over the Act and using it to attack the ministry.[42] There were also steps to

41 Thomas Perry, *Public Opinion, Propaganda and Politics in Eighteenth Century England. A Study of the Jewish Naturalization Act of 1753* (Cambridge, Massachusetts: Harvard University Press, 1962).

42 Horace Walpole, *Memoirs of King George II* edited by John Brooke (3 vols, New Haven, Connecticut: Yale University Press, 1985): 7, 240–41.

encourage a more favorable press coverage for the ministry, not least in the bitterly-contested Oxfordshire election,[43] but Fielding was no longer a warrior in this struggle.

43 Jeremy Black, "Richard Blacow and the Evening Advertiser," *Factotum*, 25 (February 1988): 23–30.

4. LONDON SETTINGS

> "She [Lady Booby] entered the parish amidst the ringing of bells and the acclamations of the poor, who were rejoiced to see their patroness returned after so long an absence, during which time all her rents had been drafted to London without a shilling being spent among them, which tended not a little to their utter impoverishing."
> *Joseph Andrews* (IV,i)

In turn, thwarted at the close of the novel,

> "She returned to London in a few days, where a young captain of dragoons, together with eternal parties at cards, soon obliterated the memory of Joseph." (IV,vi)

Country-born and educated outside the capital, Fielding, nevertheless, was a Londoner for most of his life, and increasingly so. He wrote primarily for its audiences and cultural intermediaries, notably publishers; was, subsequently, an important magistrate there; and understood the clashing cultures and disparate voices of the city, which itself was a drama in the making. Indeed, Fielding captured both the life of the city and its symbolic character. It was his theater in every respect. In modern terms, he addressed its moral economies, but, to appreciate that point, you have to understand those of the time.

Political Center

An unsought testimony to London's importance was that conspiracies and invasion schemes centered on it. In 1722, the Atterbury Plot, a conspiracy on behalf of "James III," the Stuart claimant to the throne, was blocked by prompt governmental action, including the creation of a large army camp in Hyde Park. The Jacobites had planned to exploit disaffection in the Guards and co-operation from the City Corporation, among whose senior ranks were a number of supporters, in order to seize the Tower, the Royal Exchange, and the Bank of England, an indicative choice of key points. It was then intended to raise disaffected groups of the London population: the Southwark Minters, the Westminster mob, and the Thames watermen. Once the city fell, the counties were to be raised. However, the government's firm response overawed London and thwarted the plans for rebellion.

In 1743, when planning an invasion by supporting French troops, the Jacobites again presented control of London as the crucial objective. Maldon in Essex was selected as the landing place because it would permit a march on London without having to cross the Weald, the Downs, and the Thames, each of which would offer opportunities for the defense. In the event, a Channel storm thwarted the French invasion attempt mounted in 1744, an attempt that was planned to include a landing at Blackwall. In December 1745, James's son, Charles Edward Stuart, "Bonnie Prince Charlie," the Chevalier after whom Squire Western in *Tom Jones* named a favorite horse, invaded Scotland. After success there, Charles Edward advanced on London from Edinburgh. He knew that seizing the city was crucial in order to secure the Jacobite position. Although the Jacobites never came within 150 miles of the city, this crisis threw light on the politics and anxieties of London as never before during the century. Sir Dudley Ryder, the Attorney General, noted in his diary on 3 December, "people in great pain for the City ... Papists suspected of an intended rising as soon as the rebels are near London." The following day, William, Duke of Cumberland, second son of George II and one of his leading generals, advised that "without alarming the City the infantry that is about London could be assembled on Finchley Common," as indeed were 4,000 troops.

It was unclear what London itself would do. William Hewitt suggested to William, 3rd Duke of Devonshire, a keen supporter of the government, that little could "be hoped for from the common people about London," whom, he claimed, would rather "be disposed to join in plundering than defending the property of other people." In contrast to this critical and socially-hostile view, the London weavers offered 1,000 men to the royal cause, thus exemplifying an idea of political virtue that was very different from the selfish, indeed, anti-national character of the capital's fashionable society as satirized by Fielding in his plays. George II reviewed London's militia units in St James's Park. After the Jacobites were defeated at Culloden the following April, there were popular demonstrations of loyalism in the capital, including the breaking of unilluminated windows, but the situation was less clear-cut during the crisis itself.

There was little doubt in 1745 that, if George II had lost London, his regime would have collapsed. Some of his supporters would have probably wished to fight on: it is difficult to see Cumberland accepting Jacobite success without a battle. However, without London, the logistical and financial infrastructure of the military establishment would have collapsed. Pay and supplies would have become a problem for Cumberland, doubtless encouraging desertion among his soldiers and helping to dictate his strategy. It is probable that there would have been a measure of support from the English Jacobites for Charles Edward had London fallen; although, more significantly, it is likely that the fall of London would have affected the British fleet, disrupting its supplies and influencing the determination of some officers, which, in turn, would have assisted French plans for an invasion. It was readily apparent that government finances would have been hit by a march on London. On 1 October 1745, Edward Weston, an Under-Secretary in the Northern Department, observed: "The Association of the Merchants has saved the Bank [of England] for a time, but I doubt not the first ill news will raise the same spirit again."

In the event, the bodies of Jacobite traitors were to be displayed in London after the rising as they had already been in 1696, 1716 and 1723. Many of Fielding's readers would have seen them. In 1752–53, as a further sign of London's strategic position, the Jacobite Elibank Plot focused on a coup in the city, which Charles Edward had secretly visited in 1750 in an abortive attempt to raise a rebellion in Staffordshire where Jacobite sympathies were strong.[1]

---

1   Paul Monod, "A Voyage out of Staffordshire; or, Samuel Johnson's Jacobite Journey," in Jonathan Clark and Howard Erskine-Hill (eds), *Samuel Johnson in Historical Context* (Basingstoke: Palgrave, 2000): 11–32.

The Central City

It was not only at moments of national crisis that London's role was crucial, for this significance drew on its prominence across a broad range of national activity, as well as its containing about ten percent of the population of England and Wales, and over four-fifths of those who lived in towns with populations of 10,000 or over. London's vitality and dominant position owed much to its place in politics, culture, society, trade and industry, and the world of print. Metropolitan finance was crucial, not least to government finances,[2] and London-based insurance companies, such as the Sun Fire Office, as well as the banks, were able to organize business throughout England by delegating the work to agents in other towns with whom regular contact could be maintained.

The capital also led the way in national societies and voluntary movements, such as the SPCK and the Societies for the Reformation of Manners; London parishes were more important than others in the Church of England. Indeed, in *Amelia*, Fielding presented London as "the great mart of all affairs, ecclesiastical and civil" (VII,v). The bishopric was a key position, held from 1723 to 1748 by Edmund Gibson, whose influence, aided by the weaknesses of successive Archbishops of Canterbury, was such that he was known, until they fell out in 1736, as "Walpole's Pope." In the diocese, there were many preachers, readers and lecturers, and a high level of clerical activity. Although there was non-residence and pluralism on the part of some of the clerics, levels of daily celebration and services were high, and the clergy had a pronounced view of their duty. London clergy had often driven national opinion, as in 1688 with their refusal to read the Declaration of Indulgence from the pulpit, a very public defiance of James II. London also played a central role in Dissent and in new religious developments, such as the Fetter Lane Society established in 1738 by a group of Anglicans seeking a society for religious observance, one of a number of these.

London, moreover, was the headquarters of Freemasonry, a new and rapid-growing movement, launched in 1717, that proved particularly influential amongst the Whig élite. The social élite gathered at clubs such as

2   *Craftsman*, 7 October 1727.

Whites, which is mentioned by Mutable in Fielding's *The Wedding-Day* and also in *Tom Jones.*

London's position moreover reflected the city's role as the center of government, the law and consumption, and its position in the world of print, which became even more important as a shaper of news, opinion and fashion. Most new periodicals were launched there, while it was not simply a contrivance of the plot that has Fielding in *Joseph Andrews* send Parson Adams to London in an unsuccessful quest to get his nine volumes of sermons published, for the production, sale and storage of books focused on London.[3] London magazines, newspapers and newsletters circulated throughout England, and were also crucial sources of news and opinion for the provincial press.

The energy of London was captured across the arts and provided the context for much of national culture. Amelia and her supposed friend, Mrs Ellison, go to see an oratorio conducted by Handel, and an unwilling Amelia makes "a conquest" of a male member of the audience (IV,ix). The amount of fixed, specialized investment in leisure in the city rose greatly, with the opening of theaters, pleasure gardens, picture galleries, auction houses, and the ubiquitous coffee houses. The range of establishments reflected the vitality of the metropolis, and also the intellectual and cultural ambitions at stake. In particular, the British Museum was created by an Act of Parliament in 1753 as the first national museum of its kind in the world. The Museum acted as an encyclopaedia, with the sequence of rooms, their layout, and the juxtaposition of objects within them, providing a means of understanding relationships within the world of objects and specimens. 12,000 people visited it in 1784, although the rules banned children and sought to prevent "persons of mean and low degree" from gaining access.

Under the shadow of St Paul's Cathedral, an area where the book trade was concentrated, were also published accounts of the diversions of the capital. These included travelogues, for example, attributed to Erasmus Jones, *A Trip through London: Containing Observations on Men and Things, viz.... A remarkable rencounter between a bawd and a sodomite … of a person of quality's clothes sold off his back in the Mall by auction, by his valet de chambre*

3   James Raven, *Bookscape: Geographies of Printing and Publishing in London before 1800* (London: The British Library, 2014).

... of the Exeter-change beauties ... practices of petty-foggers exposed (1728).[4]
Fielding furthermore captured a sense of the liveliness of London life in his
Life of Jonathan Wild (1743), a work that presented the attraction of
celebrity, the ability to coin it, and Londoners' interest in seeing their city
depicted. On the way to meeting his beloved Laetitia, the constantly opportunistic Wild:

> "accidentally met with a young lady of his acquaintance, Miss
> Molly Straddle.... Miss Molly seeing Mr Wild, stopped him,
> and with a familiarity peculiar to a genteel town education,
> tapped, or rather slapped him on the back, and asked him to
> treat her with a pint of wine at the neighbouring tavern....
> [T]he young lady declared she would grant no favour till he had
> made her a present; this was immediately complied with and
> the lover made as happy as he could desire." (II,iii)

Molly Straddle draws on the lively biographies of prostitutes, such as
*The Effigies, Parentage, Education, Life, Merry-Pranks and Conversation of the
celebrated Mrs Sally Salisbury* (1723), a bricklayer's daughter who was the
subject of two biographies that year. Salisbury (*c.*1690–1724) died of fever
in prison after stabbing the Honorable John Finch, one of her lovers. Such
deaths of fever were commonplace due to the crowded and insanitary conditions of prisons. Other books of this type included *Memoirs of the celebrated
Miss Fanny Mxxx* (in fact Fanny Murray, 1759) and *The uncommon Adventures of Miss Kitty Fxxxxxr* (1759).[5] The lawlessness of sex and the commerce
of pleasure extended to the marriage market focused on the area of the Fleet
to the west of St Paul's. In the 1730s and 1740s in particular, many marriages
were "solemnized" in the area which was one of the wilder parts of central
London. The roguery of London was the subject of *The Tricks of London laid
open* (1746), which was based on *The Country Gentleman's Vade Mercury*

---

4   Very popular and much reprinted, this was reprinted as *A Ramble through
    London* (1738).
5   Julie Peakman, *Lascivious Bodies: A Sexual History of the Eighteenth Century*
    (London: Atlantic Books, 2004) and (ed.) *Whore Biographies, 1700–1825*
    (London: Pickering and Chatto, 2006).

(1699). London as a source of trickery, including not only by prostitutes and gamblers, but also mock-auctions, emerged in this much reprinted work, of which a fourth edition appeared in 1755.

Images and Tensions

London was significant in influencing notions of urban life, and in providing both setting and topics for cultural activity. As a subject, it was the most striking in the country until the cult for landscape late in the century led to a marked shift in preference from urban elegance to sublime landscape, a shift that was to provide the background for a harsher view of the city as a physical environment. Throughout the century, London was not only presented as a site of liberty, trade and progress, a Whiggish account, but also in terms of moral, political and economic, disorder and dissolution. Urban living thus served, as so often, to delineate, if not define, issues and alignments.

Whigs tended to take the former view, of London as progress; and Tories more commonly the latter, of London as problem; although that was not a fixed classification. In Alexander Pope's *The Rape of the Lock* (two versions, 1712, 1714), the witty satire about a lack of values encapsulated by Belinda's expenditure, was set in London polite society. Pope was the son of a London linen-draper. In 1721, Thomas, 3rd Earl of Strafford, a prominent Tory, was urged to dine with the Lord Mayor in order to "give life to the honest part of the City. It has often been practiced by another party [the Whigs] (with too much success) in this manner to keep up the spirits and support their interest here."[6] It was not necessary, however, to be a Tory in order to criticize London. Instead, there was disquiet across the political spectrum.

While London's political support was courted or feared, the city changed physically. The expansion into the West End seen during the reign of Queen Anne (1702–14) continued, and led to the building of grand houses, as well as a larger number of those designed for the fashionable. The street-plan of the West End was filled in and also spread. As with other periods of the city's history, much of the building on the edge was speculative development, and

6   Mr Rawstone to Strafford, 26 December 1721, BL. Add. 63469 folio 137.

thus part of the froth of money, projects and image that greatly troubled commentators.

The construction of grand houses reaffirmed the aristocratic stamp on the West End. Devonshire House was built in the 1730s, Chesterfield House in 1747–52, and the new Norfolk House in 1748–56. This move of the nobility west from the Covent Garden area closer to the royal palace at St James's was an important realignment socially and politically, as well as being part of a major shift in land-use. The Haymarket, originally the source of feedstuff for horses, was cleared for development in the early eighteenth century. The churches of the West End were fashionable, especially St George's, Hanover Square, and St James's, Piccadilly.

At the same time, this aristocratic stamp caused tension within London. "Reflector" in the *London Evening Post* of 8 April 1762 condemned "that ruinous prevalence of following the fashions of the Court which now infects the citizens of London." This social tension arose in part from the uneasy neighborhood of the City and the West End, which led both to real contrasts and a perception of differences. The condescending Lord Bawble asks in *Miss Lucy in Town*: "dost thou think that men of decency are to be confined to the rules of decency, like sober citizens, as if they were ashamed of their sins, and afraid they should lose their turn of being Lord Mayor?" At the same time, there were shared areas and practices, notably Vauxhall Gardens, which was developed from 1729 as pleasure gardens that included cultural entertainment,[7] although such sharing could cause difficulties.

There was also a more light-hearted, but still edged, dimension to "town-foppery."[8] Visiting the Haymarket Theatre in 1786, Sophie La Roche noted a hostile interplay of fashionable spectators with the rest of the audience, and with the actors also responding rapidly:

"four ladies ... entered a box during the third play, with such wonderfully fantastic caps and hats perched on their heads, that they were received by the entire audience with loud derision. Their neckerchiefs were puffed up so high that their noses were

7   David Coke and Alan Borg, *Vauxhall Gardens. A History* (New Haven, Connecticut: Yale University Press, 2011).
8   *Tom Jones*, XIII,v.

scarce visible, and their nosegays were like huge shrubs, large enough to conceal a person. In less than a quarter of an hour, when the scene had changed to a market square, four women walked onto the stage dressed equally foolishly, and hailed the four ladies in the box as their friends. All clapped loud applause."[9]

Sex

In 1710, Zacharias von Uffenbach commented on the large number "walking with masks before their faces … they are generally harlots, of whom there is a vast number here especially by night in the streets." Set on "The Street" in London, Fielding's play *The Letter-Writers* (1731) shows prostitutes frightened of being sent to Bridewell by the Justices of the Peace, but also being concerned to find the right clients, not wanting "some attorney's clerk, or a haberdasher's apprentice." (II,ii). In his *Don Quixote in England* (1733), Squire Badger, in small-town England, presents the metropolis as sin-city:

"I wish, my lord, you would tell Sir Thomas the story about you and the Duchess of what do you call her. Odsheart! It is one of the pleasantest stories! about how she met him in the dark at a masquerade, and about how she gave him a letter; and then about how he carried her to a, to a, to a –

John: To a bagnio, to a bagnio [brothel].

Badger: Ay, to a bagnio…. London, where women are, it seems, as plenty as rabbits in a warren. Had I known as much of the world before, as I do now, I believe I should scarce have thought of marrying. Who'd marry, when my lord says, here a man may have your great sort of ladies, only for wearing an embroidered coat, telling half a dozen lies, and making a bow."

9   C. Williams (ed.), *Sophie in London, 1786* (1933): 94–95.

Badger is shown to be gross in action as well as word. Fielding returned to the charge in *Phaeton in the Suds* (1744), referring to London as "that great cuckolds school," which reflected social uneasiness not only about men there but also about the city's women and its impact on women. Thus, London is presented as source of seduction elsewhere in England, Lord Bawble reflecting in *Miss Lucy in Town*: "I dislike no man's wife but my own.... I know how to deal with country ladies. I learnt the art of making love to them at my election."

Venereal disease was a consequence of sexual activity in London, more particularly with both prostitutes and infected men. Later in 1775–76, commander in the early stages of the War of American Independence, Major Thomas Gage, however, in 1749 had particular peacetime problems:

> "The only way I could devise to divert myself was with a wench, who has obligingly given me a pretty play-thing to divert me in the country, in bestowing a most generous clap upon me. I call it generous from its copious flowings, which I am endeavouring with the assistance of injections and purgations to put a stop to..."[10]

This was very much the experience of Wilson in *Joseph Andrews* and, as a consequence, he provides a particularly striking image of a fall into angry railing and pointless misogyny:

> "I now forswore all future dealings with the sex, complained loudly that the pleasure did not compensate the pain, and railed at the beautiful creatures in as gross language as Juvenal himself formerly reviled them in. I looked on all the town-harlots with a detestation not easy to be conceived; their persons appeared to me as painted palaces inhabited by Disease and Death, nor could their beauty make them more desirable objects in my eyes than gilding could make me covet a pill or golden plates a coffin." (III,iii)

Londoners were angry also for other reasons. In 1744, parishioners from St James, Clerkenwell complained about the noise from those leaving

---

10   Gage to Sir Charles Hotham, no date, Hull, University Library, Hotham papers DDHo 4/3.

disorderly houses in the early hours including their "singing obscene songs," this part of a more general clash of urban lifestyles that Hogarth depicted in *The Enraged Musician* (1741). Fielding described this print in his *Voyage to Lisbon* as "enough to make a man deaf to look at."[11] This was part of his frequent references to "my friend" Hogarth's prints, including in *Tom Jones*[12] and *Amelia*.[13] Both Fielding and Hogarth aimed for a similar melding of realism and morality, the shock of recognition offered the reader or viewer providing the way to receive moral lessons.

Homosexual activity was harshly treated, not least with "molly houses" (homosexual male brothels) being raided, as in in 1698, 1707 and 1726. The raid on Mother Clap's molly house in 1726 led to the execution of three men and to the publication in 1729 of *Hell Upon Earth: or the Town in Uproar*, which attacked homosexuality in the capital. In 1750, Henry Harris reported from London about the attitude of Mary, Dowager Lady Savile to her son, Sir George, later a prominent politician:

> "We have here a young, sucking knight of the Bath, upon whom the fame of this curious taste will stick more closely. A very sober, demure, bible-faced spark he is—never misses the sacrament, and being well white-washed from all sin, but Whit-Sunday he began a new score in a stable yard with the waiter at Mount's Coffee-House."

Rural life is strikingly counterpointed as Harris added three months later:

> "Lady Savile has taken her young twig of Sodom into the country, and, by way of weaning him from that unnatural vice, takes great pains to coker him with every Abigail in her house, and all the milk maid cunts in the neighbourhood."[14]

11 Emily Cockayne, "Cacophony, or vile scrapers on vile instruments: bad music in early modern English towns," *Urban History*, 29 (2002): 45–47.
12 I,xi; II,iii; III,vi; VI,iii.
13 I,vi.
14 Harris to Sir Charles Hanbury-Williams, 6 July, 16 October 1750, Farmington, Connecticut, Lewis Walpole Library, Hanbury-Williams papers, volume 68, folios 146, 151.

The Regions of the City

Fielding saw London in terms of a corrupt Court and aristocracy at its West End, with their commerce in vice, and the more acceptable commercial metropolis. The interplay between the two was a major theme in literature and also in Hogarth's caricature series. The *Westminster Journal* of 27 February 1742 noted: "An evening politician at the Smyrna in Pall-Mall, is a quite different character to a six-o'clock-in-the-morning statesman at Grigsby's behind the Exchange," references respectively to West End and City coffee-houses. From his plays on, Fielding captured tension, as with Pierot's dance in *The Intriguing Chambermaid* (1733):

> "Were all women's secrets known,
> Did each father know his own,
> Many a son now bred to trade,
> Then had shined in rich brocade."

In *Miss Lucy in Town*, the rural wife says she wants to see "The Tower, and the crowns, and the lions, and Bedlam, and the Parliament-House, and the Abbey," only to be told that "these are only sights for the vulgar" and that she should go to "ridottoes, masquerades, courts, plays...." Adopting the usual Opposition stance, the *Champion* criticized the Walpole government for its supposed resistance to the city, defining its attitude on 5 February 1740: "It is reasonable that trade has been only under a nominal restraint in all the ports of England, except London; and that to humble the city is, in certain places, become as favourite a phrase, as Delenda est Carthago was of old."

Very differently, London, "that city where men of ingenuity can most easily supply their wants without the assistance of money,"[15] was a setting for villainy for many artists and writers, for example of the lengthily-described physical, economic, psychological and moral fall of Wilson into the pitfalls of credit, impression and vanity in *Joseph Andrews* (III,iii) and the snares that bedevil William Booth in *Amelia* (1751), Booth being modelled on Fielding and his father. And so also for other novelists, such as Tobias Smollett in *The Expedition of Humphry Clinker* (1771). Picaresque novels

15 *Jonathan Wild*, II,xiv.

involving London captured a situation in which about a sixth of the population of England and Wales had probably lived in London at some time in their lives.

A particular highpoint of the tension in *Tom Jones* was the attempted rape of Sophia Western by Lord Fellamar with the encouragement of Lady Bellaston. Whereas Tom Jones was usually the savior of threatened women in this novel, a role taken in *Jonathan Wild* by the merchant captain (II,x), in this case it was Squire Western who sums up the views of all: "You are a son of a b— ... for all your laced coat." Western provides a clear social statement that is also linked to values and place: "I will have nothing to do with any of your lords. My daughter shall have an honest country gentleman" (XV,v). Country was a key qualifier here to gentleman. Western, indeed, rejects London as a whole, not just the "Quality." Quarrelling with the "chairmen" who carry him in a sedan chair and demand far more than the proper fare:

> "He not only bestowed many hearty curses on them at the door, but retained his anger after he came into the room; swearing that all the Londoners were like the court, and thought of nothing but plundering country gentlemen. 'D—n me,' says he, 'if I won't walk in the rain rather than get into one of their hand-barrows again. They have jolted me more in a mile than Brown Bess would in a long fox chase.'" (XVII,iii)

His horse provided him with an obvious point of reference.

While counterpoints, the City and the West End were each quite varied in their circumstances. Thus, despite questions about the corruption of the City Comptroller in the early 1740s,[16] there was an apparent contrast between the world of ordered money round the Bank of England and the very different energy of the riverbank. In the increasingly populous West End, the order of the royal precincts and the new geometric elegance of Mayfair contrasted with the poverty, energy and 24–hour depravity of Covent Garden, an area which spread to include Leicester Square as well

16   Ian Doolittle, "The City's Estate in Conduit Mead and the Authorship of 'The City Secret'," *Guildhall Studies in London History*, 22 (1976): 125–35.

as Drury Lane. This was an area of brothels, gin houses, coffee shops, play-houses, artists' studios, and much else.

A male response to the pre-marital chastity expected of most women drove the sexual frenzy of male demand in this area, and led to its accompaniments, including venereal disease and crime.[17] In *Joseph Andrews*, an innkeeper reports of a villainous squire:

> "There was another, a young woman, and the handsomest in all this neighbourhood, whom he enticed up to London, promising to make her a gentlewoman to one of your women of quality, but instead of keeping his word, we have since heard, after having a child by her himself, she became a common whore, then kept a coffee-house in Covent Garden, and a little after died of the French distemper in a gaol," (II,xvii)

the French distemper being venereal disease. In Covent Garden, Wilson "shone forth in the balconies at the play-houses, visited whores, made love to orange-wenches, and damned plays. This career was soon put a stop to by my surgeon" (III,iii), which was a reference to venereal disease. Nearby, Fielding organized a large-scale raid on gamblers "in the Strand" in 1751.[18] To the south of Covent Garden, close to the Inner Temple, was the former Whitefriars, which is described in *Tom Jones* as "the scene of all mirth and jollity" (VIII,xiv). Known as Alsatia, it was an area of criminality, and it would have been present in Fielding's mind due to Thomas Shadwell's comedy *The Squire of Alsatia* (1688), which was performed several times in London in the 1730s and 1740s.[19]

To the west of the West End, very differently, there was development of suburban residences in the Thames valley where the wealthy could enjoy more space as well as hunting, which was very much Walpole's preference there. Chelsea remained a lightly-built up area at the close of the period, and, past Westminster, there was only limited development along the river, while places

17 Vic Gatrell, *The First Bohemians* (London: Allen Lane, 2014).
18 *The Gentleman's Magazine*, 21 (1751): 87.
19 George Drake, "*Tom Jones* and Alsatia," *Notes and Queries* (June 1997): 200–201.

such as Parsons Green were villages, surrounded by market gardens. The same was true south of the river of villages such as Tooting. At the same time, there was a degree of ribbon development from Lambeth, especially in Clapham, just as Kensington and Knightsbridge were characterized by ribbon development north of the Thames. Alongside farmland, especially pastures and meadows providing milk and hay, for example in Bethnal Green, Hackney and Islington, there were market gardens in this outer belt, for example in Stockwell, as well as clay and gravel pits to ensure bricks and gravel for construction and new roads. Fielding, in *The Voyage to Lisbon*, praised Enfield for having the:

> "best air, I believe in the whole kingdom, and far superior to that of Kensington Gravel-pits; for the gravel is here much wider and deeper, the place higher and more open towards the south, whilst it is guarded from the north wind by a ridge of hills, and from the smells and smoke of London by its distance; which last is not the fate of Kensington, when the wind blows from any corner of the east."

This element, of dependence on wind direction, is not one that can be grasped from paintings of the period. At the same time that the West End was being created, other areas further east were differently developed, especially Spitalfields, which was an industrial zone. In contrast, some parts of the city, such as Clerkenwell, became less fashionable, a process that was paralleled in Paris with the decline of the Marais, which was to the east of a city where the west was being built up and becoming fashionable.

While London was becoming bigger physically, the opening of routes within the city improved accessibility. Indeed, its importance and the availability of resources was shown with the building of bridges there and nearby. Several replaced ferries, in what was a major development reflecting greater human control over the environment as ferries, unlike bridges, were subject to river conditions, such as ice, as well as the weather. Although it challenged the passenger traffic by ferry, and thus harmed the watermen, the building of Westminster Bridge markedly helped development on the south bank of the Thames.

The river primarily was a place for trade, the harbor of both metropolis and empire. Arriving in 1724, the Count of Broglie, the new French ambassador, reported that there was nothing more magnificent than the innumerable number of ships he had seen on the Thames.[20] At the same time, this point underlined the dependence of the economy on the weather: aside from winter freezing, more frequent easterly winds could harm navigation from the Thames and hit employment.

A distinctive view of the river was indeed provided in *The Thames during the Great Frost of 1739–40* by Jan Griffier the younger. Until the Thames was deepened and embanked, it froze over in severe winters such as that of 1709. Griffier was the young son of an Amsterdam painter who settled in London in the 1660s and painted many Thames-side scenes, while the elder son, Robert, also painted London scenes, the family's careers reflecting the close link between London and Amsterdam, and the openness of London's culture to foreign influences.

The financial and economic importance of London indeed led to significant artistic work there. In 1725–27, Sir James Thornhill, the first native artist to be knighted, who had produced the sumptuous ceiling of the Painted Hall in Greenwich, provided painted decorations for the ceiling of the New Council Chamber in the Guildhall, offering Baroque themes and images, with the oval medallion in the center providing a personification of the City of London as a young woman attended by Pallas Athena (symbolizing wisdom), Peace, Plenty, and two cherubs. George Dance the Elder, Surveyor to the Corporation of London, designed the Mansion House begun in 1739, and the Excise Office in Broad Street.

The directories of the period underline the strength of the commercial range of London. Henry Keat's *The Directory; or list of principal traders in London* (1734) was rapidly followed by W. Meadows, L. Gilliver and J. Clarke's *The Intelligencer or, Merchants Assistant* (1738). It listed 2,000 merchants and traders as well as the list of stage coaches and carriers from London, the distances from London to major towns, and, with the fairs of England and Wales, economic information at the national level. Others played a role, including J. Fox's *Universal Pocket Companion* (1741), which included 2,300 merchants and retailers as well as transport information.[21]

---

20 Broglie to Charles, Count of Morville, French Foreign Minister, 29 June 1724, AE. CP. Ang. 348 folio 56.
21 Peter Atkins, "Eighteenth Century London Directories," *Factotum*, 28 (March 1989): 12.

Religion

Although not generally seen as a period of religious energy, this view is mistaken. Paterson's *Pietas Londinenses* of 1714 gave a list of all Church services in London and claimed that at no time of any day was London without one or more services. The period left London with an important legacy of churches, in addition to the completion of Wren's St Paul's, with the balustrade added, against his wishes, in 1718. It is true that when the Commission for Building Fifty New Churches in London and Westminster, established in 1711, was abolished in 1758, owing to the inadequacy of its principal source of funds, the coal duty, it had authorized the construction of only twelve churches. Nevertheless, several architects produced major works, including St Mary-le-Strand, St Peter's Vere Street, St George-in-the-East, and St Martin's-in-the-Field by James Gibbs, St John's, Westminster by Thomas Archer, and St Botolph's, Aldgate, St Luke's, Old Street, and St Leonard's, Shoreditch by George Dance the Elder. The sums involved could be considerable. St Giles-in-the-Fields (1731–34) by Henry Flitcroft cost £10,000, and his St Olave, Southwark (1737–39), £5,000. The churches were linked with a vibrant religious culture in London, for example the music produced by organists and the performance of oratorios, notably by Handel, whose *Samson* (1743) was performed eight times in its first season, a considerable triumph.

Houses and Squares

Within the existing built-up area, the physical creation of London was an evolutionary, not a revolutionary, process, with development taking place out of existing housing types and traditional layouts. Moreover, looking toward the current situation, the ability to change and upgrade the structure of new houses, plus the high level of maintenance houses required, especially in the painting of woodwork, made houses perfectly suited to a consumer society geared toward the continued renewal and replacement of products. As with the situation today, this continued renewal and replacement was also a process of change that reflected and sustained social distinctions.

The nature of these distinctions was also seen in open spaces within London. Squares, such as Hanover Square, laid out between 1717 and

1719, were a key element in the development of the West End, the setting of much of Fielding's London action. They tended to be public, rather than private, arenas until the 1720s. Then the emphasis came to be on exclusivity, with the open spaces enclosed, laid out as gardens (an instance of rustic taste in an urban setting), and restricted to residents; and this change helped further a process of social exclusion.

In turn, social exclusion was lessened by the range of activities and organizations where people could meet, albeit within boundaries of rank or income. Fielding covered some but not all, not for example engaging with Freemasonry. However, his characters took part in masquerades, as in *Tom Jones*, although Booth does not wish Amelia to go to one at Ranelagh without him (VI,v); or attended oratorios, as in *Amelia*. In the latter novel, Booth, having wandered around for almost two hours:

> "dropt into a coffee-house near St James's, where he sat himself down. He had scarce drank his dish of coffee, before he heard a young officer of the guards cry to another, 'Od, d-m me Jack, here he comes—here's old honour and dignity, faith....' Upon which, he saw a chair open, and out issued a most erect and stately figure indeed, with a vast periwig on his head, and a vast hat under his arm. This august personage, having entered the room, walked directly up to the upper end, where having paid his respects to all present of any note, to each according to seniority, he at last cast his eyes on Booth, and very civilly, though somewhat coldly, asked how he did."

This is Colonel Bath who asks Booth to fill the chair next to him in the coffee-house (V,i). The nearby Birdcage-walk in St James's Park is also, in *Amelia,* a place where people of different rank can meet (Vi,ix).

Pressures

A very different issue was posed by the nature of the drinking water: river water in London was often muddy, while pump water there was affected by sewage. Typhus was one result; the disease was partly responsible for a rise in winter mortality in the first half of the eighteenth century. More generally, the proximity of dunghills to humans was dangerous for health. Privies with open soil pits lay directly alongside dwellings and under bedrooms, and excrement flowed on, and beneath, the surface into generally porous walls. The smell would have been terrible. Mary Scarth, the raker of the parish of St Giles-in-the-Fields from 1705 to 1723, was paid £400 by the parish and employed twenty horses, four carts and five men in moving the excrement from cesspits to farmers seeking manure; a trade that underlined London's varied significance for the surrounding region.

Disease was not the sole killer. Dearth was also a problem. High grain prices tended to increase the incidence of epidemic diseases and deaths among middle and older age groups. The London printer Edward Owen noted in 1757: "Bread is getting so excessive dear … which makes it go very hard with the poor, even in the City."[22] The issue of food prices serves as a reminder that, although London developed as a center of consumption and leisure, the living conditions of much of the population was far from easy. Cases heard in the Guildhall Justice Room included those of leaving babies on the doorstep of local constables.

Monitoring London

Ministers and indeed monarchs monitored London politics, while there were also attempts by government to control or limit disaffection. These reflected both awareness of the political importance of the city and knowledge of its strong political divisions.[23] Ministerial steps included those against the freedom of the press, such as the Juries Act of 1730, as well as moves to manage the political system. The latest in a series of measures to control elections, the City Elections Act of 1725 defined the freeman franchise as narrowly as possible, and imposed an aldermanic veto on the actions of the more popular and Tory-inclined Common Council in order to limit the volatility and independence of popular London politics. However, the Common Council, which remained an independent body, often sought to restrict the authority of the aldermen.

22 Weston-Underwood papers.
23 Walpole to Charles, 2nd Viscount Townshend, Secretary of State for the Northern Department, 20, 28 June 1723, NA. SP. 43/4.

There was an underlying volatility in the city that spilled over into political complaint, in words and deeds. In 1736, William Pulteney, a leading opposition Whig politician, reported on such complaint directed against George II's mistress, Madame Walmolden:

"One Mrs Mopp, a famous she bone-setter and mountebank, coming to town in a coach with six horses on the Kentish Road, was met by a rabble of people, who seeing her very oddly and tawdrily dressed, took her for a foreigner, and concluded she must be a certain great person's mistress. Upon this they followed the coach, bawling out, 'No Hanover Whore, no Hanover Whore.' The lady within the coach was much offended, let down the glass, and screamed louder than any of them, she was no Hanover whore, she was an English one, upon which they all cried out, 'God bless your Ladyship,' quitted the pursuit, and wished her a good journey."[24]

Mrs Mopp was a character almost designed for Fielding and Hogarth.

London in 1733, when Fielding was a resident, played a key role in the opposition to the government's proposal for changes in the excise regulations. The nature of excise powers challenged suppositions about the constitution and the character of British liberties, as excise officers and commissioners were seen as arbitrary figures unconstrained by jury trials, and, indeed, demonstrators paraded wooden shoes, the symbols of supposed French slavery. Henry Goodricke observed "The rising tempest of an excise makes a furious roar in this town,"[25] and, on 10 April, the government majority fell to seventeen on what turned out to be the key division, an opposition motion to hear by counsel a petition from the City of London critical of the scheme. Next day, the legislation was dropped. London was illuminated in celebration, and Walpole was burned there in effigy.[26] Indeed, although Walpole sought to build up support in London, he did not have any particular feel for London politics, still more the ability to woo metropolitan opinion

24 Pulteney to Jonathan Swift, 2 December 1736, BL. Add. 4806 folio 178.
25 Goodricke to Edward Hopkins, 6 February 1733, BL. Add. 64929 folio 81.
26 Paul Langford, *The Excise Crisis* (Oxford: Oxford University Press, 1975).

successfully. London took a major role in organizing opposition activities to his government in 1733 and 1738–42. The range of disaffection in London was considerable. In 1736, in an instance of a persistent anti-Irish fear, workers rioted against the employment of cheaper Irish labor and had to be dispersed by the militia. In 1740, Walpole was informed about City clubs being centers of anti-ministerial propaganda, with one printing thousands of Opposition pamphlets.[27]

An emphasis on politics or the economy does not capture the flavor of London life in this period. Instead, the earthy quality of manners emerges frequently, and in a fashion that Fielding captured, notably in *Jonathan Wild*. The *London Mercury* of 11 February 1721 reported:

> "A certain last-maker in Butcherhall-Lane being resolved to divert himself after a new method ran into the Sign of the Three Birds, and called for the landlady, who, immediately attending, he called her a bitch and fell a laughing. The woman, surprised to know his meaning, stood mute, while Dick persisted in his tone, calling her bitch and bitch of bitches, and as she kept such a house, ought to stand the censure of her customers; the woman, who was infinitely, above the saucy language of his scandalous tongue, resenting his ill manners by calling him rascal. Dick to prove to the contrary before forty people, pulls down his breeches to stand search. The gentlewoman of the house absconded with great confusion; but a lusty butcher woman broiling her supper, having more courage than the former, she swore she would try the event, and catches hold by his trickstaff with a pair of steak tongs with which she was turning her meat, and shook him while he roared out like a bull, and ran away as fast as he came, and hath been seen no more. The woman swore she believed he was a rascal by her manner of feeling."

The sense of town-country tension repeatedly captured by Fielding was a comment, moreover, on London even if that was not the town explicitly

27 A. Mann to Walpole, 4 December 1740, Cambridge, University Library, Cholmondeley Houghton papers, correspondence, no. 3007.

in question. Thus, in *Joseph Andrews*, Lady Boothby "was a woman of gaiety, who had been blessed with a town education, and never spoke of any of her country neighbours by any other appellation than that of the brutes."[28] In *Tom Jones*, it is implicitly the example of London of which Fielding was writing when he qualifies the "character of lewdness" ascribed:

> "to these times. On the contrary, I am convinced there never was less love of intrigue carried on among persons of condition than now. Our present women have been taught by their mothers to fix their thoughts only on ambition and vanity, and to despise the pleasures of love as unworthy their regard; and being afterwards, by the care of such mothers, married without having husbands, they seem pretty well confirmed in the justness of those sentiments; whence they content themselves, for the dull remainder of life, with the pursuit of more innocent, but … more childish amusements … the true characteristick of the present *Beau Monde*, is rather folly than vice, and the only epithet which it deserves is that of *frivolous*." (XIV,i)

That was a criticism of London as a source of moral failure, one seen as destructive of all happiness and of the family basis of society. Fielding scarcely originated this criticism, but he worked with it and kept it fresh and relevant.

---

28 *Joseph Andrews*, I,iii.

5. TRAVEL AND TRAVELLERS

Fielding's life saw a major change in the context of travel, one that both affected contemporaries and offered a new context for the travels of fictional characters. Throughout, however, London was central and the turnpike and postal systems radiated from the city. Stagecoaches regularly left London inns, such as the George at Southwark, a new stage of Southwark's role as a terminus for overland journeys, as with Geoffrey Chaucer's fourteenth-century pilgrims en route to Canterbury. Written in the early 1720s, John Macky's *A Journey Through England* (1732) commented that a stage coach ran to London from Salisbury in a day in the summer.[1] Although not on the scale of what was to come, Fielding's lifetime was already seeing significant development, and this was affecting the general perception of society. Travel was made faster as a result of the road improvements carried out by turnpike trusts, as well as the replacement of leather straps by steel coach springs, and the introduction of elliptical springs.

By 1750, a sizeable network of new turnpikes radiating from London had been created. The new and improved roads made it easier for Londoners to travel, and for others to reach London. London and North-West England were well linked, with the road to Chester and both roads to Manchester turnpiked for most of their length. The frequency of links also increased: London to Bristol and Birmingham services became more frequent in the 1740s, and, thanks to such measures, "transport productivity" rose markedly.

River links, however, remained important for freight. For example, it cost 33sh 4d (£1.67 in modern currency) a ton to move goods by road from London to Reading in 1792, but only 10sh (50p) by water, although that was a slower means, which had implications for perishable products, let alone discouraging passengers. Improved communications by road and

1   Macky, *A Journey Through England* (2 volumes, London, 1732), II, 41.

canal during the century led to a greater uniformity of prices for goods, with these being set in London, so that, alongside a series of regional markets, there was a national one. A letter in the *Newcastle Journal* of 19 July 1740 referred to "London which place governs the value of all grain in England."

Transport and Trade

Infrastructure was crucial to agricultural and industrial development, as, without effective transport systems and viable financial structures, regions could not benefit from the diffusion of new methods or from new demands. Economic activities had different requirements, and the spread of competition brought by improvements in infrastructure did not benefit all; but most of the country was affected by changes in communications and by improvements in banking facilities.

Whether in terms of the movement of people or of goods, of transport with speed or in bulk, of regular or of intermittent links, poor communications were a serious problem, magnifying the effects of distance and imposing high costs on economic exchange. Land communications were generally slow, variable and unreliable to an extent that it is difficult for modern readers, accustomed to carefully-modelled and maintained roads and bridges, and mechanised transportation, to appreciate. Arriving in Fielding's *The Intriguing Chambermaid* (1733), Goodall complains: "This cursed stage-coach from Portsmouth hath fatigued me more than my voyage from the Cape of Good Hope." In Fielding's *Miss Lucy in Town*, Mrs Midnight is told by a servant "a gentleman and lady to enquire for lodgings; they seem to be just come out of the country, for the coach and horses are in a terrible dirty pickle." They would have been spattered with mud. In *Tom Jones*, Mrs Western "had lately remitted the trespass of a stage-coachman, who had overturned her post-chaise into a ditch" and she had been robbed by a highwayman (VII,ix). As so often, Fielding is blunter in *Amelia*: "by the overturning of a chaise … her lovely nose was beat all to pieces" (II,i), which was a major event for the protagonist, rather than being an aside for a minor character.

The quality of roads reflected the local terrain, in particular drainage and soil type. Road construction and maintenance techniques were of limited effectiveness in marshy regions, or in areas with a high water table, such as the heavy clays of the English Midlands, South Essex and the Vale of Berkeley in Gloucestershire. Travelling into Cornwall in August 1702, John Evelyn found "dirty or stony lanes."[2]

Mountainous terrain increased the need for draught animals and limited the speed of transport. The need to travel up or down added greatly to distance, and thus increased the time and cost of travel. Even in lowland areas, a small hill often affected road and rail routes, and steep climbs limited the value of wheeled vehicles. Furthermore, many mountains were difficult to cross. It was not until the nineteenth century that advances in transport engineering, especially bridge-building and the use of dynamite, nitro-glycerine and gelignite in tunnel construction, helped overcome some of the problems posed by the terrain.

Marshy areas were particularly hazardous, as were fords. Between Chester and Hawarden in 1698, Celia Fiennes "crossed over the marshes, which is hazardous to strangers." On her return from Wales, she:

> "forded over the Dee [estuary] when the tide was out … the sands are here so loose that the tides do move them … many persons that have known the fords well, that have come a year or half a year after, if they venture on their former knowledge have been overwhelmed in the ditches made by the sands, which are deep enough to swallow up a coach or wagon."[3]

More generally, poor roads led to long and unpredictable journeys that strained individuals, damaged goods, and tied up scarce capital in goods in transit. A wagon drawn by four horses pulling 4,000 lbs could rarely cover more than 20 miles daily. Poorly-constructed roads led often to a reliance on light carts with only two horses, which increased the number of carts necessary to move a given load, with resulting costs in manpower and forage. Still more often, burdens were limited to 2.5 cwt. (280 lbs) or so, which could be carried in panniers on a horse or mule, against the 10 cwt. (1,120

2   Evelyn journal, BL. Evelyn papers 49 folio 21.
3   C. Morris (ed.), *The Illustrated Journeys of Celia Fiennes c. 1682–c. 1712* (1982): 157–59.

lbs) which could be drawn by a single horse over good roads. The construction of good roads could therefore offer a fourfold increase in loads. Heavy wide-wheeled wagons were not quicker than pack-horses, but they were less expensive to operate, and, as a result, increasingly replaced pack-horses on the main routes to South-West England.

More generally, there were important improvements in carrying services. The increased speed and frequency of deliveries enhanced the integration of production and consumption, and furthered the development of the market; it became easier to dispatch salesmen, samples, catalogues, orders and replacements. The development of the turnpikes was central to the creation of regular long-distance horse-drawn wagon services, which also benefited from the construction of bridges. Whereas Kendal in Westmorland had been served by regular pack-horse trains moving goods as far as Bristol, London and Southampton from the fifteenth century, in the eighteenth century horsedrawn wagon services, with their greater capacity for moving goods, took over long-distance and regional routes to and from Cumbria. Similarly, wagon access to Liverpool began in the 1730s and a direct coach service thence to London in 1760.

Yet, pack-horses were still very common in Britain's advancing areas, even in the 1800s, and were even more so elsewhere. Pack-horses represented a decision not to rely on wheels, and wheeled vehicles were not widely used in many areas, so that it was not until the late 1760s that the first coach in Falmouth, the most important Cornish port, was recorded. Pack-horses and carriages alike contributed greatly to a ubiquity of horses, and significance of horsemanship and horse management that is all too easy to forget, and that was frequently referred to by Fielding. It was a major difference between rural and London society.

Even when roads were improved, there were still major problems. Wagons and carts often provided merchandise only inadequate shelter, and the methods of packing and of moving heavy goods on and off carts were primitive, although not necessarily seen as such by contemporaries. Due to limitations in transportation methods, droving was the principal way of moving livestock, although it was both slow and the animals used up much of their energy on the move: cattle from Scotland and Wales, and turkeys (shod with tarred feet) from East Anglia, all walked to London, the wholesale markets of which were crucial for the agriculture of much of the country.[4] Other settlements were similarly served, so that, at any one time, large numbers of animals were on the move.

The ability and determination of local communities to keep the roads in good repair was important because, under the Statute for Mending of Highways of 1555, each parish in England and Wales was responsible for road upkeep. However, as the resistance of the surface, usually loose and rough, to bad weather or heavy use, was limited, there was a need for frequent repair. Expensive in money and manpower, this duty was generally not adequately carried out, certainly not to the standards required by heavy through-traffic, let alone for any increase in traffic. In *Joseph Andrews*, much of which was a guide to the many and unpredictable travails of travel, Adams "came to a large water, which, filling the whole road, he saw no method of passing unless by wading through, which he accordingly did up to his middle" (II,ii). There was no technological or engineering innovation to transform the road surface. Because narrow wheels dug ruts, commentators from the 1750s advocated broader wheels for carriages and wagons, and an Act of 1753 stated that wheel rims on wagons had to be at least nine inches wide. However, there was no significant improvement until the early nineteenth century when John McAdam and Thomas Telford improved road surfaces with new construction techniques. Nevertheless, alongside the deficiencies, it would be mistaken to ignore the extent and effectiveness of the pre-turnpike road system.

In the eighteenth century, major road improvements occurred not as a consequence of technological transformation, but as a result of organizational changes, specifically the role of turnpike trusts, bodies authorised by Parliament to raise capital in order to repair and build roads and to charge travellers to these ends. The capital was raised as loans which were to be repaid through income from tolls on travelers and goods, which helped explain opposition, as in 1740 when the inhabitants of Hedworth and Monkwearmouth petitioned for exemption from the tolls for a proposed turnpike from Durham to Tyne Bridge.[5] Four years later, the proposed Newcastle-Alnwick turnpike, part of any route to Edinburgh, faced "many

4   Colin Smith, "The wholesale and retail markets of London, 1660–1840," *Economic History Review*, 55 (2002): 33.
5   Durham, CRO, Strathmore papers, D/St/C1/3/201–2.

difficulties" as a result of private interests.[6] This was not an issue with which Fielding engaged.

Initially, trusts were given powers and responsibilities for twenty-one years, but this was subsequently extended. The decision to establish trusts reflected confidence in the financial return, and thus in the economic prospects, of transport links. The availability of investment capital was crucial. In many respects, therefore, turnpike trusts were a consequence of economic health and a testimony to a confidence in the future that came from local communities, and a good example, to use modern language, of public/private enterprise. As later with canals and railways, not all turnpike schemes were implemented, while some were not effective. Nevertheless, turnpiked roads benefited from more expenditure than their counterparts, and were therefore often far better.

The co-operation between parliamentary authorization and local charge-levying bodies, reflected the absence of a national road policy, let alone a transport ministry. Unlike elsewhere in Europe, for example France, Prussia, Russia and Spain, the government played only a small direct role in road construction. This role was particular to the Scottish Highlands, where the army built about 250 miles of road between 1726 and 1738 to aid a rapid response to any Jacobite rising. As with the enclosure of agricultural land, the possibility of creating turnpike trusts was thus a permissive national policy, not a prescriptive one. Rather than following some master plan, the road system came in large part to reflect the degree of dynamism of individual trusts, and the ability of particular routes to produce revenue. The last was essentially a consequence of the strength of the regional economy and the role of the route in intra-regional communications. Although trusts reflected local initiatives, a process on which Fielding's plays and novels throw ironic light, notably with the presentation of corrupt corporations (town councils), a national turnpike system was created, but this was due to commercial opportunity in defining necessary and profitable links, not national planning.

The desire of local merchants and manufacturers for growth was important, but turnpikes were not just commercial ventures: the trusts were

6   Sir Henry Liddell to Matthew Ridley, 26 April 1744, 14 February 1745, Ashington, Northumberland CRO, Ridley of Blagdon papers, ZRI 25, 2.

dominated by noblemen and the squirearchy, and the turnpikes were seen as a form of social improvement. Parliament oversaw the system through renewal and amendment Acts that reflected the strength of local interests.

The first turnpike trust was created in 1663, and the first section of the London-Norwich road was turnpiked under an act of 1696. Early trusts dealt largely with repairs, rather than the construction of new roads. Many trusts, such as the Bath Trust, which was established in 1707, had considerable success in improving the situation. By 1750, three routes from Yorkshire to Manchester were turnpiked, as were the routes from London to Bath, Canterbury and Portsmouth. In Lincolnshire, the Great North Road was turnpiked from Grantham northwards in 1726 and from Grantham to Stamford in 1739.

Nevertheless, compared with what was to come, the 1730s and 1740s were decades of limited progress. In contrast, there was substantial expansion in the 1750s and 1760s, so that by 1770, when there were 15,000 miles of turnpikes in England, most of the country was within 12.5 miles of one. After 1751 it became easier to obtain Turnpike Acts. The first turnpike from Chichester was begun in 1749, and, by 1779, the city was the junction of four turnpikes, which led to an increase in overland trade from West Sussex to London, and a relative decline in the longer sea route. The first Devon trust, the Exeter Trust, was established in 1753, and was rapidly followed by many others, leading to major improvements. The first trust in Cornwall, to turnpike the Falmouth-Truro road, was established in 1754. By 1770, a network of turnpikes radiated from major provincial centers: Birmingham benefited from the convergence of improved routes: the Bromsgrove (1726), Hagley (1753) and Dudley (1760) turnpikes.

Non-turnpike roads remained important, crucially so in local economies, and much of the dense network of local routes changed little during the century, in quality, direction or use. For example, North Devon had poor land links and was largely dependent on shipping. In Fielding's play *An Old Man taught Wisdom* (1734), the lawyer Wornwood reaches Goodwill's rural house through roads that "are very dirty." In Squire Western's Somerset neighborhood, the bad roads deter visiting by coach (VII,iv). In his play *She Stoops to Conquer* (1773), Oliver Goldsmith wrote of a rural journey, "it is a damned long, dark, boggy, dirty, dangerous way." Many roads essentially remained bridleways.

The weather very much affected both the roads and travellers. Thus, in *Tom Jones*, Mrs Waters and Ensign Northerton set off from Worcester "on foot; for which purpose the hardness of the frost was very seasonable" (IX,vii). As with the two lawyers who sought shelter in *Joseph Andrews*, "a violent shower of rain" could lead horsemen to seek shelter (II,iii). The multiplicity of factors that could affect travellers was seen when Dowling pressed Tom Jones:

> "to go no further that night; and backed his solicitations with many unanswerable arguments, such as, that it was almost dark, that the roads were very dirty, and that he would be able to travel much better by day-light." (XII,ix)

Jones insists on setting out for Coventry by night, only for the guide to get lost and rain to come on. If not walking, riding horseback rather than in a carriage was still normal, as at the end of *Joseph Andrews*:

> "The company were ranged in this manner: the two old people, with their two daughters, rode in the coach; the Squire, Mr Wilson, Joseph, Parson Adams, and the pedlar proceeded on horseback." (IV,xvi)

There was also the continued impact of social distinctions. Thus, in *Joseph Andrews*, there is a dispute over who can gain entry into a stagecoach:

> "Mrs Graveairs insisting, against the remonstrance of all the rest, that she would not admit a footman into the coach, for poor Joseph was too lame to mount a horse. A young lady who was, as it seems, an earl's grand-daughter, begged it, with almost tears in her eyes ... but all to no purpose. She [Miss Graveairs] said she would not demean herself to ride with a footman: that there were waggons on the road; that if the master of the coach desired it, she would pay for two places, but would suffer no such fellow to come in. 'Madam,' says Slipslop, 'I am sure no-one can refuse another coming into a stage-coach.' 'I don't know, madam,' says the lady; 'I am not much used to stage-coaches; I seldom travel

in them.' 'That may be madam,' replied Slipslop; 'very good people do; and some people's betters for aught I know.'" (II,v)

Those who could not afford to travel by carriage and who did not find wagons available, had to resort to a variety of means that focused on walking.[7] Fielding described one at length, possibly because some of his readers did not know of it, but also so as to make a moral point:

"To ride and tie—a method of travelling much used by persons who have but one horse between them, and is thus performed. The two travellers set out together, one on horseback, the other on foot: now as it generally happens that he on horseback outgoes him on foot, the custom is that when he arrives at the distance agreed on, he is to dismount, tie the horse to some gate, tree, post, or other thing, and then proceed on foot; when the other comes up to the horse, he unties him, mounts, and gallops on till, having passed by his fellow-traveller, he likewise arrives at the place of tying. And this is that method of travelling so much in use among our prudent ancestors, who knew that horses had mouths as well as legs, and that they could not use the latter without being at the expense of suffering the beasts themselves to use the former. This was the method in use in those days when, instead of a coach and six, a Member of Parliament's lady used to mount a pillion behind her husband, and a grave sergeant-at-law condescended to amble to Westminster on an easy pad with his clerk kicking his heels behind him."[8]

Tom Jones is not alone in being happy to walk:

"Mrs Waters was not of that delicate race of women who are obliged to the invention of vehicles for the capacity of removing

7   See, for example, John Wells to Lydia Grey, 29 July 1723, S.M. Hardy, "An Eighteenth-Century Love Affair," *Buckinghamshire Record Office. Annual Report and List of Accessions* (1994): 22.
8   *Joseph Andrews*, II,ii.

themselves from one place to another, and with whom consequently a coach is reckoned among the necessaries of life. Her
limbs were indeed full of strength and agility, and as her mind
was no less animated with spirit, she was perfectly able to keep
pace with her nimble lover." (IX,vii)

This provides a positive account of female activity.

From the mid-eighteenth century, the road system was further enhanced by a marked increase in the number of bridges, the most marked
for several centuries. Stone bridges replaced wooden ones and ferries, improving the load-bearing capacity and reliability of the system. Existing
bridges were widened, and new and wider bridges erected with large spans.
The importance of London and the availability of resources were shown
with the building of bridges there and nearby. Several replaced ferries.
Across the Thames, bridges were built in Fielding's lifetime at Putney
(1729), Westminster (1738–50), Walton (1750), and Hampton Court
(1753). Bridge building was not restricted to the London area, although
the second half of the century was far more important than the first, and
no new bridges were built across the Severn between 1540 and 1772. In
1754, Cambridge's Great Bridge was rebuilt in stone, as was the Old Bath
Bridge. The significance of bridges contributed to the prominence of nodal
points in the transport system, for example Upton on Severn in *Tom Jones*;
a novel in which alternative routes for the protagonists played a major role.

Although Fielding's characters stick to the roads, ferries remained important, for example over the Trent north of Newark, or the Witham between Lincoln and Boston. They also continued to be very significant across
estuaries, such as the Humber and the Tamar. This importance led to a continued focus on earlier routes, and thus transport nodes, should not be for-
gotten when new developments, such as turnpikes, are discussed. Ferries
across the Bristol Channel—from Sully near Cardiff to Uphill in Somerset,
and from Beachley to Aust—continued to move cattle and other products.
Many settlements were best approached by sea. Water—both the sea and
inland waters—had far more of an impact on people's lives than is the case
today. Many towns that now lack quays were ports. As late as the nineteenth
century, Wales was more accessible by coastal traffic than road: the Bishop
of St Davids went from Carmarthen to St Davids by boat.

Where bridges already existed, however, they were often poorly maintained, and alongside lists that suggest steady improvement, it is worth noting episodes that lead toward a different conclusion. Thus, the group of bridges over the watercourses of the River Otter at Fenny Bridges on the major route east of Exeter, were reported as in a poor state of repair to the Quarter Sessions in 1704. The parishioners of Gittisham were able to show that the parish was too poor to carry out the necessary repairs, and when the Sessions provided £15, requests from other parishes for their bridges led the court to rescind the money. A report was ordered, but none was made until 1711 when the court was told that a nearby landowner, Lady Kirkham, had conveyed nearby land in trust to provide funds for bridge repairs. However, the trustees declared that the profits from the land were insufficient and claimed to be responsible for the bridges in Feniton parish and not also in Gittisham, an interpretation that was challenged. The court took the charity into its hands, but it was not until 1723 that the trustees provided the accounts ordered in 1714. Deciding that they had money in hand that should have been used for bridge repairs, the magistrates ordered the trustees to pay it into court, but the trustees refused and the administration of the trust was not settled by the High Court of Chancery until 1750, the year in which Dr. Richard Pococke recorded being delayed several hours by the road flooding. A new brick arch bridge was not built at Fenny until 1769.[9]

This situation could be repeated elsewhere for bridges, roads, and other transport improvements, and throws light on Fielding's portrayal of local government, which includes his discussion of JPs. As with business and individual bankruptcies, such problems have to be recalled rather than the uncomplicated account of progress that is too often offered. The focus on action after 1750 is also instructive. Yet, allowing for deficiencies, it is still appropriate to stress change. Thus, within towns, access and routes were improved, although not with the purposefulness that was to characterize the Victorians. In order to improve access, Nottingham's last surviving medieval gate was pulled down in 1743.

Better links were used to transport both people and goods, and it became easier to move between major centres. Travel was made faster by the

9   D.L.B. Thomas, "Fenny Bridges in Fenton and Gittisham," *Devon Historian*, 50 (April 1995): 5–10.

cross-breeding of fast Arab horses, and made easier by the improvement of facilities. Old inns were rebuilt or extended, and new inns were built. Fielding responded to circumstances: the action in *Don Quixote in England* takes place in an inn serving both stage coaches and locals, and this, characteristically, obliged innkeepers to face in two directions as they pursued business.

Travel narratives offered much of a role for inns and innkeepers, and therefore for contrasts between them, inns providing both the causes of actions and the setting for action, and Fielding ran a full range in both, from brawls to conversation. Inns were particularly significant in his stories as providing opportunities to bring together people of different backgrounds and beliefs and thus for his mastery of a narrative of contingencies. The whole was policed by innkeepers some of whom were presented as rogues, or, at least, far from being considerate hosts. In *Tom Jones*, the landlady in Upton on Severn is shown as very concerned with her reputation:

> "At a house of exceedingly good repute, whither Irish ladies of strict virtue, and many northern lasses of the same predicament, were accustomed to resort in their way to Bath. The landlady therefore would by no means have admitted any conversation of a disreputable kind to pass under her roof. Indeed so foul and contagious are all such proceedings, that they contaminate the very innocent scenes where they are committed, and give the name of a bad house, or of a house of ill repute, to all those where they are suffered to be carried on." (IX,iii)

Explaining her harsh treatment of Mrs Waters, the landlady remarks:

> "where gentry come and spend their money, I am not willing that they should be scandalized by a set of poor shabby vermin, that wherever they go, leave more lice than money behind them; such folks never raise my compassion: for to be certain, it is foolish to have any for them, and if our justices did as they ought, they would be all whipt out of the kingdom." (IX,iv)

Inns provided horses for travellers, but, as Tom Jones discovered at Upton, these could be taken up by those who came first, obliging the others to wait or walk (XII,iii), and thus providing more space for the narrative. Separately, in *Jonathan Wild*, Fielding refers to travelling near Bath, at length arriving at: "some vile inn, where he finds no kind of entertainment nor conveniency for repose" (I,xiv). Inns were also important for highwaymen and other criminals, two of the former being seized while in bed at the Bear in Burwash, Sussex in 1749.[10]

Improvements on land did not prevent a major development in water transport. The difficulties and costs of road transport had for long helped to ensure that much was moved by river or sea, or both. Water routes were particularly favorable for the movement of heavy or bulky goods, for which road transport was inadequate and/or expensive. Thus, the Severn was the major north-south route for freight in the West Midlands, and was particularly important for the movement downriver of coal from the East Shropshire coalfield. Goods carried upstream included products from outside Britain, such as wine, Baltic timber, and, from further afield, tea, sugar, spices, tobacco and citrus fruit, most of which had been transhipped at Bristol (although Gloucester was also a transhipment point), including from elsewhere in Britain. Tributaries, such as the Warwickshire Avon for the Severn, further extended river systems, while also ensuring the need for bridges, ferries, or fords.

The river system had many deficiencies, and was weak in the areas with which Fielding was most familiar. Rivers did not always supply the necessary links, for example between Somerset and both Devon and Dorset, many were not navigable, transport was often only easy downstream, and many rivers were obstructed by mills and weirs. Moreover, the un- or poorly-controlled flow of water ensured that spring thaws and autumn floods could bring problems, by sending rivers into spate, while, in the summer, due to lower rainfall, they could be too shallow to use; this was a particular problem in the upper parts of rivers. Thus, in the North Riding of Yorkshire, the navigable rivers—the Tees, Ouse and Derwent—were all on its boundaries, while the Swale, Esk and Rye were too swift, shallow or liable to flood for navigation. As a result, lead from the western dales had to be moved overland to the Tees ports, an expensive process.

The response to such problems—the canalization of rivers and the

10 *Sussex Weekly Advertiser*, 19 February 1749.

construction of canals—represented a determined attempt to alter the environment and to make it operate for the benefit of man. As with the turnpikes, and again unlike elsewhere in Europe, private enterprise and finance were crucial. The result, notably with canals, was a costly and inflexible transport system, but it cut the cost of moving bulky goods, increased the comparative economic advantage of particular areas or interests, and was therefore actively supported.

Until the 1750s, when a period of canal construction began, the improvement of rivers took precedence, with peaks of activity in the late 1690s and in 1719–21. The improvement in the Aire and Calder navigation to Leeds and Halifax in 1699–1700 was a major step. The Yare was made navigable for quite large ships between Great Yarmouth and Norwich, helping Norfolk's grain exports and the movement of coal from North-East England to Norwich. Work on the Mersey to improve navigation to Manchester began in 1724, the Avon was fully navigable between Bath and Bristol by 1727, the Douglas between Wigan and the sea was opened to navigation in 1742, and improvements in the Weaver helped Cheshire's economy. Built by the Romans, the Fossdyke between Lincoln and the Trent was restored in 1740–44.

There were also setbacks. The Avon (a different Avon) was improved from 1675 to enable commercial navigation from Salisbury to the sea at Christchurch, but the link was not possible after 1715 and, by 1744, two unsuccessful attempts had been made to re-establish the route.[11] Aside from work on rivers themselves, for example dredging, towing paths were constructed along them to permit the replacement of human bow-haulers by horses.

Canal construction was more impressive than river improvement because it created completely new links. It was also expensive, as large numbers of "navigators" or navvies had to dig canals by hand. As a result, the construction of canals can be seen as a response to deficiencies in existing transport arrangements, to powerful new demands, and to the availability of considerable resources. As a result, landlocked counties found their relative position transformed, while the movement of bulk goods by new links

---

11   Alderbury and Whaddon Local History Research Group, *Alderbury and Whaddon* (Alderbury, 2000): 110.

created important new economic opportunities. The first canal in the South West in this period, opened east of St. Austell in about 1720, was designed to serve clay pits, although it was short-lived, ending in 1731 when the tunnel collapsed. Most canals, however, came after Fielding's death. Thus, after the failure of the short canal near St Austell in 1731, none was opened in the South West until 1794, although such points underrate interest in new links in the intervening period, and the sense of potentially profitable change that this interest reflected or created.

Coastal trade was important for a whole series of local and regional economies. It also grew with the developing economy. For example, Cornish, Irish and Anglesey copper was brought by sea to the works near Swansea, while Bristol received copper for smelting from Anglesey and Cornwall, china clay from Cornwall, and iron, coal and naval timber from the Forest of Dean. Ports were also developed for exporting raw materials. Slate was dispatched from Snowdonia via Bangor, Caerarvon, and, later, Port Penrhyn. Mineral owners developed ports in order to ship coal, for example, in Cumberland, the Curwens at Harrington and Workington, the Lowthers at Whitehaven, and the Senhouses at Maryport, which was founded in 1749. Milford Haven was developed to serve Pembrokeshire.

The widespread improvement in docks and harbor facilities benefited domestic as well as international trade. For example, an Act of Parliament of 1717 established the River Wear Commissioners in order to develop harbor facilities on the lower Wear. In place of a hazardous anchorage made difficult and dangerous by rocks, sandbanks, the passage of a difficult bar, and exposure to north-easterly gales, came buoying, dredging, lighting, pier-building and controls over the dumping of ballast. The result was a much-improved harbor entrance and navigable channel that permitted a major growth in trade with the Wear, and thus aided the development of Sunderland. This was an important example of what could be achieved, and also indicated the importance of a legislative framework. Another Act of 1749 enabled the new Port Commission of Lancaster to develop St. George's Quay (1750–55), and this was followed by a Custom House in 1764 and the New Quay in 1767. The Port Commission, in which slave traders played an active role, also promoted Lancaster's representation in commercial issues of national importance.

Nevertheless, there was scant improvement in the condition of marine transport and it still remained heavily dependent on the weather. The seasonal variation of insurance rates reflected the vulnerability of wind-powered wooden ships, which had not reached their mid-nineteenth century levels of design efficiency and seaworthiness, and, by modern standards, they lacked deep keels. Sea travel was very slow compared with what it was to become the following century. However, it was the cheapest method for the movement of goods, and the sea brought together regions such as south-western Scotland and eastern Ireland, whose road links to their own hinterlands were poor. Inland towns might be most accessible via their nearest ports rather than by long-distance overland routes.

The east coast, where Captain James Cook acquired his nautical skills, was an important route, especially for the shipment of coal from Newcastle to London and intermediate ports such as King's Lynn and Great Yarmouth, the ports for East Anglia. The average annual amount of coal shipped from the Tyne rose from just over 400,000 tons in the 1660s to well over 600,000 by 1730–31, and to nearly 800,000 tons in the 1750s. Seventy percent of this coal went to London in 1682, and King's Lynn and Great Yarmouth took half of the rest.

The Irish Sea also formed an economic zone held together by marine links based on major ports, such as Belfast, Bristol, Dublin, Lancaster, Liverpool, Holyhead, Milford Haven, Wexford and Whitehaven, as well as now-forgotten or tiny ports, such as Parkgate in Wirral, and Aberaevon. These links provided crucial supplies. Ireland's fuel shortage was met by coal from Cumbria and, to a lesser extent, Ayrshire and Lancashire.

Overall, changes in transport were limited during Fielding's lifetime, certainly compared to the following century, and the balance between land and coastal transport did not alter significantly. Nevertheless, as indicated, there was important change, and this affected government, society and the economy. The law enforcement with which Fielding was to be closely involved as a magistrate benefited from quicker, better and more predictable travel for individuals. The reduction in transport costs helped to increase and extend consumption and markets, whether local, county, regional or national. These benefits were fully understood and encouraged investment, with new and improved transport links requiring large amounts of capital. Britain was in the throes of the early stages of a transport revolution.

6. THE RURAL WORLD

> "He said he no more regarded a field of wheat when he was hunting than he did the highway; that he had injured several poor farmers by trampling their corn under his horses's heels, and if any of them begged him with the utmost submission to refrain his horsewhip was always ready to do them with justice. He said that he was greatest tyrant to the neighbours in every other instance, and would not suffer a farmer to keep a gun, though he might justify it by law, and in his own family so cruel a master that he never kept a servant a twelvemonth."
>
> *Joseph Andrews*, II,iii

Growing up in Somerset, Fielding was well aware of the nuances of rural life and was able to link them to issues of value and worth. Thus, in *Tom Jones*, he uses hunting to reflect on the nature of power, including in the broadest sense of cultural relativism:

> "Contiguous to Mr Allworthy's estate, was the manor of one of those gentlemen [Squire Western], who are called *preservers of the game*. This species of men, from the great severity with which they revenge the death of a hare, or a partridge, might be thought to cultivate the same superstition with the Bannians in India; many of whom, we are told, dedicate their whole lives to the preservation and protection of certain animals, was it not that our English Bannians, while they preserve them from other enemies, will most unmercifully slaughter whole horse-loads themselves, so that they stand clearly acquitted of any such heathenish superstition."

Although there was élite participation in popular recreations, such as bull-baiting, horse-racing, cock-fighting and fishing, hunting was restricted by the Game Laws. The Game Act of 1671 gave the exclusive right to hunt game to freeholders worth £100 a year, or leaseholders worth £150 a year. This substantial landed property qualification restricted the sport to wealthy landed gentry. There was supplementary legislation in 1707, 1771 and 1773. Such acts were supported by gamekeepers and mantraps, and both the legislation and its defence helped to make clear the nature of hierarchy and power in the rural community. Thomas Sill, Bailiff for Henry Ellison at Gateshead Park, reported on problems with poaching and the difficulty of getting any information from local people, although, in the fashion of the rural society described by Fielding, he claimed to have a good idea who they were.[1] Hunting was not only restricted by legislation. In addition, keeping horses was expensive. Furthermore, sports where there was little élite participation, such as dog-fighting, were less favorably viewed than cock-fighting where there was gentry sponsorship.

A very different ethos is offered by "the gamekeeper [Black George], a fellow of a loose kind of disposition" who does not have a strict notion of "meum and tuum": mine and yours (III,ii). Tom Jones gets into trouble not only for his specific breach of the Squire's rights but also because he is temperamentally more akin to Black George's values. Fielding shows them in practice as more honorable. Furthermore, the subsequent privations of the gamekeeper's large family "perishing with all the miseries of cold and hunger," lead Tom to sell his horse so as to provide them with funds (III,viii).

While very much associated with London, Fielding was also familiar with rural England. He lived there for part of his life, including formative years, and was engaged with its economy through his West Country background and legal practice. Moreover, although his plays were largely urban, which indeed was a pattern going back to Antiquity, rural England played a significant role in his novels. In part, this was a matter of establishing the stories of both *Joseph Andrews* and *Tom Jones*, but there was also an important counterpointing of country and city. *Joseph Andrews* begins in London, but a lot of the action while on the road is in the countryside, and the story

1   Sill to Ellison, 20 November 1741, Gateshead Public Library, Ellison papers A50 no. 1. For warrants for poaching in papers of George Bowes JP, Durham, CRO, Strathmore Papers, D/St/C1/3, 172.

ends in the country. *Tom Jones* reverses this: the first six books are in the country, the next six on the road, and the final six in London. Bar Upton-on-Severn in *Tom Jones*, small-town England largely missed out in this structure, which again went back to Antiquity. Moreover, the critical portrayal of London helped ensure that rural England had to be depicted in a certain fashion in order for a counterpointing to work.

The plays, however, were not always big-city in their setting. *Don Quixote in England* (1733) was set in "an inn in a country borough" and included reflections on rural society, Sancho noting of the "true English squire": "He eats with his hands, drinks with his hounds, and lies with his hounds; your true arrant English squire is but the first dog-boy in his house." This theme can be traced on, notably to Squire Western in *Tom Jones*.

Developments in rural England and, more particularly, the difficulties of agriculture in the second quarter of the century were not to the fore in the plots, but help explain the dynamics of the rural-urban relationship. The general fall in grain prices between 1670 and 1750 led to heavy rent arrears[2] and frequent requests for rent abatement. An item on London prices carried in the *York Courant* on 20 February 1739, itself a sign of the growing national integration of the economy, reported:

> "Last Monday [12th] … the best shipping wheat for £6 [a load] which is so low, that it is impossible farmers can live and pay their rents at such prices; and as wool likewise bears so low a price, unless some care be speedily taken, and the people eased of the present heavy taxes, most of the lands of the kingdom will be flung up into the landlords hands."

Yet, this integration ensured that when grain prices rose, as in 1740, there were riots against grain being moved and/or rising prices, notably that year in Staffordshire, Newcastle, Sunderland, Stockton and East Anglia.[3]

2   Gordon Mingay, "The agricultural depression, 1730–1750," *Economic History Review*, 2nd series, 8 (1955–56): 326.
3   Council meetings, 1, 8, 10 July, Andrew Stone report, 18 July 1740, NA. SP. 43/962.

The press spread news of such riots round the country,[4] just as it provided news of grain prices.[5] The penalties could be harsh, including transportation for seizing grain at Stockton.[6] There were also occasional food riots in the West Country into the 1750s. Other prices, such as hay, moreover, rose greatly.[7] There was also social tension, as in the dispute in 1743 over the enclosure of Simonburn Common by the Allgood family:

"thinking the land would bring in peace
Our Commons did enclose and fence
to my great loss and twenty more
And the starvation of the poor."[8]

In 1746, indictments at the Northumberland Quarter Sessions included for the destruction of hedges on the Earl of Shelburne's estate.[9] Pressures on the poor increased the significance of philanthropy, and charity by members of the élite was praised in *The History of Our Own Times*.[10]

Having shot up with dearth at the start of the decade and the concomitant hardship and rioting,[11] wheat, barley and oats prices all reached their lowest level in the period in 1743–47, after harvests improved thanks to the hot, dry summer of 1741, and exports being stopped by war. Prices fell by more than 15 percent relative to the prices of the 1720s. These falls hit the agricultural sector, but the crises of rural society was more widespread. Animal-rearing was badly hit by cattle plague in the 1740s and early

4   *Newcastle Journal*, 12 July 1740.
5   *New Weekly Miscellany*, 3 October 1741; *Cirencester Flying Post*, 19 October 1741.
6   *Newcastle Journal*, 9 August 1740.
7   Reverend Patrick St Clair to Ashe Windham, 26 June 1740, 3 April 1741, Norfolk, Norwich CRO, Ketton-Cremer Mss. WKC 6/24 Iap 401,401X.
8   Ashington, Northumberland CRO, Blackett of Matfen papers ZBL 267, 9, Allgood papers ZAL 83/29/3, and 31/1.
9   Ashington, Northumberland CRO, Quarter Sessions Order Book QSOB 8, page 148.
10 Lockwood, "New Facts and Writings": 480.
11 *Champion*, 15 May 1740; *Newcastle Journal*, 17, 31 May 1740; Council meetings, 29 May, 24 June, Andrew Stone to William, Earl of Harrington, 3 June 1740, NA. SP. 43/95.

1750s,[12] with complaints that the rural population, including many JPs, was unwilling to kill and bury infected cattle. Moreover, the "West-Country Clothier" responsible for a 1742 pamphlet complained that the cloth industry was in crisis,[13] a theme also seen in the *Champion* of 14 and 28 February 1740, and 31 October 1741. So also with the *West-Country Farmer, or, a fair Representation of the Decay of Trade, and Badness of the Times: in a Letter of Complaint from a Tenant in the Country, to his Landlord in London* (Taunton, 1731), which was a presentation not only of a squeezed rural economy but also of the problems created by London extravagance and its emulation elsewhere: "The Spinning-Turn is banished, to make room for the Tea-Table."[14] In the *Champion* of 1 December 1741, criticism of the employment of French clothing workers was focused on "our Frenchified" élite. A sense of farmers as hard-done by for the benefit of knavish cheats was expressed in the song "The Honest Freeholders Resolution."[15]

The problems of the rural economy contributed, alongside political dissidence, notably Jacobitism, in order to encourage rural lawlessness. Indeed, in 1723, the so-called Black Act introduced the death penalty for those who had:

> "in great numbers, armed with swords, firearms, and other offensive weapons, several of them with their faces blacked, or in disguised habits, unlawfully hunted in the forests belonging to his Majesty, and in the parks [lands] of divers [several] of his Majesty's subjects."

Price falls hit farmers but eased the burden on consumers. In 1741, one of the Under Secretaries wrote to a colleague, "by all the letters I receive

---

12 Cuthbert Ellison to Henry Ellison, 13 April 1749, Henry Thomas Carr to Henry Ellison, 17 January, 11 March 1749, 19 January, 9 March, 24 April 1750, Gateshead Public Library, Ellison papers A20, number 12, A30, numbers 20, 21, 25, 28, 29.

13 Anonymous, *An Impartial Review of the Opposition: and the Conduct of the Late Minister* (Dublin: George Faulkner, 1742): 4–6.

14 Anonymous, *West Country Farmer* (Taunton: William Norris, 1731): 30.

15 1733 song in Hobart papers in Norwich Record Office. See also Anonymous, *Considerations on the Present State of the Nation* (London, 1720): 3.

from the country, there is a good prospect of a plentiful harvest, and indeed provisions of all kinds begin to abate in their prices considerably; which is a good thing now we have so many mouths to feed."[16] In every area, there was the dependence on the part of farming on the weather.[17]

There were great regional variations in the nature and impact of the agricultural depression of the second quarter of the century. Faced with generally static demand for grain due to relatively stable population numbers, and with the difficulties of working their land, the open-field farmers on the heavy Midlands soils of Warwickshire, Leicestershire and Northamptonshire fared particularly badly. The rising relative profitability of animal-rearing encouraged the farmers of this region to switch to it. This process involved enclosure, which transformed land management and led to a rise in the production of meat and dairy products. Fielding was not writing about this area, and enclosure was not a topic for him.

Population growth from the 1740s, in turn, resulted in greater demand on the rural economy. Like its urban counterparts, its tensions, which included the rising price of food for landless laborers, led to a range of activity, some illegal, such as poaching, which was a longstanding issue in the rural economy, as in *Tom Jones*.

A different branch of the rural world was shown in Hogarth's election series produced to mark the bitterly contested, and very expensive, Oxfordshire election of 1754. An air of suppressed violence characterizes the opposition between Whigs and Tories in this series. So also with the extent to which electioneering erodes social distance. One of the Whig candidates is being manhandled by two drunks, the other embraced by a woman who may be trying to pick his pocket and who is being encouraged by a disreputable local man.

In the countryside, where the bulk of the population lived, rising demand for foodstuffs benefited landlords and tenant farmers, not the landless poor, for whom agricultural wages remained below fifteenth-century levels in real terms. The rural population was dominated by an economy of proprietary

16 Couraud to Edward Weston, 17 July 1741, NA. SP. 43/105.
17 Robert Banks to his father Joseph Banks II, 3 September 1740, J.W.F. Hill (ed.), *The Letters and Papers of the Banks Family of Revesby Abbey 1704–60* (Hereford, 1952): 191.

wealth: a system built around rent and poor remuneration for labor in the context of a markedly unequal distribution of land. Although foreign commentators could think them better-off than Continental peasants,[18] the rural poor were badly affected by enclosure, by the decline in some rural industries, especially textiles, and by any factor, short- or long-term, that pressed on real wages.[19] Demographic and economic change led both to a substantial increase in the numbers of those competing to work for wages, and to a related growth in those in precarious circumstances. A study of four Cheshire townships in the 1740s, while noting that each had its own distinct character, found a widespread movement from a society with a large number of small farms, occupied and run by their owners without the assistance of laborers (except living-in young people), toward one with fewer, but larger, farms often run by less well capitalized, rack-rented, tenants employing growing numbers of families of laborers. This situation may partly explain the rise of the poor rates and the growth of a rural proletariat.[20]

The tensions of rural England were overseen by the authorities of state and church, with the key element being the Justices of the Peace (JPs), most of whom were local gentry, although an increasing number were clergy. At the same time, the JPs were under pressure from local communities, some of whose members filled local offices such as constables and churchwardens. There was also oversight by the central government, and notably so through its major regional agents, the Lords Lieutenant, and also by means of altering the list of JPs. Although facing difficulties in cities, governmental oversight was strongest in towns, but contributed to a local rural situation that was far from static.[21]

As part of his general concern about the administration of the law, Fielding was frequently sceptical about the justice offered by JPs, let alone

18 Anonymous memorandum on state of Great Britain, 31 December 1728, Paris, AE. CP. Ang. 364 folio 398.

19 Keith Snell, *Annals of the Labouring Poor. Social Change and Agrarian England, 1660–1900* (Cambridge: Cambridge University Press, 1985).

20 Charles Forster, *Four Cheshire Townships in the Eighteenth Century* (Northwich: Arley Hall Press, 1992).

21 Joan Kent, "The Centre and the Localities: State Formation and Parish Government in England, circa 1640–1740," *Historical Journal*, 38 (1995): 363–404.

their understanding of the law. Thus, for Squire Western, who was already in trouble with the Court of King's Bench for some of his questionable decisions, there was a focus on the Game Laws:

> "In matters of high importance, particularly in cases relating to the game, the justice was not always attentive to these admonitions of his clerk: for, indeed, in executing the laws under that head, many justices of peace suppose they have a large discretionary power. By virtue of which, under the notion of searching for, and taking away engines for the destruction of the game, they often commit trespasses, and sometimes felony at their pleasure." (VII,ix)

Yet, for Fielding, alongside "the boisterous brutality of mere country squires,"[22] virtue was generally located in the rural sphere. So also with love: "in the air of Grosvenor-Square ... young ladies do learn a wonderful knack of rallying and playing with that passion, which is a mighty serious thing in woods and groves a hundred miles distant from London" (VI,iii).

Leaving the countryside and its values was therefore a cause of trouble for those who left permanently or temporarily. Thus, in *The Lottery* (II), Chloe takes up fine lodgings in Pall Mall from which comes out "such a procession of milliners, mantua-makers, dancing-masters, fiddlers, and the devil knows what." She subsequently tells her maid, "Mention not the country, I faint at the sound of it—there is more pleasure in the rattling of one hackney coach, then in all the music that romances tell us of singing birds and falling waters." This is followed by an air:

> "Farewel, ye hills and valleys;
> Farewel, ye verdant shades;
> I'll make more pleasant sallies,
> To plays and masquerades.
> With joy, for town I barter
> Those banks where flowers grow:
> What are roses to a garter?
> What lilies to a beau?"

22 *Tom Jones* IV,v.

Mr Stocks advises her to invest in the Charitable Corporation, "a method invented by some very wise men, by which the rich may be charitable to the poor, and be money in pocket by it" (II). In fact, it is a total fraud, and was to be revealed so in a major public scandal. Deception is the theme of this play, everyone passing themselves off in a self-aggrandizing fashion. In the conclusion, both the world and the theater are compared to lotteries, which emphasizes the central role of change, as well as the parallel between human reality and its acted presentation.

The contrast of rural and urban, and largely to the benefit of the former, was developed far more in the novels, where there was more space, more need for a narrative structure, and no obligation to show the contrast on stage. Thus, in *Tom Jones*, music was used to emphasize the character of Squire Western and his difference from his daughter, Sophia: she is rural, but less dominated by the related caricature of parochialism:

> "It was Mr Western's custom every afternoon, as soon as he was drunk, to hear his daughter play on the harpsichord, for he was a great lover of music, and perhaps had he lived in town, might have passed for a connoisseur; for he always excepted against the finest compositions of Mr. Handel. He never relished any music but what was light and airy; and indeed his most favourite tunes, were *Old Sir Simon the King, St George he was for England, Bobbing Joan*, and some others.
>
> His daughter, tho' she was a perfect mistress of music, and would never willingly have played any but Handel's, was so devoted to her father's pleasure, that she learnt all those tunes to oblige him." (IV,v)

The Squire's views were those of a caricature, as when he refuses to take his late wife to London "being well assured that all the husbands in London are cuckolds" (VII,iv). That was certainly the impression given by Fielding's plays, but was not one that was taken as essentially true other than for theatrical or rhetorical purposes. Yet, given the habitual harshness of the treatment of women in the world described by Fielding, it would have been reasonably deserved, Western telling Bilfil: "Women never give their consent, man, if they can help it, it is not the fashion. If I had stayed for her mother's consent, I might have been a bachelor to this day" (II,vi). This remark is one of many that makes Western totally deplorable.

London for the inhabitants of Somerset, which, alongside neighboring Dorset, was the part of rural England with which Fielding was most acquainted, appears an amazing alternative. Sophia Western's plans to run off there is supported by her servant Mrs Honour who "eagerly longed to see a place in which she fancied charms short only of those which a raptured saint imagines in heaven" (VII,viii). Mrs Western's maid treats her with disdain in part because, unlike Mrs Honour, she has been in London. Government commentators could indeed link the Opposition to rural ignorance, as with the *Daily Courant* of 5 July 1734:

> "It is undeniably evident, that their artifices prevailed chiefly in counties among the smaller freeholders; who having but little business in places of resort, where they might be rightly informed; and less time to canvas matters and search into the truth of facts, were too readily taken in the snares, which artful men had laid to entrap them with …; we ought rather to look for the sense of the nation from the conversable, valuable part of it; from those who understand its interests, and know the state of its affairs."

The metropolis, however, was not the sole counterpoint for the rural world, for there were also the contrasts within the latter. A classic one, that of order and disorder, ranged to include the natural and human environments, with marginals seeking the shelter and/or cover of the un-, or less, cultivated where, as a result, travellers were most at risk. There are also aesthetic contrasts, as in *Tom Jones* where the protagonist looks silently at a very steep hill before saying:

> "I wish I was at the top of this hill; it must certainly afford a most charming prospect especially by this light: for the solemn gloom which the moon casts on all objects, is beyond expression beautiful, especially to an imagination which is desirous of cultivating melancholy ideas." (VIII,x)

There are therefore hints in Fielding's work of what would later be termed the "Pre-Romantic," but, in practice, was also an echo of ideas about landscape found with some Classical authors. Typecasting writers indeed is generally a flawed process, and never more than with Fielding. To a degree, he certainly idealized the rural world, but he also presented tensions there.

7. WOMEN AND FAMILIES

"A domino soon accosted the lady … nor was it long before the he domino began to make very fervent love to the she … not indeed in the most romantic style. The lover seemed to consider his mistress as a mere woman of this world, and seemed rather to apply to her avarice and ambition than to her softer passions." Masquerade in *Amelia* (X,ii)

Fielding's plays and novels focused on human relations, and, most powerfully, on those between men and women, with the prospect and state of marriage a way to provide both narrative purpose and moral context.[1] Correspondence from the period fully vindicates his portrayal of marriage as a battleground of emotions and expectations. Four letters from 1723 found concealed under the floorboards of Westbury Manor Farm in Buckinghamshire, show the difficulties that John Wells encountered in wooing Lydia Guy. Son of a cleric, Wells did not gain appointment to clerical livings himself until 1725, which was when he married Lydia. Her mother opposed the match on the grounds that John was a rascal and that, due to poverty, any children would run about barefoot and barelegged. Cheered by the engagements he and Lydia had agreed, Wells was not prepared to marry until he could maintain Lydia "like a gentlewoman." Prefiguring the role of report and rumor in Fielding's works, John was "heartily sorry to hear what uneasinesses thou art forced to undergo upon account of some tattle tittle [sic]." He also wrote of his "longing arms" and of being "passionately" fond of Lydia.[2] This element needs to be remembered alongside all the discussion

---

1   Anaclara Castro-Santana, *Errors and Reconciliations: Marriage in the Plays and Novels of Henry Fielding* (Abingdon: Routledge, 2018).

2   S.M. Hardy, "An Eighteenth Century Love Affair," *Buckinghamshire Record Office, Annual Report and List of Accessions* (1994): 17–22.

of material circumstances and social groups: the raw emotions of individuals were at stake, an element Fielding possibly best presented in *Amelia*.

In addition. women faced environmental and demographic challenges similar to those of men, although women's biological role brought specific problems, while their treatment by society differed from those of men. Many women experienced gruelling labor and debilitating diseases identical to that of the men at their sides, but they were also in a society that awarded control and respect to men, and left little independent role for female merit or achievement.

The economy of the poor was such that employment was the essential condition for most women. The arduous nature of work, and the confining implications of family and social life, together defined the existence of the majority of women. Social and economic pressures helped drive women toward matrimony, and, whether married or not, also toward employment. Employment in agriculture, textiles and service was very important for women. Domestic service was the life of many in a society where household tasks were arduous and manual, and the contribution from machines minimal. Jobs such as the disposal of human excreta were unpleasant, although Fielding can understandably underplay this due to conventions about coverage, to his focus on the issue of emotional exploitation, and to the frequent use of servants as comic commentators — an English version of the Sancho seen in *Don Quixote in England*, for instance. Fielding put servants to the fore in his play *The Intriguing Chambermaid* (1733).

Many servants were immigrants from rural areas. Generally not members of collective groups, and lacking guilds, they were largely at the mercy of their employers. It was possible to gain promotion in the hierarchy of service, but, in general, domestic service was unskilled and not a career. Wages were poor, and pay was largely in kind, i.e. food and accommodation. This made life very hard for those who wished to marry and leave service, and married servants were relatively uncommon. For girls saving for a dowry, domestic service was far from easy, while they were often sexually vulnerable to their masters, which was a central theme in Richardson's *Pamela* (1740) and, with a male servant pursued by a female employer, Fielding's *Joseph Andrews* (1742), while, in *Tom Jones*, there is an ensign who "was son to the wife of a nobleman's butler," which means that the nobleman is really the father (VII,xii).

There was indeed appalling exploitation. The notorious Colonel Francis Charteris, the "Rape-Master General," was convicted in 1730 of raping Ann Bond, a servant, in 1729, after a trial in which much of his evidence was shown to be false, only to be pardoned by George II. Charteris is very possibly hinted at in *Rape Upon Rape*. Separately, the Chelsea bastardy examinations of claimants before a Justice of the Peace included:

> "the voluntary examination of Sarah Powell, single woman, taken 15 Oct. 1754, before Thomas Lediard esq. … Who upon oath saith that she is pregnant of a bastard child or children which was or were unlawfully begotten on her body by one James Silvester of the parish of Chelsea … with whom this examinant lived as a hired servant.… James Silvester in the month of June last, about two o'clock in the morning (being just after her mistress was gone to market) came to this examinant's bedside in his dwelling house and waked out of her sleep, and did take the advantage of getting to her in bed."[3]

Thinking that he was linked sexually with the servant Mrs Honour, Squire Western "having given Jones a hearty curse between jest and earnest, he bid him beat abroad, and not poach up the game in his warren" (V,iv).

The bastardy examinations were a way in which mothers could establish the parish and/or the putative father as responsible for the well-being of the child or children. The women who bore illegitimate children in Chelsea were mainly young, unmarried, migrant servants, while the majority of the fathers were male servants and household workers, and only about ten percent came from the middling sort, mostly employers or their friends. The arbitrary character of justice depicted by Fielding was certainly apparent in the variable nature of such examinations often with disregard for the requirements of the law linked to the personality of the presiding magistrate.

Service was not only domestic, although that was the area in which female labor was most important. Agricultural servants were also vital. Generally living with their employers, servants gave many nuclear families the

---

3   Tim Hitchcock and John Black (eds.), *Chelsea Settlement and Bastardy Examinations, 1733–1766* (London: London Records Society, 1999): 91.

quality, in part, of an extended family. The need for both men and women to go into service, and also the need for servants, varied geographically, seasonally and socially. The contradictory needs led to difficulties, such as dismissals, and migration in search of employment, producing a labor market filled with uncertainties, both constant and changeable. More generally, servants, laborers and women could not aspire to the "independence" so valued by political theorists.

Domestic manufacturing was another important source of employment for both married and unmarried women. Clothing was the biggest, though not the sole, form of employment in this area, and spinning-wheels featured frequently in household inventories. Domestic manufacture could be a crucial contribution to family income, especially in areas where agriculture was poor and in households that had limited agricultural resources. The women involved either formed part of a family in which all members worked in domestic manufacturing or supplemented family income derived from other activities. As the value added by their work and that of children was usually greater than that derived from comparable labor in the fields, women and children generally made a greater contribution to family incomes if they engaged in domestic manufacturing. However, their opportunities were limited by the restricted nature of market-oriented domestic manufacture in many areas.

The most striking aspect of the female contribution to the labor force was its variety. Although women had only a relatively small role in the churches, save with the Quakers, as Methodist preachers and in charitable works, and none in the armed forces (save the important informal role of camp-followers), they were found in most spheres of employment, including those involving arduous physical labor. Thus, women were employed as coal-heavers, taking coal to the surface, and as fish- and salt-carriers, and many worked in agriculture. Much of this employment reflected the expediency economy of the poor, and female opportunities were limited by the nature of the economy as well as the particular problems and restrictions that affected women. Literacy rates were lower for women, a result of the limited attention to their education, while women were generally given the worse-paid jobs: in many industries, such as glove-making, women were given the less skilled jobs or their employment was defined as less skilled and therefore was paid less. The majority of the poor were women, which reflected the impact of widowhood, spinsterhood, unwanted pregnancy, and differential job opportunities and rewards.

Not all women were confined to poor jobs. A tiny minority had interesting careers, some benefiting from the expansion of the commercial economy. In the theater from the late-seventeenth century, actresses took over female roles and this led to a more realistic presentation of women and of gender relationships, both becoming more relevant to women play-goers. However, women writers faced difficulties, in part possibly because they were objects of a cultural anxiety directed at "empowered" women outside their proper roles and at "feminized" men led by their emotions. Thus, Eliza Haywood, who offered frank discussions of female desire in *The City Jilt* (1726) and *The Mercenary Lover* (1726), could be seen as a threat. Haywood's *The Anti-Pamela; or, Feign'd Innocence Detected* (1742) was less successful than Samuel Richardson's *Pamela* possibly because it was more disturbing and less didactic, but also because Richardson was better able to capitalize on the market for fiction thanks to his role in the print trade.[4] *The Anti-Pamela* claimed, in the person of Syrena Tricksy, to show "the mischiefs that frequently arise from a too sudden admiration" and to be "published as a necessary caution to all young gentlemen."[5]

Fielding's sister, Sarah, an impressive writer under her own name, never achieved her brother's fame. Computer analysis suggests a measure of co-operation between the two, notably in the last chapter of *A Journey from this World to the Next* and in Leonora's letter to Horatio in *Joseph Andrews*, both of which were allegedly by female writers. The evidence, however, is less than conclusive.[6]

Women's reading troubled many (male) commentators and even biblical and devotional reading were not always considered safe for female

4   Catherine Ingrassia, *Authorship, Commerce and Gender in Early Eighteenth-Century England: A Culture of Paper Credit* (Cambridge: Cambridge University Press, 1998).
5   Kirsten Saxton and Rebecca Bocchicchio (eds), *The Passionate Fictions of Eliza Haywood: Essays on her life and work* (Lexington: University Press of Kentucky, 2000); Leslie Morrison, "Serialized Identities and the Novelistic Character in Eliza Haywood's *Fantomina* and *Anti-Pamela*," *Eighteenth-Century Fiction*, 30 (2017): 25–44.
6   John Burrows and A.J. Hassall, "*Anna Boleyn* and the Authenticity of Fielding's Feminine Narratives," *Eighteenth-Century Studies*, 21 (1988): 427–53.

readers. Imaginative literature was seen as potentially exacerbating the female imagination, and drama also raised the perils of sensibility. Reading works about science became increasingly acceptable for women, but, for many commentators with conservative inclinations, science, especially botany, remained problematic, although less so than fiction and philosophy, both of which led to informal reading bans for women and girls. Women were thought especially vulnerable to new philosophical ideas.

Despite, and, at times, because of, such strictures, many women enjoyed reading, and explicitly commented on its pleasurableness. Reading permitted critical engagement with issues of authority, although that could help accentuate the anxiety that reading could give rise to. Private libraries were generally seen as male domains, and were frequently identified with patriarchal power, and women, in contrast, favored subscription and circulating libraries, which were crucial to the "democratization" of literature. Female novel-reading possibly gave women writers a series of potent images to deal with their anxieties about, or even to fight for their rights to, literary authority,[7] a process possibly aided by the expansion of serial publication.

Women played only a minimal formal role in politics. Personal relations were such that, at the individual level, the influence of women over their husbands or lovers could be considerable, but public practice and theory were male-centered. There were no women in Parliament, although some played a part in the management of constituencies. Women also acted as political hostesses. A few individuals were prominent because of their royal position. This was particularly true of William III's wife and co-ruler Mary II (1689–94), Queen Anne (1702–14), and Queen Caroline, the wife of George II, who played an important role in Walpole's retention of power in 1727 and was formally proclaimed regent on four occasions when George visited Hanover. Several other women were also influential because of their spouses or connections. Sarah, Duchess of Marlborough, Groom of the Stole to Anne and an influential advisor to her, who became a Duchess, as wife to John, 1st Duke of Marlborough, was left the effective head of the family on his death. Intelligent and obsessed with politics, Sarah was committed to the Whig cause. Unusually for the period, Sarah was

---

7   Jacqueline Pearson, *Women's Reading in Britain, 1750–1835: A Dangerous Recreation* (Cambridge: Cambridge University Press, 1999).

allowed by her husband to manage her dowry and retain her salaries from court posts. She died the wealthiest woman in the country, but with the conviction that her sex had deprived her of political influence. Sarah was far from alone among women in making informed and perceptive remarks about politics.[8]

Yet, the use of the household as the basis for social organization led to an emphasis on the role of men, because they were regarded as heads when they were present. Furthermore, the legal rights of women were limited, not least their rights to own and dispose of property. Although the image of justice might be female, its formulators and executors were all male: there were no women judges, JPs or lawyers. Legal devices circumvented common law rules of inheritance that would otherwise have left more land inherited or held by women. Although it could be broken, the Strict Settlement was a device that encouraged patrilineal inheritance and primogeniture. It preserved estates by limiting charges for subordinate members of the family; although that did not imply that landowners lacked concern for the members of their nuclear families nor that children and wives were casually or indifferently treated. Thanks in part to the Strict Settlement, land that had been added to a great estate was likely to remain with it.[9]

It would be mistaken to minimise the role of women. For a start, it would be wrong to imagine that they lacked political consciousness. Indeed, women frequently participated in riots, and, although this may have reflected the crucial role that women played in the purchasing of foodstuffs and the sense that women would receive more lenient punishments than men, it also reflected political awareness. If this primarily took the form of hostile responses to changes in the price or availability of foodstuffs that were believed to be unfair, that was the politics of the poor in general.

---

8   Lady Cecilia Finch to Lord Malton, 4 November 1740, Sheffield Public Library, Wentworth Woodhouse Mss. M3, 81; Frances Harris, *A Passion for Government: The Life of Sarah, Duchess of Marlborough* (Oxford: Oxford University Press, 1991); Elaine Chalus, *Elite Women in English Political Life c.1754–1790* (Oxford: Oxford University Press, 2005).

9   Susan Staves, *Married Women's Separate Property in England, 1660–1833* (Cambridge, Massachusetts: Harvard University Press, 1990); Eileen Spring, *Law, Land, and Family. Aristocratic Inheritance in England, 1300 to 1800* (Chapel Hill, 1994).

Women were also of great importance as consumers, and the need to satisfy the demands and fashions of women in the middling orders comprised a major aspect of the consumer revolution. Fielding concentrated for satirical reasons on this need from élite, or would-be élite, women, but it was more widespread in practice.

Women as well as men as consumers were also at stake in the depiction of women in plays and novels. In both, aside from their independence, their desire and desirability were facets that gave them considerable agency, and thus provided issues for male characters and commentators. A fear of being cuckolded was the spur for Sir Simon Raffler in Fielding's *The Universal Gallant* (1734): "Why always running to that church where the youngest parson is?" In turn, Lady Raffler exclaims: "Must I give a husband an account of all my words and actions? Must I satisfy his groundless fears? I am no such poor-spirited wretch."

There were also instances of women playing a role as officials. Thomas Coram's Foundling Hospital in London placed the children it accepted with rural wet-nurses for the first five years of their lives. The system depended on the voluntary inspectors who identified suitable wet-nurses and then supervised them. The majority of the women inspectors had the necessary skills of literacy, numeracy, and administrative ability. The role of those women in the 1750s was striking. There was no precedent for the management and supervisory activities undertaken by women for the Foundling Hospital; neither had there been any previous recognition by a national organization of women working for it on equal terms with men.[10]

Poverty was an experience to which women were particularly vulnerable. This was different from that of men for a number of reasons, particularly the responsibility of women, both unmarried and married, for children. It was the women who were commonly held responsible for the birth of illegitimate children, while married men had a greater propensity than their spouses to abandon their families.

Seduced girls often had recourse to prostitution. The absence of an effective social welfare system, and the low wages paid to most women, ensured that prostitution, either full- or part-time, was the fate of many. The

---

10   Gillian Clark (ed.), *Correspondence of the Foundling Hospital Inspectors in Berkshire 1757–68* (Reading: Berkshire Record Office, 1994).

diseased prostitute, her hair and teeth lost in often fatal mercury treatments, was a victim of the socio-economic and cultural circumstances of the period. More generally, an economic system that bore down hard on most of the population, was linked to a social system in which the position of women, whether relatively fortunate or unfortunate, was generally worse than that of men. The breakdown of marriage and desertion by the spouse frequently featured in accounts of women vagrants.

It has been argued that male attitudes to women softened and became more sympathetic to female feelings, as a crucial part of the process by which more "polite" and genteel social norms were encouraged. The good manners implied by the term "gentleman" were thus redefined. An aspiration toward politeness was certainly a keystone of various public discourses. It fostered particular ends of moral improvement, Christian purpose, and social order, and was also a means and goal of the quest for reputation that was so important to social positioning. As the diplomat and MP Edward Finch, the son of an Earl, observed in 1740: "guarantys like young beauties with small blemishes in their character have now a fine opportunity to reestablish their reputation."[11]

Fielding repeatedly addressed these issues which, indeed, were an established part of the comic repertoire but given renewed focus by the emphasis on politeness. *Don Quixote in England* (1733), a comedy centred on the Don, also dealt at length with the claimants to the hand of Dorothea; a theme moreover seen in Fielding's farce *An Old Man taught Wisdom: or, The Virgin Unmasked* (1734). In the former, Fairlove lives up to his name, while Squire Badger's grossness thwarts the avarice of Dorothea's father, Sir Thomas Loveland, and Quixote offers the slapstick of ridiculous misunderstanding. A drunk Badger tries to kiss Dorothea not knowing she is his wife to be. Loveland intercedes: "This is my daughter," Badger replying first that he does not care whose daughter she is, and, secondly, that he is making addresses to her. Loveland then rallies: "Let me beseech you, Sir, to attack her in no rude manner." Badger's response is to say to Dorothea, "Let us send for a parson." Far from passive, Dorothea tells Badger that she hates and despises him, whereupon Badger

11 Finch to Robert Trevor, 4 November 1740, Aylesbury, Buckinghamshire CRO, Trevor Mss, volume 24.

departs; while Quixote presses Loveland on the need to marry for love as well as money:

> "Money is a thing well worth considering in these affairs; but parents always regard it too much, and lovers too little. No match can be happy, which love and fortune do not conspire to make so. The greatest addition of either ill supplies the entire absence of the other."

This was a sane response to the world as it is.

In *The Wedding-Day*, Charlotte complained of being "in the greatest distress in the world; for I am this day to be married to a man I despise" (III,viii). In turn, Millamour adds that he has to contend with a husband of his lover: "A damn'd legal tyrant, who can ravish a woman with the law on his side? All my hope and comfort lie in his age: and yet it vexes me, that my blooming fruit must be mumbled by an old rascal who hath no teeth to come at the kernel" (IV,ix), a clear sexual image. The play ends with a call for virtue.

As well as comedy, propriety and the developing cult of "politeness" were also used to help manage the symbolic authority of fathers and husbands. In their periodicals, the *Tatler* and the *Spectator*, Joseph Addison and Richard Steele had fostered and glamorised heterosexual sociability, thereby raising the prestige of those spheres which offered women a place beside their men and also the profile of the gentleman who could do a woman honor.[12] Fielding referred in *Tom Jones* "to the savage authority too often exercised by husbands and fathers, over the young and lovely of the other sex," adding a context which helped make Tom a hero who delivers an "imprisoned nymph." Indeed, bringing the light of modern reason and reflection to play, he adds:

> "I have often suspected that those very enchanters with which romance everywhere abounds, were in reality no other than the husbands of those days; and matrimony itself was perhaps the

12 Amanda Vickery, *The Gentleman's Daughter. Women's Lives in Georgian England* (New Haven, Connecticut: Yale University Press, 1998).

enchanted castle in which the nymphs were said to be confined." (XI,viii)

Later in the chapter, the tyranny of husbands is to the fore alongside the "unjust powers given by" marriage "to man" over women. Seduction by other men is a continuation of this situation. It is understood by many of the seducers Fielding presents as callous, if not cruel. Thus, Colonel James longs, like a "glutton," for Amelia:

"And sure this image of the lamb is not improperly adduced on this occasion; for what was the colonel's desire but to lead this poor lamb, as it were, to the slaughter, in order to purchase a feast of a few days by her final destruction, and to tear away from the arms of one where she was sure of being fondled and caressed all the days of her life." (VIII,viii)

Politeness in part could mean female passivity, but Fielding takes pains not always to go in that direction, although Amelia is somewhat passive. In his plays, however, the women are far from passive. Furthermore, in *Tom Jones*, the influence behind Squire Western's attempt to direct Sophia comes from his sister:

"By hatred you mean no more than dislike, which is no sufficient objection against your marrying of him. I have known many couples, who have entirely disliked each other, lead very comfortable, genteel lives.... The contrary is such out-of-fashion romantic nonsense.... A young woman of your age, and unmarried, to talk of inclinations!... You ought to have a greater regard for the honour of your family, than for your own person...." (VII,iii)

Given the horror of being sent to prison, it is instructive that the aunt is referred to twice as delivering Sophia into the arms of the gaoler, her prospective husband.

Descriptions of the culture of the period in terms of a "polite society" are insufficient. In fact, the culture was highly ambiguous. "Politeness" was part of the century's self-image, but a coarseness of utterance and indeed of thought was equally part of its image,[13] while evangelicals disliked "politeness" as leading to hypocrisy. Frequent campaigns against swearing, lewdness and profanity, and the insistence on sabbath observance, were of a piece with sexually explicit and forthright language, and prurience. The stress on sobriety and restraint can be seen as a comment on drinking levels. There was much matter-of-fact acceptance of prostitution, casual sex and venereal disease. On 2 February 1702, George Hilton (1674–1725), a Westmorland Catholic gentleman, recorded in his journal, "went to George Dix at the Sandside with Geo Wilson broke 3 of my resolutions, eat flesh, lay with a woman up till 2 o'clock in the morning."[14] An explicit sexuality was hardly remote from a society in which large quantities of self-education sex literature was printed, while prostitution was also very important. Many men may not have "internalised" the politeness that they apparently valued in public, which possibly presaged the public morality and private vice of the Victorians.

Venereal disease is brought home to readers with the comment in *Joseph Andrews* about "that part of the face where, in some men of pleasure, the natural and artificial noses are conjoined" (III,ix) and the description of Blear-eyed Moll in *Amelia* is starker (I,iii). The harshness of men was captured in *Tom Jones* with Molly's first seducer:

> "This Will Barnes was a country gallant, and had acquired as many trophies of this kind as any ensign or attorney's clerk in the kingdom. He had, indeed, reduced several women to a state of utter profligacy, had broke the hearts of some, and had the honour of occasioning the violent death of one poor girl, who had either drowned herself, or, what was rather more probable, had been drowned by him." (V,vi)

Barnes is scarcely alone in vileness. So also with Captain Hebbers, the

---

13 Kate Davison, "Occasional Politeness and Gentlemen's Laughter in Eighteenth Century England," *Historical Journal*, 57 (2014): 921–45.

14 Anne Hillman (ed.), *The Rake's Diary. The Journal of George Hilton* (Barrow: Curven Archive Texts, 1994).

bigamist in *Amelia*. Compared to Barnes, Tom Jones is a far better individual, not least because

> "the meanness of her [Molly's] condition did not represent her misery as of little consequence in his eyes, nor did it appear to justify, or even to palliate, his guilt, in bringing that misery upon her." (V,iii)

This background provides a way to consider Jones' moral "improvement" during the course of the novel.

The harsh impact of those like Barnes on women was presented in the case of the maid Mrs Honour, Mrs being a title applied to all women of a certain age whatever their marital status:

> "Tom was a handsome young fellow; and for that species of men Mrs Honour had some regard; but this was perfectly indiscriminate: for having been crossed in the love which she bore a certain nobleman's footman, who had basely deserted her after a promise of marriage, she had so securely kept together the broken remains of her heart, that no man had ever since been able to possess himself of any single fragment. She viewed all handsome men with that equal regard and benevolence, which a sober and virtuous mind bears to all the good. She might, indeed, be called a lover of men ... never carrying this preference so far to cause any perturbation in the philosophical serenity of her temper." (V,iv)

When Tom meets an army contingent, it is headed by a talented lieutenant who had been denied preferment for nearly forty years because his wife would not have sex with the colonel, Fielding capturing the hypocrisy of society by describing this as her "indiscretion" (VII,xii). When Jonathan Wild passes for: "a Gentleman of great fortune in the Funds. Women and Quality treated him with great familiarity, young ladies began to spread their charms for him" (I,vi), again a clearly sexual image.

Yet, public morality was important. If politeness was a public act, it tells us something about changes in society that such a show was thought necessary, although politeness itself could be seen as far from virtuous. Engine, a maid in Edward Ravenscroft's play *The London Cuckolds* (1681), explained:

> "This employment was formerly named bawding and pimping, but our age is more civilised and our language much refined. It is now called doing a friend a favour. Whore is now prettily called mistress. Pimp; friend. Cuckold-maker; gallant. Thus the terms being civilised the thing itself becomes more acceptable. What clowns they were in former ages."

There was also a class dimension. Politeness and gentility, or at least a discourse of their value, can be seen as "middle-class" virtues, and the discourse as characteristic of "middle-class" writers. Eighteenth-century public restraint can thus be presented as evidence of the emergence of values which defined the "middle class," and of their greater importance within society. There were also ideas of moral and social superiority implicit in the attitudes to vulgarities and the vulgar. This was an approach Fielding challenged with his emphasis on true charity between individuals and at all levels.

In his pages, there is also a contrast between the different practices that met with disapproval. Rape was castigated, and heroes acted bravely to stop it, notably so with *Joseph Andrews*. For Fielding, as for contemporaries, there was also the need to define responses to seduction, adultery, and pre-marital sex. All could meet with disapproval, but its character varied, as did responses, and these were major themes in Fielding's plays and novels.

Sexual activity outside marriage was condemned by the Church, and the proportion of illegitimate babies in baptism registers was low, although there could be "bastardy-prone subcultures." Very differently to illegitimate babies, there pre-nuptial pregnancy, which in part reflected the practice of plighting faith and troth in a formal agreement before witnesses, but without a calling of banns and marriage in church until later (or never). Thus, in Shipton-under-Wychwood, about 1.5 percent of babies were illegitimate, while about 10 percent of brides were pregnant at marriage.[15] In *Tom Jones*, a serjeant says of Mrs Waters, the wife of an army officer: "Some folks used

---

15   Tom McQuay, "Base-born in Shipton," *Wychwoods History*, 8 (1993): 21–26.

indeed to doubt whether they were lawfully married in a church or no," although she was also "very well acquainted" with "Ensign Northerton … as long as there is enough for him [Captain Waters] too, what does it signify?" (IX,vi).

Promises of marriage, however, could prove simply a means of seduction. The cynical Jonathan Wild is ironically described as being "so remarkably attached to decency, that he never offered any violence to a young lady without the most earnest promises of that kind, being, he said, a ceremonial due to their modesty, and which was so easily performed, that the omission could arise from nothing but the mere wantonness of brutality" (I,ix).

Alongside such pressure, the idea of equality between men and women was increasingly approved of, although the general notion of equality was one of respect for separate functions and development, and the definition of the distinctive nature of the ideal female condition did not entail equality by modern standards. This was true of sexuality. Women, but not men, were expected to be virgins when they married, and chaste thereafter. When in 1779, Parliament discussed the "more effectual discouragement of adultery," it was of course an all-male body, and Fielding is interesting in part because he problematizes the issues involved in female sexuality albeit within the constraints of what could be discussed.

The extent to which there were changing meanings and styles for masculinity and femininity is unclear. By European standards, British social conventions were not rigid, and the Comte de Gisors was surprised, when visiting England in the 1750s, to find young women of quality paying visits alone without loss of reputation, only for the French ambassador to tell him that it was the English habit to trust daughters to do this. In 1763, a later French ambassador was described as "not yet been long enough in England to learn that the ladies here had much rather trudge up and down the stairs by themselves, than be escorted by anybody."[16]

The fluidity of gender practices and the complexity of gender relations, indeed, undermines efforts to present a simple pattern of "separate spheres" in which the public world had a male complexion while women were largely

16 Journal du voyage de M. le Cte de Gisors, AE. Mémoires et Documents, Ang. 1 folios 25–6; George Villiers, 4th Earl of Jersey, to Lady Spencer, 2 December 1763, BL. Althorp papers, volume F101.

restricted to private and domestic spheres and roles. The public profile of privileged women was important and advancing, with these women employers and consumers, who made their devotions and took their pleasures in public. Furthermore, within the domestic sphere, women were also able to assert independence and self-control, for example in music-making, and this assertiveness was not contained by that sphere. Novelists could take this on board, showing female agency as significant, not least in the handling of money.[17]

Nevertheless, by modern standards, the situation was far from benign, and the emotional position of many women was difficult. The portrayal of marriage to a callous husband as imprisonment, one offered in Thomas Southerne's play *The Wives' Excuse* (1691), was not fanciful: Mrs Friendall, the perceptive and wronged protagonist, declared "But I am married. Only pity me," and later spoke of the "hard condition of a woman's fate." This was not fanciful. In 1712, Mary Pierrepont, was intended by her father, Evelyn, Marquess of Dorchester, for Clotworthy Skeffington, heir to Viscount Massereene. She felt she "had rather give my hand to the flames than to him," whom she described as Hell, but Dorchester, "the disposer of me," refused to accept her decision for a single life. To escape, Mary eloped.[18] This could have been a plot for a novel. In *Tom Jones*, Blifil's desire for Sophia is presented as sadistic, a form of hunting/eating of "this human ortolan," and her aversion to him raises his desire: "as it added triumph to lust; nay, he had some further views, from obtaining the absolute possession of her person, which we detest too much to mention" (VII,vi), which was presumably a reference to sodomy.

In Fielding's plays, the restraint on wives frequently came from their husband's fears of being cuckolded, fears that emerge as very justified. Thus, in *The Letter-Writers* (1731), which in some respects is a farce centered on who gets locked in closets, Mrs Softly complains, "Where's the difference, whether one be lock'd up in one's grave or one's own house?... That man

---

17 Fielding receives due attention in Mona Scheuermann's *Her Bread To Earn: Women, Money, and Society from Defoe to Austen* (Lexington, Kentucky: University Press of Kentucky, 1993).

18 Isobel Grundy, *Lady Mary Wortley Montagu: Comet of the Enlightenment* (Oxford: Oxford University Press, 1999): 46–8.

must be a most unreasonable creature, who expects a woman to abstain from pleasures for his sake." (II,xii–xiii). Mr Wisdom assures his wife that in his arms she is free from fear of hurt, only for her to add "or hope of pleasure." Jack Commons goes to London:

> "to take one swing in the charming plains of iniquity; for I am come to take my leave of this delicious lewd place, of all the rakes and whores of my acquaintance,—to spend one happy month in the joys of wine and women, and then sneak down into the country, and go into orders."

When a laughing Captain Rakel asks, "Hast thou the impudence to pretend to a call?," Commons replying, "Ay, Sir; the usual call; I have the promise of a good living," argues that he at least has sincerity before saying "Pox of preaching." Far from applauding the marriage vows, Commons sees the marriage of an old man and a young woman as a cause of cuckolding (I,ii).

In Fielding's *The Universal Gallant: or, the Different Husbands* (1734), Lady Raffler reveals that she married Sir Simon not out of fondness, but "out of obedience to my father, he thought it a proper match." When her niece, Clarinda, asks whether a wife ought not to be fond of her husband once married, the reply is: "No, she ought to have friendship and esteem, but no fondness, it is a nauseous word, and I detest it. A woman must have vile inclinations, before she can bring herself to think of it." Clarinda declares for romantic love, whereupon her aunt seeks to banish her from London: "Nor will I ever live in the house with a woman, that can own herself capable of being fond of a fellow," a Lady Bracknell remark.

In marked contrast, romance is frequently depicted, and notably so in *Tom Jones*. Yet, in *Jonathan Wild*, Mrs Heartfree is presented, in the topsy-turvy world of false values, as "a mean-spirited, poor, domestic, low-bred animal, who confined herself mostly to the care of her family, placed her happiness in her husband and her children; followed no expensive fashions or diversions...." (I,iv). Such honor and family life are shown as repeatedly under attack, as with the drugged drink that leads, after her visit to the masquerade at Ranelagh, to the seduction of Mrs Bennet in *Amelia*, a seduction in which she contracts venereal disease that she then passes on to her husband (Vii,vii–viii).

Prior to 1750, the majority of actions for divorce brought in the London Consistory Court were brought by women against their husbands for cruelty, not for a lack of love or compatibility. Expectations about what women should obtain from marriage rose and, after mid-century, the notion of romantic marriage and domestic harmony came to prevail among the prosperous, and the practice of divorce for incompatibility arose. However, the custody of any children was generally invested in the father and divorced women commonly lost touch with them.

Gender issues were also possibly affected by what appears to have been a greater assertiveness on the part of homosexuals or a stronger consciousness of their role, although this is a controversial field in which, due to the character of the relatively scanty sources, the analysis is necessarily impressionistic. Certainly in London, there was the development about 1700 of a more overt homosexual subculture whose participants, known as "mollies," were regarded as distinctive in clothes, mannerisms and speech, although coming from across society. It has been suggested that this subculture affected attitudes to relations with women as most men sought to prove that they were not bisexuals or with homosexual tendencies but, instead, were clearly heterosexual. This has been seen as leading to a greater acceptability of prostitution, and thus to a different attitude to women and to marriage. Both such claims are difficult to substantiate, and it is not always clear whether relevant documents, such as court records, note more than the keeping of mere records.

There could be a harsh treatment of homosexuals, but also ambivalence. The *Norwich Mercury* of 20 March 1742 contained an account from London of one sentenced to stand in the pillory at the Royal Exchange in London who was "most severely used by the populace; particularly by an Amazon, who tore off the greatest part of his cloaths, whipp'd him with rods for a long while, and diverted the spectators with some other extraordinary discipline." In the prison in *Amelia*:

> "Blear-eyed Moll, and several of her companions, having got possession of a man who was committed for certain odious unmanlike practices, not fit to be named, were giving him various kinds of discipline, and would probably have put an end to him, had he not been rescued out of their hands by authority." (I,iv)

Much presumably depended on the local oversight that Fielding mentions in *Tom Jones* when discussing how Jenny Jones was fingered as the mother of a bastard. In the small Norfolk town of Diss, Robèrt Carlton, a local tailor, was hanged in 1742 for sodomy with his young lodger and for poisoning Mary Fuller, the latter's fiancée. Carlton had been "notoriously guilty of that abominable sin," but it was the death through poisoning that led to action being taken. In accordance with the very public nature of punishment, the execution was followed by the body being put in chains, hung from a tall gibbet, and left for the crows to eat.[19]

Families

It has been argued that the period witnessed the rise of a pattern of family life that placed more weight on the wishes of individual members, and in which affection, rather than discipline, and emotion rather than patriarchalism, bonded families together. This shift has in part been explained by a rise in the life expectancy of both children and women allegedly encouraging a greater degree of emotional commitment. In turn, these changes have been linked to a range of developments, including the growth of distinctive clothes and the toy industry for children, the literary cult of the sentimental family, and new pedagogic fashions that placed greater weight on the individuality of children and the need to socialize them without treating them as embodiments of original sin.

Discussion of these suggestions is complicated as the overwhelming majority of the population did not keep journals or leave correspondence. Furthermore, it is unclear how to assess, let alone measure, affection and changes in it, for it is important not to mistake changes in style, such as modes of address within the family, for changes in substance. Certainly, if marital experiences and expectations were related to economic circumstances, then it is difficult to see much reason for major change. Work on sixteenth- and seventeenth-century family life, moreover, has revealed that many of the suppositions supporting the ideas of subsequent periods as different were actually false. The idea that romantic love as a reason for, and

19 David Stoker, "The Tailor of Diss: Sodomy and Murder in a Norfolk Market Town," *Factotum*, 31 (April 1990): 18–21.

aspect of, marriage was an eighteenth-century invention, whether a consequence of modernization or not, has been rejected, as has the notion that children were brutally treated until then as a matter of course. Rather, it seems clear that in this period, as earlier, parents of all social and religious groups loved their children, and in much of the literary work it is nephews and nieces that are the butt of authority, for example Fielding's *The Universal Gallant*. In bringing children up, parents saw the need to teach them basic skills, but regarded this, correctly, as for the benefit of children as much as parents. This was particularly the case when children were to follow the occupations of their parents, a tendency that was made desirable by the nature of inheritance practices and by the limited opportunities faced by most people. Furthermore, the absence of state-provided education placed a burden of responsibility on parents and, failing them, other relatives. The same was also true of health, housing and social welfare. The deaths of children were a cause of grief, as when the thirteen-year old elder son of John Collier died of smallpox,[20] and also the deaths of his infant brothers for Edward Gibbon.

The degree to which the individual family lived together in close proximity led to a need for co-operation and mutual tolerance that necessarily affected the nature of patriarchal authority. Thus, the inculcation of deference, discipline and piety by authoritarian parents was not incompatible with affection, and the tension between individual preferences and family pressures was scarcely new. The basic unit of society was the nuclear family: a married couple and their generally non-adult children, although nuclear families were also nodes within closely connected networks of kin. Other than those headed by widows or widowers, there were few one-parent families.

The structure of individual families was not constant. Birth, ageing and death ensured that the life-cycle of families was continually changing. It was necessary to adapt in order to survive periods when the family altered to include dependants, young children and invalid adults. As these groups consumed without working, they posed a challenge to the economy of individual families, just as they created formidable problems for society in general, and for many other functions, such as education.

20   Richard Saville (ed.), *The letters of John Collier of Hastings, 1731–1746* (Lewes: Sussex Record Society, 2016).

The responsibilities of social welfare were left to families, communities, and private and religious charity, but communal and charitable support focused on families rather than single adults. There was also the question of safety: an isolated individual could be in a vulnerable position.

Families coped with the problem of feeding children by defining childhood so that it included employment as far as possible and in so far as it was necessary. Many agricultural and industrial tasks, such as tending livestock, were undertaken by children, and were part of a family economy. Publicists approved of child labor, arguing that it prevented idleness and begging, educated children to useful employment, and, through a system of domestic apprenticeship, accustomed them to work. Most families needed no such encouragement; their problem was to find employment for the children and to feed them until they were able to work.

The employment of as many family members as possible was essential not only to its well-being, but also to its very existence as a unit. Parents who could not cope left children to foundling hospitals, which were established from mid-century. Unmarried mothers sometimes turned to abortion and infanticide, but both were treated as crimes and the former was hazardous to health. The women, often very young, who were punished as a result of these desperate acts, suffered from the limited and primitive nature of contraceptive practices; as did those exhausted from frequent childbirth. Unwanted children were not only an economic liability, but also, when born to unmarried mothers, the source of often severe social disadvantages, moral condemnation and legal penalties. In a society where women sought marriage as a source of precarious stability, the marital prospects of unmarried mothers were low, with the significant exception of widows with children of a first marriage, especially if they possessed some property. As a consequence, unmarried mothers frequently became prostitutes, or were treated as such.

Fielding, significantly, was careful to attribute flaws more widely, as with Betty, an inn chambermaid in *Joseph Andrews*:

"An ensign of foot was the first person who made an impression on her heart: he did indeed raise a flame in her which required the care of a surgeon to cool. While she burnt for him, several others burnt for her. Officers of the army, young gentlemen travelling the western circuit, inoffensive squires, and some of graver character, were set afire by her charms."

Thus responsibility for venereal disease was spread widely. However, in society as a whole, there were double standards for men and women, both in terms of the treatment easily available and with reference to social attitudes. This was more generally true of the position of women, one that Fielding handled with considerable sensitivity.

8. SOCIETY

> "She ran with all speed to hasten the surgeon, who was more than half dressed, apprehending that the coach had been over-turned and some gentleman or lady hurt. As soon as the wench had informed him at his window that it was a poor foot-pas-senger who had been stripped of all he had, and almost mur-dered, he chid her for disturbing him so early, slipped off his clothes again, and very quietly returned to bed and to sleep."
> *Joseph Andrews*, I,xii

"In Society alone, Men can mutually enjoy the Benefit of that vast variety of talents with which they are severally endowed." Fielding's argument, in *A Plan of the University Register Office* (1751), was amplified by an approach in which charity was seen as a crucial social good:

> "If any society ever hath been, or ever can be so regulated, that no talent in any of its members which is capable of contributing to the general good should lie idle and unemployed, nor any of the wants of its members which are capable of relief should re-main unrelieved, that society might be said to have attained its utmost perfection."

This was at once a deeply Christian vision and an understanding of meritocracy. The morality of human interdependence in society was a key element of Fielding's journalism and fiction, but society was much more the setting and topic of the storyteller, and the source of fun for playwright and novelist. Fielding's plays and novels, indeed, not only captured links between social ranks, but also relied on them for context, plot and character. In doing so, the plays and novels reproduced the closeness of social milieux, notably those of households including servants, but also of inns and other places of work. This closeness meant a constant jostling and arbitration of relations, one in which convention and employment vied with individuality and friendship. In part, this jostling was expressed in tensions over space, both that of access, notably intimate access, to the senior figures in the household and workplace, and that within a building. Fielding captures this with the placing of people in his plays and novels, notably in terms of compartments that may serve to be secret, and the entire issue of overhearing which was a frequent engine in the plots. Favor, patronage, friendship and companionship were intermingled in access.[1]

Moreover, Fielding saw these factors as found across society, and part of his skill was to display the universality of what he discussed. As he observed in *Tom Jones*:

> "The great are deceived, if they imagine they have appropriated ambition and vanity to themselves. These noble qualities flourish as notably in a country church, and church-yard, as in the drawing-room, or in the closet. Schemes have indeed been laid in the vestry, which would hardly disgrace the conclave. Here is a ministry, and here is an opposition. Here are plots and circumventions, parties and factions, equal to those which are to be found in courts.
>
> Nor are the women here less practised in the highest feminine arts than their fair superiors in quality and fortune. Here are prudes and coquettes. Here are dressing and ogling, falsehood, envy, malice, scandal; in short, everything which is common to the most splendid assembly, or politest circle." (IV,vii)

The basic social framework throughout Fielding's life was clear. Social relationships and attitudes reflected both a clear cultural inheritance and the prevalent economic and technological environment. The Judaeo-Christian inheritance, clearly enunciated in the laws and teachings of the churches, decreed monogamy, prohibited marriage between close kin, stipulated procreation as a purpose of matrimony while condemning it outside,

---

1   Amanda Vickery, *Behind Closed Doors: At Home in Georgian England* (New Haven, Connecticut: Yale University Press, 2009).

denounced abortion, infanticide, homosexuality and bestiality, made divorce very difficult, enforced care of children, venerated age, and ordered respect for authority, religious and secular, legal and law-enforcing. Other issues that would be more regulated today, such as spousal abuse and rape within marriage, however, were largely ignored.

The economy was technologically unsophisticated, and much of it was agrarian. Economic productivity was low, there was little substitute for manual labor, and the value accrued through most labor was limited. The situation could be very harsh, the *Daily Post* of 30 January 1731 carrying a Durham report of four days earlier:

"Great numbers of the wives and children of the coal-pit men are begging about in all the neighbouring towns, by reason their husbands have not their usual work, and are forced to draw coals about for small pay, to prevent starving. We are in great dread of them, for their numbers are very large, and no body will trust them, which makes them desperate. It is said some of the coal-owners have agreed not to deliver more coals till Feb. 20, which will not only make them dear, but ruin hundreds more of working men."

Most of the population neither controlled nor produced much wealth, and the principal means of acquisition was by inheritance, which repeatedly was to the fore in Fielding's work, in terms of both context and narrative. The dominant ethos was patriarchal, hierarchical, conservative, religious, and male-dominated; although each element involved both tensions and a variety of means of expression.

The Orders of Society

To consider the orders of society is not to move to the static and the structural, because social patterns were more the product of dynamic relationships, especially the daily reiteration of status and the continuous interaction between, and within, groups, than of any fixed caste-like rigidity that left no role for social mobility. Nevertheless, the weight of the past was very apparent in the distribution of wealth, status and power. The influences that affected this distribution were similar to those of the previous century, and there was little change in the methods by which the social position of individuals was determined or could be altered; yet there was also considerable diversity of views about the nature of hierarchy in the eighteenth century. Furthermore, certainly in comparison with the following two centuries, the rate of social change was low, although that does not imply that there was little social change. In addition, although it cannot be measured with precision, social mobility was greater than on the Continent, including France, which was generally considered the antithesis of England.

Status and power were linked to wealth, although not identical with it. This was generally regarded as appropriate, although there was a degree of tension over the definition of wealth, and, in particular, the legitimacy of money as opposed to landed wealth was a matter of controversy. Great wealth could be made in London: Sir Francis Child, a goldsmith banker who came from a clothier family in Devizes, became Lord Mayor in 1698 and an MP, and was able to purchase the Osterley estate in 1713. His grandson, Francis, was able to spend £17,700 buying Upton as a country seat for hunting in 1757, as well as £1,200 on his election as an MP in 1761.

Many saw such wealth as disruptive. Jonathan Swift offering a classic critique of financial activity and speculation, in his strongly anti-governmental pamphlet *The Conduct of the Allies* (1711), in which he referred to:

> "undertakers and projectors of loans and funds. These, finding that the gentlemen of estates were not willing to come into their measures, fell upon those new schemes of raising money, in order to create a moneyed interest, that might in time vie with the landed, and of which they hoped to be at the head."[2]

Similarly, in his pamphlet *Thoughts on the late Transactions respecting Falkland's Islands* (1771), Samuel Johnson referred to "the sudden glories of paymasters and agents, contractors and commissaries, whose equipages shine like meteors and whose palaces rise like exhalations."[3] This criticism looked back on a rich tradition, and underlay Squire Western's resentment of his sister, but was also in many respects outdated in a society where such

2   H. Davis et al (eds.), *The Prose Works of Jonathan Swift* (16 vols., Oxford, 1939–68): VI, 10.

3   Samuel Johnson, *Political Writings*, ed. Donald Greene (New Haven, Connecticut: Yale University Press, 1977): 371.

activity and wealth were of growing importance. Legislation was passed to ensure that only those with a certain amount of land could become Justices of the Peace (JPs), Acts of 1732 and 1744 decreeing that JPs possess freehold or copyhold land with an annual value of £100 above all encumbrances, or other land of a yearly value of £300, but this legislation reflected the failure to maintain such criteria.

The relationship between capital and income greatly favored the former, and the ability to create income without capital was limited. Nevertheless, opportunities for self-advancement from imperial expansion or industrialization existed, although such newly-minted wealth was still uncommon, sufficiently so for there to be grave suspicion about the wealth produced by "nabobs" who had made their money in India. However, these men began to make their mark. James Dawkins from Jamaica, a slave plantation economy, purchased the Oxfordshire estate of Over Norton in 1726, spent at least £1000 standing, unsuccessfully, as MP for Oxford in 1734, and was elected unopposed for New Woodstock on the interest of Sarah, Duchess of Marlborough, sitting for the constituency from 1734 until 1747.

Such new wealth offended many, especially if it were derived from India and enabled "nabobs" to engage in upward social mobility. Fielding as a playwright, was one of those who expressed disquiet; but the care taken by the newly-affluent to buy status helped ensure that they did not undermine notions of social hierarchy, although, in doing so, they did emphasize a financial and transactional character to this hierarchy. The very existence of social distinctions was seen as obvious, and as arising from the natural inequality of talents and energies. Although the Christian message was inherently egalitarian, egalitarianism found favor with few writers on social topics, and social control by the élite was a fact, not an issue, in politics. These assumptions pervaded society, encouraging ranking by birth and snobbery, and affecting the choice of friends and marriage partners — the son of a Wakefield linen-draper, John Potter, Archbishop of Canterbury from 1737 to 1747, disinherited his eldest son for marrying a domestic servant. The desire to preserve family status and wealth in part lay behind Hardwicke's Marriage Act of 1753, which increased the power of parents, by outlawing clandestine marriages in England. Social differentiation, or at least an awareness of distinctions of rank and status, may, indeed, have become more acute in response to social mobility and to the pressures of commodification that commercialism created. Heredity and stability were regarded as intertwined.

At the same time, there was a sense that status should be a matter of conduct not lineage. This stress on civil, rather than social, virtue was particularly evident in urban settings, and contributed to the importance of conduct judged polite. Fielding focuses on this contrast in *Amelia* when Harrison intercedes with an aristocratic friend in favor of preferment in the army for Booth, only to find that he is pressed in return to support Colonel Trompington in an election. Harrison replies that he, instead, must support his old friend, the aptly-named Fairfield:

> "… the one being a neighbouring gentleman of a very large estate, a very sober and sensible man, of known probity and attachment to the true interest of his country; the other is a mere stranger, a boy, a soldier of fortune, and, as far as I can discern from the little conversation I have had with him, of a very shallow capacity, and no education."

In return, the lord resolves not to support Booth and rejects Harrison's emphasis on merit as a "mere Utopia." Harrison warns that if Britain is as corrupt as the lord argues, British liberty will collapse as that of Rome did, while Britain would also become contemptible to its neighbors (XI,ii). Fielding is excellent in showing the nature, frequently harsh and arbitrary, of dependence in a variety of contexts, including army patronage in *Amelia*.

Fielding's remedy is that of a broad-based government of probity and national interest, the remedy advanced by the political group to which he was aligned and later by George III (r. 1760–1820). Fielding argues for a first minister who would:

> "please to consider the true interest of his country, and that only in great and national points…. Will engage his country in neither alliances nor quarrels but where it is really interested … raise no money but what is wanted nor employ any civil or military officers but what are useful … he shall either have no

opposition to baffle, or he shall baffle it by a fair appeal to his conduct. Such a minister may, in the language of the law, put himself on his country." (XI,ii)

Social differentiation was reflected in a range of activities and spheres, such as sport and dress. The seating arrangements in churches and the treatment of the dying and their corpses also reflected social status and differences, as did the provision of health, with wealthy subscribers recommending poor dependants for admittance to infirmaries. Those with pretensions to social status wore wigs, while the poor wore their own hair. Patterns and practices of crime and punishment, credit and debt also reflected social distinctions. The trial, hanging and dissection of Laurence, 4th Earl Ferrers in 1760 for the shooting dead of his steward, John Johnson, was cited as evidence of the universality of the law, but it was rare for members of the élite to suffer execution or imprisonment unless involved in treason, as with those active as Jacobites. Ferrers was particularly difficult and possibly mentally unwell. A heavy drinker and womanizer, his wife, Mary, had obtained a separation from him for cruelty in 1758.

Aristocratic debtors escaped the imprisonment for debt that was a frequent consequence of the role of credit in society, a theme very much seen with Fielding who frequently handled credit and debt in varied meanings, as did Johnson with an essay in the *Idler* on imprisonment for debt. The impact of social differences was also clear at the hiring fairs where employers scrutinized the men and women who sought employment, and in housing where there was increasing social segregation.

Religion offered a degree of contrast, because the churches remained a career open to the talent of the humbly born, as was demonstrated by several bishops of the Church of England. Nevertheless, connections and patronage generally worked to the benefit of the well-born. Clergy from a gentry background received a disproportionately high share of the good livings.

Fielding had no time for these views in Church or State. In *The Intriguing Chambermaid* (1733), the criticism is firm. Lord Pride observes: "Damn me, there's a pleasure in ruining these little mechanical rascals, when they presume to rival the extravagant expenses of us men of quality," and Lord Puff replies: "That ever such plebeian scoundrels who are obliged to pay their debts, should presume to engage with us men of quality, who are not!" Both like the opera. In *Amelia*, the villainous peer, a noted seducer, dies of venereal disease "by which he was at last become so rotten that he stunk above-ground" (XII,ix).

Educational access and provision also reflected social power and assumptions. Because so many children worked, their access to formal education was limited, even if it was available free. Attendance at school was far lower in summer, the highpoint of agricultural work, than in winter. Education in England had to be paid for by the pupil's family, which was generally the case in grammar schools, or by a benefactor, dead or alive. There were many "petty" charity schools, often known as "dame schools" although most were small. However, some took more children in return for payment. Some grammar schools were also free. Education was not supported by taxation, central or local, but could be helped by charities, although these, as Fielding noted, could display the faults of the rest of society. Thus, George Trend, the son of a single mother in Covent Garden, with the implication that she is a prostitute, goes to a charity-school between the ages of 8 and 14:

> "without making any great proficiency in learning. Indeed it is not very probable he should; for the master, who, in preference to a very learned and proper man was chosen by a party into this school, the salary of which was upwards of a hundred pounds a year, had himself never travelled through the Latin Grammar, and was, in truth, a most consummate blockhead." (XI,iii)

In *Joseph Andrews*, the squire who makes false promises, encourages poor people to have pretensions for betterment that he then thwarts, and he drives home the message by noting that the education he has encouraged has made those in question unsuited for the position in which they will have to remain: "your other son, who can hardly write his name, will do more at ploughing and sowing, and is in a better condition" (II,xvii). This is a very public display of the problems facing social mobility.

Educational provision, nevertheless, expanded over the century. The Society for the Promotion of Christian Knowledge (SPCK), established in

1698, encouraged the foundation of charity schools; and 63 schools were founded in Lincolnshire alone in the first quarter of the eighteenth century. As part of the widespread philanthropy of the period, in which charity, paternalism, dependence and deference were all linked, local worthies and the clergy played a major role in the foundation of schools. Land was donated as sites, money provided for construction, and rentals were used to guarantee the salary of the schoolmaster (most schools had just one). In 1720, the SPCK offered premiums to towns to set up charity schools and workhouses. In 1723, the Workhouse Test Act was sponsored by the SPCK, so that the worship and schooling offered was Anglican, and Anglicans had priority in adopting workhouse boys and girls as apprentices. The London workhouse school was established in 1698 and the *Account of the Workhouse* (1725) indicated that schools were an integral part of workhouses. Besides charity schools, probably the biggest number of ordinary (not those from an affluent background) children were educated in workhouses.

However, the situation remained very uneven. The vicar of the Yorkshire rural parish of Brandesburton reported to a diocesan visitation in 1764:

> "Mrs Frances Barker of York left the interest of £100 to this parish towards the maintenance of a schoolmaster, who should teach poor children to read and write *gratis*, till a convenient purchase could be made with the principal. This sum is now laid out in lands at Sutton. Besides these poor children there are about 30 taught from this and the neighbouring villages in reading, writing and arithmetic by Thomas Ryley. Care is taken to instruct them in the Christian religion according to the Church of England and to bring them to church,"

but, for every child who acquired some education, there were many others who received none. In particular, girls and the rural population had fewer educational opportunities than boys and town-dwellers. In 1706–12, there was schooling only in about sixty parishes in Buckinghamshire and a surprising number of the county's parishes had no regular charitable endowments. The replies to the episcopal visitations of Surrey in 1725 and 1788 reveal that, by explicit statement or implication, more than a third of the parishes responding had no educational provision.[4] In 1778, only about 5 percent of the children in Cheshire attended school.

More generally, literacy levels reflected the degree of economic freedom enjoyed by families and their occupational aspirations. Contrasting with higher literacy rates in the towns, illiteracy in the rural parishes of Dorset in 1750–1800 appears to have been an average of 56 percent, with Worcestershire as 50 percent and Cambridgeshire and Huntingdonshire as 58 percent. Male was higher than female literacy. In a sample of communities in West Sussex, the general literacy level for brides was between 15 and 25 percent lower than that of the grooms in the second half of the century. In the Sussex towns surveyed, "totally illiterate marriages" seldom formed more than one fifth to one quarter of the total in any decade, but literacy levels were lower in the rural parishes. The highest rates of illiteracy were to be found amongst those without land, trade or skill,[5] which provides Fielding with the opportunity for a joke in *Tom Jones*:

> "Three countrymen were pursuing a Wiltshire thief through Brentford. The simplest of them seeing the Wiltshire House written under a sign, advised his companions to enter it, for there most probably they would find their countryman. The second, who was wiser, laughed at this simplicity; but the third, who was wiser still, answered, 'Let us go in, however, for he may think we should not suspect him of going amongst his own countrymen.' They accordingly went in and searched the house, and by that means missed overtaking the thief, who was, at that time, but a little way before them; and who, as they all knew, but had never once reflected, could not read." (VI,iii)

---

4   J. Broad (ed.), *Buckinghamshire Dissent and Parish Life, 1669–1712* (Aylesbury, 1993); W.R. Ward (ed.), *Parson and Parish in Eighteenth-Century Surrey. Replies to Bishops Visitations* (Guildford, 1994); C. Annesley and P. Hoskin (eds.), *Archbishop Drummond's Visitation Returns, 1764. I. Yorkshire A-G* (York, 1997).

5   G.J. Davies, "Literacy in Dorset, 1750–1800," *Notes and Queries for Somerset and Dorset*, 33 (1991): 21–28; D.E. Smith, "Eighteenth Century Literacy Levels in West Sussex," *Sussex Archaeological Collections*, 128 (1990): 177–86.

The poor who were educated were offered less than the children of the better-off. Reading, writing and arithmetic were provided in the "dame schools," where inexpensive teaching was offered by widows and elderly women, although sometimes only the reading was available for free. The Classical teaching in the grammar schools was not available in most other schools, but nor also in many was free mathematics. There was a general assumption in charity schools that the pupils should be provided with a vocational education, which meant teaching employable skills as well as the morality that contributed to good conduct. These requirements were laid out in the terms of the bequests under which charity schools operated. Thus, spinning, weaving and knitting were taught to girls. Morality was provided by discipline and by the teaching of the fundamentals: the Catechism, the Creed, the Commandments and the Lord's Prayer.

Education and printing exacerbated social divisions, including the limitations on the poor expressing themselves, and gave an extra dimension to the flow of orders, ideas and models down the social hierarchy. Printing and books emphasized the dependence of the poor and illiterate on the literate.

The social élite favored boarding schools for boys, Eton and Westminster being the most popular. Pupils who wished could move on, without difficulty to Oxford and Cambridge, the only universities in England and Wales, but most of the élite did not bother to take degrees, while some had the right to a degree based on status. Degrees, instead, were generally taken by students who hoped to follow a career as clergymen in the Church of England, although many dioceses relied on clergy from the grammar schools. Girls from this background received far less formal education: most were educated at home, and universities were not an option. Fielding did not tackle university life in his fiction.

Medical attention, poor relief, philanthropy and moral admonition can be considered as forms of control, the Reformation of Manners movement being seen as an attempt to police popular pastimes and mores, as well as vice and impiety. This movement, which flourished from the early 1690s to the late 1730s, with later revivals in the late 1750s and late 1780s, led to the foundation of Reformation of Manners societies that raised funds to bring prosecutions for offences such as breach of the Sabbath regulations and streetwalking (prostitution).

However, the idioms and symbols of reformation provided a rhetorical theme that could be used by a variety of groups, and to varying ends, and in different contexts. Far from being restricted to, or in some respects defining, a middle-class consciousness, the theme of the Reformation of Manners had a longer tradition, back to Puritanism and beyond, that was not exclusive to the middling sort, as well as a powerful religious dimension that looked forward to reforming and evangelical movements at the close of the century.[6] Similarly, although philanthropy reflected social norms and hierarchies, its ideology was more complex than any focus on social ordering and policing might suggest.

"Politeness" was more socially exclusive as a concept than the Reformation of Manners, with its religious dimension; although it would be misleading wholly to separate the two. "Politeness" had a public and a private side, but both were characterized by an emphasis on an orderly sociability that was defined in a socially excluding way that in part contributed to a sense of shared values and identity among the middling orders. Furthermore, two social institutions that developed in this period, the male club and the mixed assembly, have been seen as spheres for an important redefinition of social consciousness that led toward the idea of a middle-class culture.[7] The political equivalent to "politeness" was the distinction between appropriate and dangerous activism:

> "I believe there is no sober man doubts but there is a difference, a very material one, between liberty and licentiousness, and that the latter ought to be restrained … the ruin of free governments has been owing to nothing more than to the degenerating of liberty into licentiousness."[8]

---

6   Joanna Innes, "Politics and Morals: The Reformation of Manners Movement in Later Eighteenth-Century England," in Eckhart Hellmuth (ed.), *The Transformation of Political Culture. England and Germany in the Late Eighteenth Century* (Oxford: Oxford University Press, 1990): 57–118.

7   John Smail, *The Origins of Middle-Class Culture: Halifax, Yorkshire, 1660–1780* (Ithaca, New York: Cornell University Press, 1994).

8   Anonymous, *The Treaty of Seville and the measures that have been taken for the four last years, impartially considered* (London, 1730): 30.

The distinction generally had a social dimension: those who pursued liberty were "polite," while the "mob," to use a contemporary term, were licentious. It would be mistaken, however, to assume that individuals and groups should be seen in terms of a simple and single position. As with social positions, actions and aspirations, those focused on culture reflected multiple interests, possibilities, commitments and anxieties. Analysis in terms of social groups is only helpful if their openness to many and varied cultural pressures is understood, as for example with gardening.

The Social Élite

> "Fortune segregates from the vulgar, those magnanimous heroes, the descendants of ancient Britons, Saxons, or Danes, whose ancestors being born in better days, by sundry kinds of merit, have entailed riches and honour on their posterity."
> *Tom Jones,* XIII,ii

Power and wealth were concentrated. The hierarchical nature of society and of the political system, the predominantly agrarian nature of the economy, the generally slow rate of change in social and economic affairs, the unwillingness of governments composed of the social élite to challenge fundamentally the interests of their social group, or to govern without their co-operation, and the inegalitarian assumptions of the period, all combined to ensure that the concentration of power and wealth remained reasonably constant. The old order was under scant threat from popular protest. Furthermore, despite Tory claims to the contrary, the Whigs were a party made up primarily of great landowners, not of bankers, Dissenters, and the urban interest. The recipients of Walpole's letters seeking political support in Parliament were members of this élite.[9]

Across Europe, those who enjoyed power and wealth tended to be nobles by birth or creation. In Britain, however, the ownership of a significant amount of land was not an indication of noble rank; although those of the

9   For example, Walpole to Sir James Grant, 5 November 1741, Edinburgh, National Archives of Scotland, GD 248/48/1; Walpole to Sir John Ramsden, 5 November 1741, Carlisle, Cumbria CRO, D/Pen 234.

(non-aristocratic/noble) gentry who did have much land, such as Allworthy in *Tom Jones*, enjoyed considerable social status as in effect untitled nobility. Indeed, the major landowners are the most appropriate point of comparison with the continental nobilities, although special privileges (and relatively few of these) were attached only to the peerage. Creations helped to keep the number of peerages up: there were 43 peerage creations by William II, 42 by Anne, 66 by George I, and 74 by George II. The size of the peerage was far smaller than on the Continent, but gradations in the peerage remained vital to individual and family status and aspirations. Yet, although affected by political divisions, the relatively small size of the English aristocracy helped make it far more socially coherent than Continental counterparts. Nevertheless, in *Love in Several Masques*, Sir Positive Trap bases his "fantastic pride" on the "antiquity of his family" (I,i), and argues that "an old English baronet is above a lord. A title of yesterday! An innovation!" (III,vii).

There was an active land market, and status could be readily acquired, but marriage and inheritance remained the crucial means by which land was transferred. The pattern of estates also did not alter. Thus in Oxfordshire, the estate of the Dukes of Marlborough could be created only because there was a royal manor (Woodstock) to use, which affected the nearby parliamentary constituency of New Woodstock. The Dukes became the hereditary high stewards, claimed the right to appoint the Recorder of the borough (an influential figure at election time), and selected many of the MPs, including family members, such as the heir, the Marquess of Blandford, in 1727, and John Spencer, grandson of John, the 1st Duke, in 1732, 1734, 1741 and 1744. Such individuals regarded membership of the Commons as a right. They were also the prime catches in the marriage market and thus best able to preserve and increase their wealth by marriage. A remodelling of the local power hierarchy comparable to that produced by the creation of the Churchill estate was unusual in England where there were no changes similar to those suffered by Catholic landowners in Ireland. The Tories suffered political proscription under George I and George II, but were not driven from the land.

The small size and relatively closed nature of the peerage helps to make aristocratic/noble rank too narrow a specification for any analysis of the élite. The inheritance of noble status only by the eldest son was an important limiting factor, although other children were not released destitute into the world. All adult, male, non-Catholic English peers were members of the House of Lords.

The absence of serious tension between nobility and gentry was an important feature of English society, and a crucial aspect of stability. They generally formed a homogeneous group that intermarried and socialized together. There were moments of tension, for example in 1745 when there was some opposition to the idea that peers receive government pay for the volunteer regiments they were raising and officering. However, an absence of contention was far more common. The divide between peers and gentry did not usually operate as a political fault line and did not usually reflect political or social divisions.

Central and local government were dominated by the élite of nobility and gentry, although not in the major towns. Command of local government reflected supremacy in local society. Justices of the Peace (JPs) were the crucial figures in local government and law and order, and the Bench of JPs was dominated by the gentry. As commissioners, they were also the crucial figures in the local allocation of the Land Tax. This was paid by all landowners, including peers, unlike the considerable tax immunities of much of the Continental nobility.

The dominance of both center and localities by the landed élite was expressed by enclosure Acts which facilitated a reorganization of the rural landscape to enhance the control and profits of landlords. As freehold tenure became more important, the sense of place and identity of others who worked on the land was challenged, which was taken furthest where settlements were moved. Enclosure Acts were part of a more general process by which in parts of the country landholding was concentrated in fewer hands.

As Fielding showed, the gentry could use their resources and the law to harm other groups. Sir George Downing (c. 1685–1749), a Suffolk landowner and MP for the rotten borough (parliamentary seat with very few voters) of Dunwich, employed his wealth to buy most of Dunwich, took a lease of the right to collect taxes for the Crown there, had the freemen who could not pay imprisoned for debt, and allowed his tenants to fall into debt while requiring them to enter into bonds on the understanding that they would support him at elections. If most of the landed élite preferred to gain their ends in a more consensual fashion and managed their localities in a more reciprocal manner, they, nevertheless, did so in their interests. Consensualism and reciprocity were only taken so far, and many were excluded from its scope.

Fielding was accurate in *Tom Jones* in detecting difference within the élite. Thus, when considering a partner for Sophia Western, her Tory father who draws on Joseph Addison's portrayal of the Fox-hunter in *The Freeholder*, reflects:

> "… there be larger estates in the kingdom, but not in this county, and I had rather bate something, than marry my daughter among strangers and foreigners. Besides most o' such great estates be in the hands of the lords, and I hate the very name of *them-mun*." (VI,ii)

The character of Western-like figures was captured by John Tucker in referring to a fellow Dorset MP, George Richards, in 1743:

> "It is a most unaccountable thing that country gentlemen will spend great sums of money even to the hurting their fortunes to get into Parliament and when they are chosen think every moment of their time lost and thrown away that is passed in the attendance on that duty. Mr Richards and near 50 others of that stamp have not vouchsafed to make their appearance this session by which the court have made the formidable figure you have seen in the late divisions. It is hoped however they will be driven up at the meeting after the adjournment from the shame and regret some of them must feel already by the reproaches of their own consciences as well as the stinging reflections of their friends and acquaintance by letters etc."[10]

Although he took care to emphasize that some were honorable, Fielding could be very hostile to the social élite, as in *Joseph Andrews*:

> "By those high people, therefore, whom I have described, I mean a set of wretches, who, while they are a disgrace to their ancestors, whose honours and fortunes they inherit (or perhaps

10   John to Richard Tucker, 17 December 1743, Bod. Ms Don.c.106 folio 121.

a greater to their mother, for such degeneracy is scarce credible), have the insolence to treat those with disregard who are at least equal to the founders of their own splendour. It is, I fancy, impossible to conceive a spectacle more worthy of our indignation than that of a fellow who is not only a blot in the escutcheon of a great family but a scandal to the human species, maintaining a supercilious behaviour to men who are an honour to their nature and a disgrace to their fortune." (III,i)

Soon after in the novel, he provides an instance of the cruelty of the élite when the pet dog of Wilson's eldest daughter is killed by the son of the lord of the manor, who is described as an absolute tyrant who tramples down hedges and rides over crops and gardens (III,iv). This cruelty is taken further, when the local hunt indulge the master's hobby of hunting men (III,vi). A confusion between humans and animals, one that emphasizes Fielding's more general concern with what is natural is also seen with Squire Western in *Tom Jones*. While liking Tom:

"He did indeed consider a parity of fortune and circumstances, to be physically as necessary an ingredient in marriage, as difference of sexes, or any other essential; and had no more apprehension of his daughter's falling in love with a poor man, than with any animal of a different species." (VI,ix)

There is also a sense of corruption spreading from élite values, and in small as well as large matters:

"nor did the landlady condescend to wish him a good journey: for this was, it seems, an inn frequented by people of fashion; and I know not whence it is, but all those who get their livelihood by people of fashion, contract as much insolence to the rest of mankind, as if they really belonged to that rank themselves." (VIII,vii)

Fielding repeatedly challenges this process, as in *Amelia* when Mrs Bennet observes:

"We rob the lower order of mankind of their due. I do not deny the force and power of education; but, when we consider how very injudicious is the education of the better sort in general, how little they are instructed in the practice of virtue, we shall not expect to find the heart much improved by it. And even as to the head, how very slightly do we commonly find it improved by what is called a 'genteel education.' I have myself, I think, seen instances of as great goodness, and as great understanding too, among the lower sort of people as among the higher."

This conversation is pushed home when Amelia reflects on the "monstrous" character of considering "our matching ourselves the least below us in degree, as a kind of contamination" which Mrs Bennet, in turn, argues is not only inhumane but also "unchristian" (VII,x). This is a powerful challenge to the assumptions not only of society as a whole but, more particularly, of the élite.

In one sense, Fielding's work was an attempt at public reproach and reflection, a classic feature of satirical moralists. He seems at times to despise the nobility as self-regarding exploiters of their status and wealth quite as much as Western does.

The Middling Orders

Those who can be variously termed the "middling orders," "middle class" or "bourgeoisie" are not easy to define, as they tail off into the élite and the poor, and were far from uniform. However, as a whole, although they did not have a common economic interest, the middling orders were a distinct social group. They tended to emphasize values of professionalization, specialism and competence that helped to define their social function and presence. A stress on such factors was necessarily one of the individual, rather than the family or dynasty.

Yet the latter were also very important. It would be mistaken to focus on function, for example as doctors or lawyers, both of whom were extensively dealt with by Fielding in his plays, and to ignore the concern of the middling orders with hierarchy and background. Such considerations also played a major role for them, and snobbery, as much as function, helped to define social presence, as with the lower social status of surgeons compared to doctors (physicians). Moreover, alongside the desire for betterment, there was a widespread aspiration to gentry status.

The expansion and growing profitability of the commercial and industrial sectors of the economy led to a growth in the middling orders, although, at the individual level, there was much fragility in status and position, a fragility that led to display, pretension and debt, the last being a central issue in *Amelia*. The protection offered today by largely reliable systems of insurance and pensions, and by relatively secure investment and credit, was absent. Attempts to associate together in order to provide a measure of security could offer only limited protection. This fragility was also captured by novelists with their emphasis on prospects and on turns of fate. In Defoe's *Moll Flanders* (1722), wealth comes and goes, it is difficult to find emotional and financial constancy, and crime, marriage and inheritance are ways to acquire capital. The sense of precariousness was unsurprising given the traumatic financial crash of 1720, the South Sea Bubble. Moll's third husband "finding his income not suited to the manner of living which he had intended, if I had brought him what he expected, and being under a disappointment in his return of his plantations in Virginia, he discovered many times his inclination of going over to Virginia to live upon his own."[11]

Nevertheless, at the general level, and in a period of only modest inflation, the percentage of households with annual incomes between £50 and £400 rose from 15 percent in 1750 to 25 percent by 1780, and that in a period of rapidly growing population. The middling orders, moreover, were increasingly difficult to locate in terms of a social differentiation based on rural society and inherited position. Many lived in the towns, but still, despite differences, shared the inegalitarian and hierarchical character of rural society. Thus, the wealthy and prominent in towns derived their power from their ability to organize others, generally economically and often politically. Moreover, the oligarchical nature of urban government corresponded to that of the countryside, although there was less of an emphasis on lineage. Rural commentators might group townsmen above the rank of artisan in terms of "trade," but, in fact, there were many distinctions in terms of wealth and status.

11   Daniel Defoe, *Moll Flanders* (London, 1722; 1978 edn.): 98.

There was also an important middling order in rural society: tenant farmers, the agents of landlords, and rural professionals such as parsons, a group greatly affected by the movements of the agrarian economy. Many encountered particular problems during the agrarian difficulties of the 1720s and 1730s, although the fate and fortune of tenant farmers varied greatly. From mid-century, the rise in grain prices due to the growing population brought more wealth into the rural economy, but its distribution within rural society was very uneven. The beneficiaries of rural industrialization were another instance of this unevenness and of the rural middling order.[12]

The middling orders, especially those in towns, played a considerable role in public affairs, generally co-operating with the landed élite to achieve their socio-political objectives. Their property and interests were as much protected by the general emphasis on liberty and property, and by the ethos and direction of parliamentary government, as were those of the landed order. Property qualifications for many posts were relatively low, enabling the lower middling orders to participate in the government of the localities.[13] Subscription associations also gave them an important role, as, more generally, did the full range of public politics.

The middling orders did not seek political change. Rather than seeing themselves as the flag-bearers of a "rising middle class," they displayed little sign of what would later be termed class consciousness. There were signs of a new ethos, especially in books and plays that portrayed a way of life emphasising the value of industry and discipline, and castigating supposedly aristocratic habits of self-indulgence, but such ideas were neither new, nor politically pointed and significant, and much of the landed élite would have accepted them.

The middling orders were affected by a porosity of social boundaries that was greater than that on the Continent, although less than in Britain's North American colonies. Social mobility was helped by primogeniture (undivided inheritance by the eldest son), and the consequent need for

12 David Rollinson, *The Local Origins of Modern Society, Gloucestershire, 1500–1800* (London: Routledge, 1992).
13 Paul Langford, *Public Life and the Propertied Englishman 1689–1798* (Oxford: Oxford University Press, 1991).

younger sons to define and support their own position, and also by the relative openness of marital conventions. Despite snobbish disdain for "trade," these conventions allowed the sons of land to marry the daughters of commerce, and, less frequently, led to the daughters of land marrying the sons of commerce. Partly as a result, the social élite in England was far less exclusive and far more widely rooted in the national community than was the case in most Continental countries. In some counties, such as Durham, estates were frequently acquired by purchase, and acquisitions by previously non-landed men were frequent. More generally, there was an active land market, and status (though not peerages) could also be readily acquired. The notices in the *London Journal* of 27 November 1725 included one for Thomas Rogers, "Agent for Persons that Buy or sell Merchandises, Estates etc," who was willing to meet customers at the Rainbow coffeehouse in London, and that very much presented a society where land and money were easily exchanged:

> "Any person that has twenty thousand pounds to lay out, may be informed where a good estate in land very improvable, may be purchased at a price considerably less than land now usually sells for.... A person wants to buy a large estate with a seat, fit for a gentleman in any pleasant healthy country. Another an estate from about £6000 to £8000 value not far from Bath. Another a good house with some farms near Reading of from £200 to £500 a year. Another an estate of £2,000 value, or upwards, in Middlesex, Essex or Hertfordshire...."

The market that was discussed was not particularly place-specific, and, alongside the strong sense of place seen in *Tom Jones*, many sought the right property rather than a specific location.

Marriage and land purchase were not the sole links, as urban and rural groups also shared cultural and leisure interests, such as visiting spas, which became more popular in this period, while they were linked by myriad patterns of subscription and other forms of social intercourse. For example, the Birmingham Bean Club acted as a dining society to bring the town's leaders and the local gentry together, and, more generally, towns were a social focus for the surrounding countryside. Chester had important race meetings in midsummer and autumn, as well as the Lent and summer assizes. Towns competed to make themselves attractive to wealthy country visitors, this competition being another stage in that which had led them to compete as centers of the rural economy with rival fairs.

At the same time, to the benefit of Fielding's plots, for both plays and novels, the urban/rural divide could remain strong, and there was rural resistance to urban influences.[14] Differences remained, not least in politics and religion, and the landed magnates visited towns on their own terms. It is too easy to assume that rural society responded rapidly or evenly to urban developments, or that rural values and opinions were determined by those of the towns. Yet, there was a degree of interchange based on shared values that was arguably greater than that of the previous two centuries.

The countryside was not cut off from the towns; the latter played a major role as markets for the countryside, and as centers of, and for, consumption, while road links improved with the spread of turnpikes. Peddlers from towns brought wares, while rural readers read newspapers, acquiring information about urban opinions, fashions and products. Alongside signs of tension between urban and rural interests and consciousnesses, the two were also different aspects of the life of the élite, and related or unified in a new sensibility.

More generally, fashions were rapidly transmitted between social groups and made accessible and affordable, and this mobility strengthened, rather than weakened, the social hierarchy. There were fewer signs of social tension than at the close of the nineteenth century, but, as Fielding reflected, a degree of criticism of the values associated with the élite. In both plays and novels, he could give a bite that was variously social, cultural and sexual. In *Tom Jones*, the protagonist comes across the husband of the landlady of the inn in which he was staying, an individual who does no work:

> "He had been bred as they call it, a gentleman, that is, bred up
> to do nothing, and had spent a very small fortune, which he in-
> herited from an industrious farmer his uncle, in hunting, horse-
> racing, and cock-fighting, and had been married by my landlady

14 Carl Estabrook, *Urbane and Rustic England: Cultural Ties and Social Spheres in the Provinces 1660–1780* (Manchester: Manchester University Press, 1999).

for certain purposes, which he had long since desisted from an-
swering: for which she hated him heartily." (VIII,vii)

The last was a key undercurrent in Fielding's work. The sexual viciousness
of rapacious members of the élite reflect a desire to capture, control and
humiliate sexually, by seduction, prostitution, purchase and violence, that
it is implicit is a matter not only of depravity, immaturity and "unnatural"
cruelty, but also of an inadequacy that extends to sexual desire and performance.

The Poor

"The stagnation of foreign trade begins already to affect our
manufactures at home: Those tradesmen who used to pay 40
or 50 £ per week, journeymen's wages, now not paying above 5
or 6: whence it is easy to account for the daily increase, both of
the numbers and calamities of the poor."
Champion, 9 February 1740

Social welfare was limited, even though it was more generous than provision
in most of the world in this period. Alongside signs of a sympathetic treatment of the poor,[15] including in Fielding's *Proposal for Making an Effectual
Provision for the Poor* (1753), they could be regarded as objects, or a problem, and not as equal participants in the community. As the *Citizen* pointed
out on 5 April 1757, "They are called the vulgar, the mob, the rabble ...
and treated as if they were of some inferior species, who are designed only
for labour." The poor were particularly harshly treated if they could not
earn their keep. Thus, John Locke proposed to the Board of Trade that the
poor should be made to work, and that those who refused should be
whipped and, if necessary, mutilated. His suggestions were not adopted,
but should not surprise us from an individual and society that profited from
the slave trade. John Wesley conspicuously adopted a different viewpoint,
seeing the poor as industrious and a source of spiritual renewal, and the

15 Joan Howard-Drake, "The Poor of Shipton under Wychwood Parish 1740–
1762," *Wychwoods History*, 5 (1989): 4–31.

beggar as an image of the suffering Christ, although his view that the Devil made work for idle hands meant that he supported six days a week working and no leisure on Sundays. Moreover, in order to try to avoid the birth of children who would be a burden on the rates, a frequent theme in Fielding's work, parish vestries sought to dissuade the poor from marrying, or to persuade or force unmarried mothers to go elsewhere.

The largest urban group[16] was the poor, who tended to lack political weight. Their poverty stemmed from the precarious nature of much employment in even the most prosperous of towns. Most workers lacked the skills that commanded a decent wage, and many had only seasonal or episodic employment. Day-laborers, servants and paupers were economically vulnerable and often socially isolated. A large number were immigrants from the countryside. Fielding was prepared to introduce his readers to poverty, inviting them, in the preface to *Joseph Andrews*, "to enter a poor house and behold a wretched family shivering with cold and languishing with hunger," which was particularly appropriate in the early 1740s. Indeed, his depiction of poverty was far more pointed than that of Richardson, and was no mere add-on to his work.

Due to poverty, the poor, both rural and urban, were very exposed to changes in the price of food, as in 1740,[17] and generally lived in inadequate housing. As they could not afford much fuel, the poor were often cold and wet in the winter, and were more commonly in the dark. Candles, as Fielding reminds us, cost. The circumstances of the life of the poor, paticularly families sharing a bed, made them prone to disease, notably infectious disease, though disease was also a social leveller. Malnutrition stunted growth, hit energy levels, and reduced resistance to ill-health. Poor diet encouraged colon parasitic infection, hepatitis and salmonella.

Commentators generally distinguished between the "mob" and the "people." The former comprehended the bulk of the poor; while many of the latter had a more settled income and were artisans, their economic interests and social cohesion frequently expressed through membership of fraternities of workmen. The "small tithes" records for the Oxfordshire

16 The rural poor are discussed in chapter six.
17 Diary of Dr Richard Wilkes, Wellcome Library, pp. 85–86, 91.

living of Shipton under Wychwood reveal that nearly half the households were poor, with particular issues for some families due to bereavement.[18]

There was scant understanding of the problems posed by unemployment and under-employment, and such hardships were treated as self-inflicted and thus deserving of neglect or punishment. The standard precept of care was that it should discriminate between the deserving and the undeserving. This religio-moral principle tended to be applied on grounds of age, health and sex, rather than on socio-economic criteria relating to income and employment. The sick, elderly, young, and women with children, were the prime beneficiaries of relief; while, on a longstanding pattern, the able-bodied, whether in low-paid employment or unemployed, were denied it.

A well-established system of poor relief was available through the Poor Law, and the majority of the population relied on it at some time during their lives. Compulsory poor rates had been introduced in England and Wales in 1572, and in 1598 the relief of poverty was made the responsibility of the individual parish, but able-bodied men unable to find work were treated as rogues and vagabonds. The financial and administrative system organized in the Elizabethan Poor Law Acts remained until the 1834 Poor Law Amendment Act, although supplementary legislation was of importance. The Poor Relief Act of 1662 made the right to relief dependent upon the pauper being settled in the parish, a practice that led to the expulsion of paupers deemed non-resident. Individuals could only remain in a new parish if they had a settlement certificate stating that their former parish would support them if they became a burden on the poor rate, and others were liable to be driven away unless they could find work, generally harshly treated and frequently whipped as vagabonds, as in County Durham. The removal orders from Bradford-on-Avon, a leading centre of the West Country cloth industry, show the expulsion of married men with families, together with single women, wives, and a small number of widows. Clearly there was concern to limit the number of dependent children in the community. The chances of removal from Bradford increased considerably from

18 Anthea Jones, Joan Howard-Drake, Sue Jourdan and Tom McQuay, "Eggs for the Vicar. A Study of the Small Tithes in Shipton under Wychwood 1727–1734," *Wychwoods History*, 11 (1996): 4–27.

the 1750s. In many English parishes a "P" stitched on clothes denoted those in receipt of poor relief.

A growing institutionalization of poor relief was seen in the eighteenth century. It involved specific facilities and also taking forward the provision under the Elizabethan Poor Law Acts that "overseers of the poor" should try to find them work. "Corporations for the poor" were established in Bristol, Exeter, London, and other cities, to distribute poor relief through a system of workhouses, the first, John Carey's central workhouse, established in the Mint in Bristol in 1697 and later named St. Peter's Hospital, which represented a major development in the treatment of the able-bodied poor. Carey was a merchant, a devout Anglican and a Whig. An increase in the number of the poor led Worcester in 1703 to establish a workhouse in which "Beggars and idle people" could be compelled to work.

The Workhouse Test Act of 1723 encouraged parishes to found workhouses to provide the poor with work and accommodation. All Nottingham's parishes built workhouses under the Act in the 1720s, Lancaster built one in 1730, and Birmingham another in 1733. In 1740, the vestry of Nazeing in Essex decided that a workhouse should be built to control the costs of poor relief because there had been complaints from the parishioners that they were "oppressed by the exorbitant assessments annually raised for relief and maintenance of the poor." In Banbury, the Council used charity money to repair the workhouse and support poor people "which are out of the workhouse in spinning jersey."[19] In 1751, Charles Gray argued, in his *Considerations on Several Proposals lately made, for the better maintenance of the poor*, that the key need was for the poor to be found "right employment."[20]

However, over the country, too few workhouses were founded to deal with the problems of poverty, and many workhouses were badly underfunded. Some workhouses were purpose-built, while others were converted from existing properties. The poor set to work in workhouses generally were

19 Nazeing History Workshop, *Five Miles from Everywhere. The Story of Nazeing, part 1* (Nazeing, 2000): 91; R.K. Gilkes, "The Banbury Journal, 1722–1761," *Cake and Cockhorse*, 16 (2004): 102.
20 Gray, *Considerations* (London, 1751): iii.

given tasks involving textiles, such as combing wool, spinning and clothes making.[21]

Workhouses, however, remained less important than "out relief": providing assistance, and sometimes work, to the poor in their own homes. This had the virtue of flexibility, not least in dealing with the seasonal problems of unemployment, under-employment and dearth that the variations of work in agriculture, industry and transport produced. A seasonal need for relief was best served through outdoor relief rather than through institutionalization.

Far from the Old (pre-1834) Poor Law being necessarily ineffective or repressive, it could be an adaptable system offering a satisfactory response to the needs of many communities. As with the political and ecclesiastical institutions and practices of the period, it is important, alongside contemporary criticism and subsequent replacement, to note the longevity and general success of the system. Variety remained the keynote of the provision of poor relief, as more generally with administrative practice. Some parishes had "poorhouses," but did not provide work. Others provided the poor as cheap labor for employers, but did not house them.

The general problem was the same everywhere: an absence of resources not only to deal with the poor *in situ*, but also with issues created by migration. There was neither wealth nor tax income sufficient to provide a widespread and comprehensive welfare system, but, as the government was not seeking to abolish poverty, but rather to alleviate it, or at least allay the fears created by the depiction of the poor, it is perhaps anachronistic to criticise it for failing to create an adequate system, or for treating the effects of poverty, rather than dealing with its causes. Government, both nationally and locally, succeeded for most of the time, in containing poverty.

Fielding could be harsh about some of the poor, but was more usually critical of the system. In the prison in *Amelia*;

> "Mr. Booth took notice of a young woman in rags sitting on
> the ground, and supporting the head of an old man in her lap,
> who appeared to be giving up the ghost ... father and daughter

21   David Avery, *Edmonton Workhouse Committee, 1732–37* (Edmonton: Edmonton Hundred Historical Society, 1967).

... the latter was committed for stealing a loaf, in order to support the former, and the former for receiving it, knowing it to be stolen." (I,iv)

At the same time, in his *Enquiry into the Causes of the late Increase of Robbers* (1753), which reflected his work as a JP, Fielding employed the standard classification of worthy and unworthy poor, adding that "much the most numerous class of poor, are those who are able to work, and not willing." He pressed the need to compel the idle to work and to enforce the law in order to do so, adding:

"The behaviour of the wretches brought before me; the most impudent and flagitious of whom, have always been such as have been before acquainted with the discipline of Bridewell ... usually treated with ridicule and contempt by those who have already been there."[22]

It was difficult for the poor to improve their condition. Despite the development of charity schools, they had only limited access to education, especially if they were female. Although the political process was not impervious to public opinion and pressures, it was closed to any attempt to redistribute wealth and opportunities. Labor had only limited possibilities of improving its conditions, although there was widespread trade unionism, for example among the West of England clothworkers and the framework knitters of the East Midlands. Indeed, there were many industrial disputes, frequently as a result of defensive action against unwelcome changes, as in the Wiltshire cloth industry in the late 1720s. In 1752, the combers in the Norwich textile industry struck in order to gain better wages and to prevent the employment of blackleg labor.

At the same time, there was the downward pressure on wages arising from the competitive situation across Europe, which affected both industrial and agricultural prices. Thus, in 1735, Martin Bladen, an expert on trade, observed, with reference to the production of cambrics:

22 Fielding, *Enquiry*, section four.

"As for England, provisions and labour are in most places too dear either for that undertaking, or for the manufacture of thread, and indeed the excessive expense of provisions and labour in general, carry us to foreign markets under a heavier load, than our neighbours bear, in almost all sorts of manufactures."[23]

Conclusions

Despite Fielding's sarcasm, notably, but not only, in *Jonathan Wild* (1743), it would be misleading to suggest either that there was widespread criticism in his work of the existence of a hereditary hierarchical society, or that tensions were only apparent between, rather than within, social groups. Social tension anyway is difficult to assess, and a relatively open society, in which people sought to create their own identities, was noticeable. This openness can be seen in the clubs of the period: the numerous social clubs for the affluent were matched by many others for laborers. These fulfilled recreational functions, although some, the friendly societies, also offered welfare. Clubs for laborers were self-regulated and part of a world of sociability that was only lightly supervised by government, and then largely in the form of licences for public houses (pubs). Some women accompanied their husbands to pubs and there were female clubs, but the overwhelming complexion of organized sociability was male, and the same was true of sociability in public places, such as street activities. The openness of society (although not to the illiterate) was captured by the critical "Lilliputian" in the *Newcastle Courant* of 24 December 1743:

"Your mathematical corespondents grow so numerous of late that, unless some task be assigned them, we shall know no end of their debates. it is but too common in these our days for a young student to commence pedant before he thoroughly understands his common arithmetic, and to fancy himself a philosopher as soon as he has gained a smattering of Euclid's Elements. To carry on an epistolary correspondence in a private

23 Bladen to Waldegrave, 15 April 1735, Chewton Mendip, Chewton Hall, Waldegrave papers, papers of James, 1ˢᵗ Earl Waldegrave.

manner, for the sake of instruction, or for finding out the truth is commendable enough; but to pester the public with common questions in navigation, which every school boy can solve, is most intolerable ... each of them seems to value himself upon his own abilities,"

a situation that was encouraged by the culture of print. At the same time, there was also a measure of popular resentment that should not be ignored; although it would be misleading to present successive governments as presiding uneasily over a seething mass of discontent, or of Fielding or other commentators heeding or ignoring such discontent.

Like Fielding, food rioters appealed to biblical notions of charity as well as to ideas of what humans owed each other in time of need, rather than to a language of political rights. More generally, riots can be seen both as community politics—showing discontent with establishment practices—and as direct action. There was an element of desperation, seen most clearly in food riots: seizing food was more important than staging a protest, let alone regulating markets. But, there could also be political currents in popular agitation, even though Fielding's depiction of electoral demonstrating is that of a farce. During the 1722 elections, John, 1ˢᵗ Earl of Egmont, a Whig, reported, "The mob which is generally High Church have where they are strongest been insufferably rude, as at Westminster, Reading, Stafford etc." In July 1736, when London workers rioted against the employment of cheaper Irish labor, and were dispersed by the militia, Walpole wrote to his brother, Horatio:

> "I sent several persons both nights to mix with the mob, to learn what their cry and true meaning was, and by all accounts their chief and original grievance is the affair of the Irish, and so understood by the generality of the mob, but in several others, the Gin Act was cried out against, in some few words of disaffection were thrown out, and one body of men of about eight were led on by a fellow that declared for Liberty and Property."[24]

24   Egmont to Daniel Dering, 27 March 1722, Robert to Horatio Walpole, 29 July 1736, BL Add. 47029 folio 110, 63749A folios 249.

Two months later, troops were deployed in London to prevent disturbances over the Gin Act, the hostile response to which helped cause Fielding's play *Eurydice* (1737) to fail due to a relevant but poorly-received joke.[25] Fielding as a magistrate was involved in 1749 in the case of Bosavern Penlez, a wig maker convicted and executed for rioting at a brothel in the Strand, in an episode that arose from cheated seamen attacking brothels. Fielding examined the prisoners taken by the watchmen and was to be criticized for Penlez's execution which led him to publish a pamphlet, *A True State of the Case of Bosavern Penlez*. The entire episode reflected the precarious nature and the often arbitrary character of the administration of justice. The use of the Riot Act was heavy-handed.

Despite Walpole's fears,[26] disturbances were contained in the 1730s, and, more generally, the absence of serious radical political pressure from the lower and middling orders in the 1740s, when the political nation was divided and the state was vulnerable, suggests a need to put such pressure in perspective. Had there been such a challenge from below, it is doubtful whether the non-Jacobite élite could have afforded the bitter political disputes that occurred. Instead, the absence of a social challenge on the part of the unpropertied allowed the élite to pursue their divisions.

To Fielding, it was the similarities between people that were noticeable. In *The Modern Husband* (1731), Bellamant declares: "It is a stock-jobbing age, everything has its price; marriage is a traffick throughout; as most of us bargain to be husbands, so some of us bargain to be cuckolds; and he would be as much laughed at, who preferred his love to his interest, at this end of the town, as he preferred his honor to his interest at the other" (II,vi).

Two decades later, the lesson was driven home harder in *Amelia* as Fielding seeks to rescue his protagonist from the possible criticism of his readers, a means that enables him to guide the latter clearly as well as to refer to his ability to use images:

"… it is not because innocence is more blind than guilt that the
former often overlooks and tumbles into the pit which the latter

25   Bertrand Goldgar, "Why Was *Eurydice* Hissed?," *Notes and Queries*, 38 (1991): 186–88.
26   Robert to Horatio Walpole, 30 September 1736, BL. Add. 63749A folio 262.

foresees and avoids. The truth is, that it is almost impossible guilt should miss the discovery of all the snares in its way, as it is constantly preying closely into every corner in order to lay snares for others. Whereas innocence, having no such purpose, walks fearlessly and carelessly through life, and is consequently liable to tread on the gins [mechanical spring-operated traps to catch animals or people] which cunning hath laid to entrap it. To speak plainly and without allegory or figure, it is not want of sense, but want of suspicion, by which innocence is often betrayed. Again, we often admire the folly of the dupe, when we should transfer our whole surprise to the astonishing guilt of the betrayer. In a word, many an innocent person hath owed his ruin to this circumstance alone, that the degree of villainy was such as must have exceeded the faith of every man who was not himself a villain." (VIII,ix)

9. RELIGION

"As to the character of Adams ... as the goodness of his heart will recommend him to the good-natured, so I hope it will excuse me to the gentlemen of his cloth, for whom, while they are worthy of their sacred order, no man can possibly have a greater respect. They will therefore excuse me, notwithstanding the low adventures in which he is engaged that I have made him a clergyman, since no other office could have given him so many opportunities of displaying his worthy inclinations."
Preface to *Joseph Andrews*

To the casual observer of today, the period may not appear a particularly religious age. Urban building is not generally recalled for its churches,[1] no more than the British painters of the period are remembered for religious works.[2] Confessional warfare is seen as largely something of the more distant past, and the period is viewed as one of growing toleration. Although almanacs continued to be very popular, it is presented as a period of enlightenment, and the Enlightenment is presented as a secular movement. Faith is generally ascribed to superstitious conservatism or irrational religious enthusiasm. The serious anti-Catholic Gordon Riots of 1780 are seen as an anachronism.

Yet, there was also a strong religious faith, one that was part of an understanding of the natural world as including a strong role for divine providence, and that could extend to a belief in the occult. Fielding in *The*

---

1   Although see Terry Friedman, *The Eighteenth-Century Church in Britain* (New Haven, Connecticut: Yale University Press, 2011).

2   For an important recent re-evaluation of a key painter, Matthew Craske, *Joseph Wright of Derby: Painter of Darkness* (New Haven, Connecticut: Yale University Press, 2020).

Intriguing Chambermaid (1733) has great fun with the chambermaid's idea of deterring a visit by pretending that the house is:

> "haunted with the most terrible apparitions that were ever heard or beheld! You'd think the devil himself had taken possession of it! … all the wild noises in the universe; the squeaking of pigs, the grinding of knives, the whetting of saws, the whistling of winds, the roaring of seas, the hooting of owls, the howling of wolves, the braying of asses, the squalling of children, and the scolding of wives, all put together, make not so hideous a concert. This I myself have heard; nay, and I have seen such sights! One with about twenty heads, and a hundred eyes, and mouths and nose, in each."

A skeptical Goodall is convinced of this haunting by noises within the house. In nighttime confusion in *Joseph Andrews*, Adams thinks Slipslop a witch giving "suck to a legion of devils." Indeed, despite his mistake, "He often asserted he believed in the power of witchcraft notwithstanding, and did not see how a Christian could deny it" (IV,xiv). In this context, alongside Wesley's belief in ghosts, it is instructive to turn to an item in the *Cirencester Flying-Post* of 21 March 1743:

> "From Limpley-Stoke, in the parish of Bradford in the county of Wiltshire, we have the following story, which, however incredible it may seem, is insistent upon to be really fact. vis. That one of the bells of the parish aforesaid, was, in the nighttime, between eleven and three, conveyed from thence to a village called Winsley, about two miles distant, and over a river about a stone's throw. The ringers coming in the morning to ring for a wedding, to their great surprise found a bell more in the steeple than usual—By whom or by what means the said bell could most probably be removed, is matter of much debate among the people; some will have it to have been removed and fixed up by a body of fairies; others say it certainly was carried away by a North-West wind; and others (the more wise part of them) conclude it to have been removed by the spirits of some deceased ringers."

Joseph in *Joseph Andrews* does not "absolutely disbelieve" in ghosts, while Adams asks about "evil spirits" walking in the neighborhood and considers exorcism; although the light Joseph sees is in fact that of sheep-stealers (III,ii). In *Tom Jones*, aside from Partridge's response to the ghost in *Hamlet* (XVI,v), the frightened guard responds with fear to the injured Tom's nighttime appearance: "His imagination being possessed with the horror of an apparition, converted every object he saw or felt, into nothing but ghosts and spectres" (VII,xiv). Nevertheless, a landlady comments: "As the parson told us last Sunday, nobody believes in the devil now-a-days" (XII,vi). To an extent, the devil had become a matter of phrasing, as in *Amelia* when Betty, a dishonest servant, explains to a JP, "It must have been the devil that put me upon it" (XI,vii).

The quality of the religious experience of the bulk of the population is hard to assess, as is the source and depth of their faith. It is similarly difficult to establish how far such personal and communal experience was affected by the politico-ecclesiastical changes of the period. Religious antagonism provided a key to past, present and future, such antagonism, while also about society, politics and culture, being rooted in the need to protect the faith, provide for salvation, and thus save souls.

In England, the "Glorious Revolution" of 1688–89 had ensured that the monarch would be a Protestant, but had also loosened Anglican hegemony. Under the "Act for Exempting their Majesties Protestant Subjects, Dissenting from the Church of England, from the Penalties of certain Laws," the concessionary but restrictive formulation of what is better known as the Toleration Act (1689), Dissenters (Protestant Nonconformists who believed in the Trinity) who took the oaths of Supremacy and Allegiance and accepted thirty six of the Thirty-Nine Articles, and made the Declaration against Transubstantiation, could obtain licences as ministers or schoolmasters, although these had to be registered with a bishop or at the Quarter Sessions, tasks which posed problems for both.

The Act was followed by the registration of numerous Dissenting meetinghouses: at least 113 in Devon alone by 1701. The Presbyterians, Independents (Congregationalists), Quakers and Baptists were the leading Dissenting churches. In Exeter, two Dissenter meeting houses were opened in about 1687 (and others by 1715 and 1760), followed by a Quaker meeting house in 1715, a Baptist church in 1725, an Independent chapel by

1744, and a synagogue in 1763. An Independent meeting house was opened in Norwich in about 1693, followed by a Quaker meeting house in about 1699 and a Baptist chapel in 1745. In Coventry, where a large Quaker meeting house was opened in 1698, a new Presbyterian chapel in 1701, and one for the Particular Baptists in 1724, Anglicanism declined in the face of a strong challenge from the Presbyterians and the Unitarians.

Unitarians, Catholics and non-Christians (mostly Jews) did not officially enjoy rights of public worship under the Act of Toleration; while Catholics were subject to penal statutes, as were Unitarians under the Blasphemy Act. There was no Toleration Act for Unitarians until 1813. Indeed, Trinitarian orthodoxy was strong and united Catholics and Protestants.

Aside from clashes between different churches, there were also tensions within them, as with the Church of England. Some of its clerics were more hostile to other Protestant groups and inclined to see a threat in toleration toward them, a threat not only to church attendance and religious orthodoxy, but also to the moral order and sociopolitical cohesion that the Church was seen as sustaining. The Toleration Act thereby contributed to a sense of malaise and uncertainty. The lower clergy were frustrated that William III did not allow Convocation (the clerical assembly; there was one for each archdiocese) to meet until the last year of his reign. It was prorogued (postponed) continually from the reign of George I on (from 1717 with the exception of a brief session in 1741–42), as was the Convocation of the Church of Ireland. Dr Henry Sacheverell, a high Anglican Cleric and a Tory, felt able to argue controversially in 1709 that the Church was in danger under the Revolution settlement, as interpreted by the Whigs. The Occasional Conformity (1711) and Schism (1714) Acts, designed respectively to prevent the circumvention of communion requirements for officeholding by Dissenters communicating once a year, occasional conformity, and to make a separate education for them illegal, measures both passed by Anne's Tory ministry of 1710–14, were both repealed by the Whigs under George I in 1719. The Reverend Benjamin Robertshaw, Rector of Amersham 1728–44, recorded the tension in Anglican attitudes to Dissent:

> "About the year 1721 I was so unfortunate as to fall under the displeasure of my diocesan, Bishop Gibson [a Whig].... The

occasion was my refusing to bury a Presbyterian's child, sprinkled in their unauthorised way, in my parish at Penn. Upon my absolute refusal the parents ... carried it to Wycombe, where it was buried by one who I suppose would have given Christian burial even to Pontius Pilate himself, provided he had but in his lifetime used to cry 'King George forever!'"[3]

Conversely, the Tory Squire Western would "rather be anything than a courtier, and a Presbyterian, and a Hanoverian too" (VI,ii), the linkage, a jumble, really looking back in its concern about Presbyterians, for, although the Hanoverians were Lutherans, their supporters were mostly Anglicans.

Indeed, attempts during the years of Whig ascendancy to repeal the Test and Corporation Acts failed. These Acts, of 1673 and 1661 respectively, obliged members of borough corporations and office holders under the Crown to take oaths of allegiance and supremacy, and to receive communion in the Church of England, and these remained in force until 1828, although the Corporation Act was much diluted in 1719 so that many Dissenters were able to play a role in local government. The Test Act, however, remained much more effective at the national level. Fielding was happy to make fun of Dissenters, as in *The Letter-Writers* (1731) in which the linkboy offers Jack Commons a light to guide him through London at night, earning the reply: "Do you take me for a Dissenter, you rascal? Do you think I carry my light within, sirrah? I travel by an outward light. So lead on, you dog, and light me into darkness" (II,ii).

The Tories retained their control of the University of Oxford, where many clerics were trained. Once the male line of the Stuarts had been driven out in 1688–89, the dynasty became a convenient symbol for conservatism and, alongside Tories who did not seek contention,[4] several prominent eighteenth-century Oxonians were Jacobites.[5] The University had two MPs,

3   G. Eland (ed.), *Shardeloes Papers of the 17th and 18th Centuries* (Oxford: Oxford University Press, 1947): 50.
4   Nigel Aston, "Thomas Townson and High Church Continuities and Connections in Eighteenth-Century England," *Bulletin of the John Rylands Library*, 97 (2021): 57.
5   David Greenwood, *William King: Tory and Jacobite* (Oxford: Oxford University Press, 1969).

elected by its doctors and masters of arts, and all the MPs elected were Tories, including such prominent Anglican champions as Henry Hyde, Viscount Cornbury (MP 1734–50) and Sir Roger Newdigate (MP 1750–80); as the crown did not possess the power of creating honorary doctors, by which a Whig majority was secured at Cambridge. In *The Jacobite's Journal* of 23 July 1748, Simon Supple complains about "a grave clergyman from Oxford" who becomes a boarder and persuades his wife and children to become Jacobites.

The Whig party had traditionally been associated with Dissenters, such that the Tory Squire Western regards his pro-government sister as "a Presbyterian Hanoverian b–" (VII,v), but, in practice, many Whigs were Anglicans and were sometimes referred to as "Church Whigs."[6] Whig Anglicans were mostly Low Church, and the bulk of the Presbyterians who were absorbed into the Church of England after 1689 swelled the numbers of the Low Church. From 1722, a small *regium donum* (king's gift) was given annually to trustees from the Baptist, Independent and Presbyterian churches, the funds used to supplement the incomes of their indigent clerics. Tory propaganda accused the Whigs of being anti-Church: "The Church of England and her clergy were ever objects of my most implacable aversion," declared a Whig in a Tory pamphlet of 1724,[7] while Whig commentators argued that the views of "our parsons ... undoes all notions for liberty...." In practice, government control of ecclesiastical patronage—the Crown appointed the archbishops, the bishops and about a tenth of the parish clergy—greatly influenced the senior ranks of the Church of England, and ensured that it was in alliance with the secular power.[8] However, the cautious Whig administrations of Walpole and his successors did not fulfil Tory fears and tamper with religious fundamentals, not least because of the considerable groundswell of opinion in defense of the Church.

More generally, there was a close relationship between the Church of England and the landed élite. The appointment of the majority of the parish

---

6   Edward Carteret to Charles, 2nd Viscount Townshend, 2 July 1725, NA. SP. 35/57 folio 9.

7   Anon., *The True Character of a Triumphant Whig both in his Religion and Politics* (London, 1724): 7–8; George Tilson to George Whitworth, 30 August 1722, BL. Add. 37389 folio 138.

8   Newcastle to William, Lord Harrington, 18 July 1740, NA. SP. 43/92.

clergy, about 53 percent, was directly controlled by the latter. In addition, one third of English tithes were held by lay impropriators, although that could lead to frequent clashes, for example between George Vane and the Reverend James Douglas over the titles of Long Newton, Durham.[9] Moreover, church properties tended to be rented on favorable terms by the laity, as most tenants being too powerful to be exploited. Indeed, resistance to episcopal rent increases was effective.

There was a degree of anticlericalism in the early Whig ascendancy, but, from the 1720s, the hierarchies of Church and State moved closer together in England. Some prominent Whig politicians were personally devout. Thomas, 1st Duke of Newcastle, a Secretary of State from 1724 until 1754, and subsequently First Lord of the Treasury, read a lesson every day and followed a course of theological reading. Philip, Lord Chancellor Hardwicke listened to daily prayers, and, in February 1754, blaming crime in part on "a gross neglect of religion," he urged the judges to emphasize the danger to hopes of salvation posed by perjury.[10] Horatio Walpole, the brother of Sir Robert, referred to the prospect of order coming from chaos "which is entirely in the hands and power of Providence."[11]

High Churchmen moved toward the Whigs as they responded to the piety of Whig patrons. Newcastle, the minister who was most influential in ecclesiastical appointments in 1742–62, was concerned to ensure that effective and able men were appointed to positions of responsibility, although concern about the political consequences led him in the 1740s and 1750s to oppose the introduction of bishops into the American colonies. Though, from 1726, Walpole obtained Indemnity Acts, protecting the Dissenters from malicious prosecution, especially office-holders who had failed to take communion, each year bar 1730 and 1732, and they were repeated frequently until 1757 and regularly thereafter, moves to repeal the Test and Corporation Acts were defeated in 1736, 1739, 1787, 1789 and 1790.

The division between Anglicanism and Dissent that had played such a major role in the dynamic of Whig-Tory struggle, especially in 1689–1720,

9   Durham, CRO, Londonderry papers, P/Lo/F, 203, 751.
10   BL. Add. 35870 folios 241–43.
11   Walpole to Reverend John Milling, 20 January 1741, BL. Wolterton papers, volume 187.

was still important thereafter. As the Test and Corporation Acts survived the 1689–1720 period of controversy and change, so Anglican prerogatives and privileges became a permanent feature of the Whig state; unlike in the mid-seventeenth century, it was possible to remove the Stuarts without overthrowing Anglicanism. It also proved possible in 1714 to install a Lutheran monarch (George I) without apparent danger to the Church of England, with which he was in communion, a situation that remained the case under George II. As a consequence of the Church's maintenance of its position, pressure for the repeal of the Acts, the prime political thrust of Dissent, itself came to denote opposition to the dominant system. If the defeats of attempts to repeal the Test and Corporation Acts reaffirmed the identification of religion and state, in the form of government protection for the Church of England, they also sustained local tensions. In England and Wales, animosity between Anglicanism and Dissent was a basic political axis, although the two rivalries were different in important respects and, in addition, there is much evidence that the fit between religious and political divisions was far from neat and uniform. In England, Dissenters tended to support more radical political positions, especially prior to the 1720s and after mid-century, and their urban locale ensured that their activism was predominantly middle class and had only limited reference to aristocratic leadership and interests. Whether the Church was in danger or not at the national level, Anglicans felt it necessary to protect it in the localities. Furthermore, in the absence of a modern structure of party organization, ecclesiastical links provided the basis of community and sociability that was so important in the development of political alignments and the mobilization of political support.

Alongside humor, such as the bawdy tale in the Tory *London Evening Post* of 12 March 1743 of a London publican finding his wife in bed with a Presbyterian cleric, this was a society in which disagreements over how (not whether it was) best to worship God and seek salvation, how to organize the Church, and the relationship between Church and State, were matters of urgent concern. "Polite" and "religious" are not mutually incompatible, but the image of Hanoverian Britain as a "polite" society is misleading if that is taken to imply the marginal nature of religious zeal. In fact, despite the claims of other Protestant groups, the established churches were not devoid of energy, and their congregations were not sunk in torpor.

The Societies for the Reformation of Manners indicated the strength, social awareness and social conservatism of Anglican piety. Language was suffused in religious imagery, as in Fielding's play *The Letter-Writers* (1731), in which Risque says of Captain Rakel: "Go thy ways, young Satan; the old gentleman himself cannot be much worse" (II,i), while, in *Amelia*, Colonel James declares, "I am of the Church of England and will fight for it to the last drop of my blood" (IX,iii).

As a concrete example of religious activity, one that greatly affected particular communities, hundreds of churches were built, or significantly altered, during the century. Although few new parishes were created, new churches were built in areas of expanding population, including Manchester, Lancaster, Birmingham, Bath and Leeds, and, if many growing towns, such as Leeds and Hull, lacked sufficient church accommodation, the problem of providing for population growth did not become very serious for the Church until the 1780s. New churches included the new London churches of Queen Anne's reign, as well as Thomas Archer's baroque St Philip's in Birmingham (1711–24), and St Michael's (1734–42) and St James's in Bath (1768–9), All Saints, Gainsborough (1736–48), Holy Cross, Daventry (1752–8), and St Paul's in Liverpool (1765–9). Churches were built at new fashionable watering places, such as Bristol Hot Wells. Many churches were rebuilt, for example five in Worcester in 1730–72, and St Nicholas's in Bristol in the 1760s. Most churches were kept in good repair. The creation of side aisles and the erection of galleries increased the seating in many churches, as at Saddleworth.

"The clergy are men, as well as other folks," remarked Slipslop in *Joseph Andrews* (II,vi), while in *Amelia*, a much harsher work, a visit to Vauxhall leads to rude treatment of a clergyman: "Here's the fellow that eats up the tithe-pig. Don't you see how his mouth waters at her? Where's your slabbering bib?" (IX,ix). In practice, this is a highly inaccurate account of Harrison who is described more appropriately later by one of the mob: "The clergyman is a very good man, and acts becoming a clergyman, to stand by the poor" (XII,vi). Moreover, the JP to whom that case is referred has a proper respect for the cloth.

In practice, indeed, much recent work has stressed the dedication and diligence of clergymen, and the relative effectiveness of the Church's ministry. Clerical diaries of the period indicate faith and an attempt at self-examination.

There is also much evidence of clergymen fulfilling the standards of clerical life. For example, the diary of 1759–62 of James Newton, rector of Nuneham Courtney, shows his daily attendance at morning and evening prayer, his care to find replacement clergy when he was absent, and his concern to provide food for the poor.[12] Other sources provide similar evidence.

Thanks to toleration, the Church of England had to operate more effectively if it was to resist the challenge of other churches. Some bishops consciously responded to the idea of competition from Dissent. The duty of the Church to teach the faith was much emphasized: religious activism for clergy and laity alike was stressed in Anglican propaganda, not the soporific complacency of a stagnant establishment. The Church continued the themes established at the Reformation of strengthening piety and education. Moral and institutional reform was a major element. Correspondence with officialdom, or visitation returns, might give an over-optimistic view on the part of incumbents, but they also reveal what the clergy wanted to happen.[13]

The range of religious practice was extensive, but, although Wilson in *Tom Jones* had belonged to a London club of them, a club he discovers to be full of dishonest and transactional individuals, there were very few professed atheists. Moreover, they could suffer prosecution under the Blasphemy Act, while profane books were criticized.[14] Indeed, there was no necessary dichotomy of enlightenment and faith, the secular and the religious, scientific and mystical. "Freethinker" critics of the Church of England should not be seen in a secular context, but rather as advocates for a reforming civil theology. Deism, which was influential in intellectual circles, was not anti-religious. Instead of being a clear intellectual position or a movement, for it had neither creed nor organization, Deism was a vague term used by polemicists that had a wide range of religious connotations. Eschewing the notion of a God of retribution, deistic writers, such as John Toland, in his *Christianity not Mysterious* (1696), suggested a benevolent God that had created both a world and a humanity capable of goodness,

12 Gavin Hannah (ed.), *The Deserted Village: The Diary of an Oxfordshire Rector, 1731–86* (Stroud: Alan Sutton, 1992).

13 Jeremy Gregory, *Restoration, Reformation and Reform, 1660–1828, Archbishops of Canterbury and the Diocese* (Oxford: Oxford University Press, 2000): 8.

14 *Universal Spectator*, 24 October 1741.

and that did not intervene through revelation or miracles. The universe therefore had origins, order and purpose, but there was no need for a priesthood, which helped to encourage anti-clericalism. This was very much a minority view, however, and Fielding uses the account in *Joseph Andrews* of Wilson's history to provide what is presumably a portrayal of a difficult passage in his life including as a Deist. Square, the philosopher in *Tom Jones*, is unimpressive, self-interested, and a hypocrite.

Amelia is far more orthodox when she argues that she has "been guilty of many transgressions. First, against that divine will and pleasure without whose permission, at least, no human accident can happen" (VIII,iv). Fielding's latitudinarianism comes out in his protagonists' rather differently expressed belief in good works rather than justification by faith alone. This helps explain why Fielding disliked Whitefield and made Thwackum, the cleric who holds these views in *Tom Jones*, so dreadful.

Literacy, relative wealth, and an urban environment, enabled some to respond to new intellectual and spiritual currents, although it would be wrong to suggest that, in contrast, rural religion was necessarily unchanging, while it is unclear how far shifts in religious sensitivity in intellectual and clerical circles affected popular Christianity. There was, as in practically every period, widespread concern about irreligion. In 1738, John Hildrop, a country cleric, published *A Letter to a Member of Parliament containing a Proposal for bringing in a Bill to revise, amend, or repeal certain obsolete Statutes commonly called the Ten Commandments*, a satirical pamphlet that argued that they should be abolished because they were little regarded by fashionable society. This had parallels with Fielding's style, and the latter uses Adams to provide an account of true Christianity. When asked by Wilson why he is so familiar with Joseph, Adams replies:

> "I should be ashamed of my cloth if I thought a poor man who is honest, below my notice or my familiarity. I know not how those who think otherwise can profess themselves followers and servants of Him who made no distinction, unless, peradventure, by preferring the poor to the rich."

With a salutary image, the listener reflects that, "He was not yet quite certain that Adams had any more of the clergyman in him than his cassock"

(III,ii). Indeed, Wilson reveals that the local parson thinks him a Presbyterian because he will not drink with him (III,iii).

There is copious evidence, nevertheless, both of massive observance of the formal requirements of the churches and of widespread piety. Sunday schools and devotional literature, such as the chapbooks read by relatively humble people, fostered sanctity, piety, and an awareness of salvation. Popular piety was internalized, and there was a high level of introspective or "internalized" faith. Concerns over the frequency of receipt of communion were caused by feelings of unworthiness; one reason for the infrequency was that many people felt unworthy of it. Private prayer was frequent and Fielding shows some of his characters participating:

> "Amelia was retired above half an hour to her chamber, before I went to her. At my entrance, I found her on her knees, a posture in which I never disturbed her. In a few minutes she arose, came to me, and embracing me, said, she had been praying for resolution to support the cruellest moment she had ever undergone."[15]

Devotional literature was extensively purchased. The *Whole Duty of Man* by Richard Allestree (1619–81), Regius Professor of Divinity at Oxford (1663–79), which was first published in 1658, appeared in its 25th edition by 1690, was revised by 1743, and was widely recommended, especially by Gibson in his *Pastoral Letters. The Church Catechism explained by way of question and answer, and confirm'd by Scripture proofs* (1700) by the Kent cleric John Lewis (1675–1747) went through 42 editions by 1812. Lewis also wrote a series of defences of the position of the Church of England. William Law's *A Serious Call to a Devout and Holy Life, adapted to the State and Condition of all Orders of Christians* (1728) enjoyed huge sales, and was influential in the development of Methodism. 1728 also saw the publication of an edition of the sermons of John Tillotson (1630–94): the theft of an edition leads Thwackum to anger in *Tom Jones* (III,ix). Wesley's "Christian Library" was a selection of cheap religious works sold by preachers and was hugely popular and profitable.

15 *Amelia*, III,ii.

John Bunyan's *Pilgrim's Progress* (1678) was widely read, and the journey to an earthly perdition and a hellish end was extensively rehearsed by commentators, both the explicitly religious and the "secular"—for example the popular mid-eighteenth century morality series of engravings by Fielding's friend Hogarth, including *The Rake's Progress, Industry and Idleness,* and *Before and After*. Such works depicted and offered guidance on the routes of life from within a Christian context. This was even more true of explicitly religious admonitory prints.

Based on Fielding's friend, William Young, Adams, who was very much in the Latitudinarian tradition of the Church of England, pressed for acceptance of the unknowable will of an unseen God, telling a Joseph in despair: "You are to consider you are a Christian, that no accident happens to us without the divine permission, and that it is the duty of a man and a Christian to submit…. [T]he same power which made us, rules over us, and we are absolutely at his disposal" (III,xi). The contrast between Adams and Thwackum is a reminder that Fielding, like the generally-sympathetic Austen, avoided any one characterization of the clergy.

The Church of England, as always, faced serious problems, especially in the distribution of its resources, but was in a less parlous state than is sometimes suggested. Standards of pastoral care were as good as in earlier periods, and were encouraged by the vigilance of the hierarchy. Thomas Herring, Bishop of Bangor, in 1737–43, regularly toured his diocese in order to ordain and confirm, and to exercise a pastoral ministry among the clergy. Translated to York in 1743–47, Herring was again an energetic and conscientious diocesan who ordained and confirmed with regularity. More generally, the vigilance of the Anglican hierarchy in supervising the parochial clergy promoted pastoral commitment.

The nonresidence of clerics could be a difficulty, and certainly became more common. Herring's visitation return indicated that 393 out of the 836 parochial benefices in the diocese of York in 1743 had non-resident clergy, while 335 out of 711 of the clergy were pluralists. In 453 out of 836 parishes, the required two Sunday services were not provided. Moreover, there was a lack of large enough churches, notably in Hull and Leeds. Pluralism (holding more than one living) often arose due to lay impropriation (the revenues being in the possession of a lay owner of the living) or from clerical poverty stemming from major discrepancies in clerical income and the inadequacy of many livings, but this did not necessarily lead to inadequate pastoral care because non-resident incumbents frequently lived nearby and, in general, there were resident stipendiary curates. Pluralism was more common in areas where many parishes had poor endowments, for example on the Essex coast. In the diocese of London, there were many preachers, readers and lecturers, and a high level of clerical activity and, although there was non-residence and pluralism, levels of daily celebration and services were high, and the clergy had a pronounced view of their duty.[16]

Greater profits from agriculture from mid-century and opportunities for pluralism helped ensure a rise in the social standing of the clergy and in their general educational standard, with increasing clerical income meaning better-educated clergy. Yet, as Fielding repeatedly showed, for example in Mrs Bennet's account of the curate in *Amelia* (VII,iv), the ruthless selfishness, blatant hypocrisy and evil unfairness he dissected in civil society was also present in the Church. Indeed, as with the military, Fielding was repeatedly very sarcastic about the reward of merit in the Church. Of Adams, the curate, he wrote:

> "His virtue and his other qualifications, as they rendered him equal to his office, so they made him an agreeable and valuable companion, and had so much endeared and well recommended him to a bishop that at the age of fifty he was provided with a handsome income of twenty-three pounds a year; which, however, he could not make any great figure with because he lived in a dear country and was a little incumbered with a wife and six children."[17]

Adams was poorly treated in part as a result of the difficulties in lay-clerical relations in that parish. Sir Thomas and Lady Boothby:

16 Viviane Barrie-Curien, *Clergé et Pastorale en Angleterre au XVIIIe Siècle: le Diocese de Londres* (Paris: CNRS, 1992); John Guy (ed.), *The Diocese of Llandaff in 1763, The Primary Visitation of Bishop Ewer* (Cardiff: South Wales Record Society, 1991); L. Butler (ed.), *The Archdeaconry of Richmond in the Eighteenth Century: Bishop Gastrell's "Notitia" – The Yorkshire Parishes 1714–1725* (Cambridge: Cambridge University Press, 1990).
17 *Joseph Andrews*, I,iii.

"both regarded the curate as a kind of domestic only, belonging to the parson of the parish, who was at the time at variance with the knight; for the parson had for many years lived in a constant state of civil war, or, which is perhaps as bad, of civil law, with Sir Thomas himself and the tenants of his manor."[18]

Subsequently, Lady Boothby threatens to have Adams deprived of his living if he calls the banns for the Joseph-Fanny wedding (IV,ii). In contrast, in *Tom Jones*, Squire Allworthy, hearing of the learned nature of Jenny Jones, a local girl, intended her, "together with a small living," for a neighboring curate" (I,vi). Fielding later adds, with reference to Mrs Honour:

"This is the second person of low condition whom we have recorded in this history, to have spring from the clergy. It is to be hoped such instances will, in future ages, when some provision is made for the families of the inferior clergy, appear stranger than they can be thought at present." (IV, xiv)

In the end, Allworthy, having broken at last from the dishonest Thwackum, takes Adams into his house. Adams' difficulties drew on those of Fielding's friend William Young, curate of East Stour from 1731 and 1740 and headmaster of the Free School in nearby Gillingham.

The role of the churches in worship was but part of a wider mission, notably in education and social welfare, that helped to enhance their importance. Yet, that mission faced issues, including self-interest and snobbery: Peter Pounce tells Adams that charity was "a mean parsonlike quality, though I would not infer many parsons have it."[19] Public morality was another aspect of the clerical role. Parson Supple dislikes Western's readiness to swear, but does not dare to rebuke him, a choice ironically presented as the "manners" already qualified by "the parson submitted to please his palate at the squire's table." Supple however:

18 *Joseph Andrews*, I,iii.
19 *Joseph Andrews*, III,xiii.

"paid him off obliquely in the pulpit; which had not, indeed, the good effect of working a reformation in the squire himself, yet it so far operated on his conscience, that he put the laws very severely in execution against others, and the magistrate was the only person in the parish who could swear with impunity."
(VI,ix)

Swearing was also a target of the Societies for the Reformation of Manners.

Dissatisfaction reflected the importance of, and widespread commitment to, religion, the Church and the clergy. Few believed that they could or should be dispensed with, or doubted the close relationships of faith and reason, church and state, clergy and laity, religion and the people. Nevertheless, the very nature of established churches that sought to minister to all, in an age when religion was a social obligation, as well as a personal spiritual experience, posed problems for some of those, both clergy and laity, who criticized anything that might compromise the latter. Believers sure of their faith could find the compromises of comprehension abhorrent. Yet, the determination of the clergy as a whole, as opposed to the foibles of individuals, to ensure standards of religious knowledge and observance ensured that these compromises were not those of the lowest common denominator.

Methodism was one consequence of religious enthusiasm. It was initially a movement for revival that sought to remain within the Church of England,[20] supplementing the official parochial structure by a system of private religious societies that would both regenerate the Church and win it new members. However, after Methodism's institutional founder, John Wesley, died in 1791, it broke away completely, and his decision to ordain ministers on his own authority in 1784 marked a point of real division between Methodism and the Church of England. Wesley had begun his evangelical campaign in England in 1738, although George Whitefield, Howell Harris and Daniel Rowlands were already preaching a similar message. They used the same methods as Wesley, but preached Calvinism, while Wesley preached Arminianism which was easier to reconcile with the Church of England.

20 As was made clear in an anonymous French memorandum of August 1739, AE. Mémoires et Documents, Ang. Volume 8 folios 209–12 at 209.

Many "Methodist" clergy and worshippers probably thought of themselves as Anglicans throughout the century, although Methodism can be seen both as a revival movement within the Church of England and Dissent. Methodists used methods and practices that were quickly adopted by (and thereby encouraged) Dissenters, and they developed a theology that placed them closer to Dissent, for example Wesley's emphasis on conversion and the stress on the importance of works. Wesley combined concern for the church establishment with first-hand contact with Continental Protestants, particularly the revived Moravian Brethren based at Herrnhut, a German religious community, developed by the Pietist Count Zinzendorf, that established a permanent presence in England. Methodism, initially intended by Wesley as a means to reawaken Anglicanism, was thus part of the "Great Awakening," a widespread movement of Protestant revival in Europe and North America, and it employed many of the organizational features of European Protestant revival, including itinerant preaching and love feasts, both of which could have provided Fielding with settings for description and action in his novels.

Seeing his mission as one of saving souls, Wesley urged men to turn to Christ to win redemption, and promised they would know that they had achieved salvation. Wesley's Arminianism led him to stress that salvation was open to all. He rejected predestination, asserted justification by faith, and offered an eclectic theology that was adapted to a powerful mission addressing itself to popular anxieties. Wesley combined religion with traditional Enlightenment thought processes. His belief in religion as an epic struggle, with providence, demons and witchcraft all present, and his willingness to seek guidance by opening the Bible at random, all found echoes from a growing popular following in many, though not all, areas. This was facilitated by the energy of the preaching mission, and the revivalist nature of Methodism, with its hymn-singing, watch-nights and love feasts. In his *Enthusiasm of Methodists and Papists Compared* (3 parts, 1749–51), the hostile George Lavington, Bishop of Exeter, claimed that Methodism imitated the enthusiastic excesses of medieval Catholicism, with visions, exorcisms and healing; although Wesley, in fact, argued against excessive emotionalism and enthusiasm. He was both flexible in his approach, and well-aware of the value of print, producing many tracts and much serial material. Wesley was also tolerant, accepting men and women of all denominations for membership, and, from the mid-1740s, using lay preachers because he could not obtain enough support from ordained ministers. The use of lay preachers, especially as some of them were female, helped to increase clerical opposition, as did unease about Wesley's theology.

Wesley had much sympathy for the poor, although not enough to allow them leisure time: he disliked the idea of the poor having time away from work or worship. Wesley criticized some aspects of society, but was loyal to the dynasty and the political society. Thus, although its energy and place to a degree were to draw on the gap left by the failure of Jacobitism, Methodism did not pose a threat to the political order or élite. Wesley's loyalty, concern about personal and social disorder, and belief in divine intervention were reflected in a letter he sent Matthew Ridley, Mayor of Newcastle, during the Jacobite rising of 1745. He felt bound to write, by the fear of God, love of his country, and zeal toward George II, as he had been pained by "the senseless wickedness, the ignorant prophaneness" of the city's poor and the "continual cursing and swearing, and the wanton blasphemy" of the soldiers, and feared this conduct would endanger divine support.[21]

Methodism was particularly popular among artisans (though not so much among unskilled workers) and servants, and was responsive to the religious needs of such groups. In Nottingham, its following was mostly among artisans, particularly those working in the important stocking industry. Methodism was also very popular among Cornish tinners and fishermen, both dangerous jobs. It developed rapidly in England and Wales, especially in manufacturing and mining areas, such as the West Riding of Yorkshire, where the parochial structure was weak. Methodism was an important development, but it is necessary not to exaggerate its numerical significance.

Fielding was unimpressed. In his play, *Miss Lucy in Town*, Jenny Ranter, the best prostitute at Mrs Midnight's brothel, is turned Methodist, and married to one of the brethren:

"Lord Bawble. O, if that be all, we shall have her again.
Mrs Midnight. Alas! I fear not; for they are powerful men."

21 Wesley to Matthew Ridley, 26 Oct. 1745, Ashington, Northumberland CRO, ZRI 27/5.

In the *True Patriot* of 8 April 1746, Fielding was unimpressed by a Methodist sermon, and reports the preacher as having "got his living many years by collecting articles of news for one of the public papers," which is a double-handed way to damn both. In *Tom Jones*, there was widespread suspicion of Methodist inclinations as with Captain Blifil (I,x). Moreover, as a clear linkage of villainy and Methodism, Blifil's son turns "Methodist, in hopes of marrying a very rich widow of that sect" (XVIII,xiii), and, to different ends, Wesley certainly cultivated wealthy women whom he called the "mothers in Israel." Earlier in the novel, Fielding had referred to "the pernicious principles of Methodism, or of any other heretical sect" (VIII,viii). In the prison in *Amelia*, Cooper, a Methodist, presents crime as an opportunity for grace to operate, an approach Fielding describes as "cant" (I,iv). While thus "searching him [Booth] to the bottom," the Methodist is revealed to be a pickpocket in practice, as well, subsequently, as a total hypocrite. In combination with the Deist Robinson, this is a repeat of Thwackum and Square from *Tom Jones*, but in grimmer circumstances and with more harshness in their conduct. Cooper is a clearer villain.

Methodist meetings sometimes met with a violent response, as in Walsall (1743), Sheffield (1744), Exeter (1745), Leeds (1745), York (1747), and Norwich (1751–52), although the degree to which the Church of England did not respond to Methodist activity in an official fashion is striking. Wesley was not expelled from the Church. Thus, there was an effective toleration of Methodism at the national level that was not always matched locally, although the local experience varied greatly. If Bishop Lavington of Exeter was very hostile in the 1750s, Bishop Ross was very friendly in the 1770s. Lavington, like Gibson, was also hostile to the Moravians, but the majority of Anglican bishops did not see them in the same light, and, in 1749, supported the passage of the Moravian Act, which recognized the Moravian church.

Baptists, Quakers, Presbyterians and Independents (Congregationalists) were the major categories of Dissenters. Aside from theological and organizational differences, not least over Trinitarian and predestinarian principles, both of which came under increasing criticism in this period, and also over baptism, these congregations also varied socially and geographically. For example, Baptists were more commonly rural and Presbyterians urban.

The laity played a bigger role in Quaker and Baptist worship than in that of the Independents and Presbyterians. Anglican clergy regarded Quakers in a more hostile fashion than they treated Presbyterians, some of whom partially conformed to Anglicanism. In *Tom Jones*, a Quaker is revealed to be a nasty, mean hypocrite (VII,x), which prepares the way for the depiction of the Methodist in *Amelia*. In this period, Quakers were more likely than other Dissenters to fall foul of the law.

There were very strong continuities between areas where Dissent was strong and those that had earlier been characterized as Puritan. Dissent itself appears to have contracted and become increasingly urban from mid-century. The complex pattern of Dissent was part of the variety of religious life in Britain that undermines clearcut descriptions. At the same time, alongside the conventional term for variety, a mosaic, it is important to note that the individual pieces were linked, by organizational and other ties. The interaction between varied local circumstances and these links helped give the period much of its dynamism.

Toleration in religious life must not be exaggerated, as religious issues were "real," indistinguishable from political and social issues, and worth fighting over, literally so as the riots against Dissenters in England in 1710, 1715 and 1791, and against Catholics in England in 1780, indicated all too clearly. Anti-Catholicism was a powerful force, throughout the period at the popular level, and at least until mid-century, at that of the élite. Prior to then, it was widely believed that Catholicism was on the increase in the British Isles and on the advance in Europe; the latter was certainly true until Frederick the Great of Prussia's invasion of Austrian-ruled Silesia in 1740. Suspicions of Catholic disloyalty were greatly increased by the Jacobite threat. There was an enormous amount of anti-Catholic material both in the culture of print-newspapers, pamphlets, prints and books—and in the public culture of anniversary celebrations, for example of the defeat of the Armada in 1588 and the discovery of the Gunpowder Plot in 1605, and of other public rituals. The representation of Catholics was generally crude and violent[22]: their intentions were seen as diabolical, while their strength and deceit were frightening. The public ritual lent immediacy to

22 For Catholic cruelty in Kent, *Weekly Journal, or, British Gazetteer*, 21 September 1723.

the material in print, and both were further linked by sermons, as for the anniversary of the Gunpowder Plot. The wish of William Wake, Archbishop of Canterbury from 1716 until 1737, for closer Anglican relations with the French Catholic Church (as well as with the Orthodox and Continental Protestants) was unrealistic, and evidence of divergence between popular and clerical religion.

Fielding is most clearly anti-Catholic in *The Old Debauchees* (1732), where the context provides an undercutting for the remark made by the credulous and wicked Jourdain, who reproaches his wiser and honest daughter, Isabel, for being critical of the Catholic Church: "You owe these wicked thoughts to your education in England, that vile heretical country, where every man believes what religion he pleases, and most believe none" (III,ix). Never, thereafter, does he devote so much space or energy to the issue. On 1 May 1740, the *Champion* brought together Catholicism, authoritarianism, and deceit:

> "In what great ignorance, with regard to public affairs, the subjects of arbitrary princes are kept, is effectually proved by the Spanish prisoners taken in the *Princessa* who report that Port Mahon is as good as taken … being all lies of the first magnitude; and yet as glibly swallowed by them, as transubstantiation: or any other thundering imposture of the Roman Church."

Port Mahon was the British base on Minorca, which was not in fact captured by the Spaniards. In *Joseph Andrews*, Fielding comments on a Catholic priest concealing his Catholicism: "Those who understand our laws will not wonder he was not overready to own it" (III,viii). The aftermath of the '45 led to a harsher note in *Tom Jones*. Thus, with reference to the ghastly Blifil, whom Sophia Western is expected to marry, he:

> "departed home, having first earnestly begged that no violence might be offered to the lady by this haste, in the same manner as a Popish inquisitor begs the lay power to do no violence to the heretic, delivered over to it, and against whom the Church hath passed sentence." (VII,vi)

Tom declares "I love my King and Country, I hope, as well as any man in it, yet the Protestant interest is no small motive to my becoming a volunteer in the cause" (VII,xii). Newspapers, such as the *Whitehall Evening Post* of 14 April 1752, continued to report the persecution of Protestants abroad.

It has been argued that anti-Catholicism diminished during the period, especially after the suppression of Jacobitism in the 1740s;[23] but it is unclear that this was so, especially at the popular level, and concerns about Catholic disaffection continued to be expressed to prominent figures.[24] However, there is little doubt that, at the level of the élite, social relations between Protestants and Catholics improved. This was helped by the extent to which most English Catholics proved loyal in the crisis of 1745–46. The stone with which the nave of York Minster was repaired in mid-century was the gift of a Catholic, Sir Edward Gascoigne, although Catholic landowners were hit by a double land tax.

Anti-Catholicism was not static, but an ideology that could be flexible and influenced by its local environment and by political developments. Where landowners were Catholic, the Penal Laws against Catholics were generally not enforced. Separately, the Jacobite rebellion in 1745 led to a serious, albeit temporary, upsurge in anti-Catholic activity, as with the demolition of a Catholic chapel at Stokesley by local sailors.

Religious antagonism had other manifestations. The small Jewish community grew by immigration, but met prejudice. In *Miss Lucy in Town*, Zorobabel, a secretive dealer in lottery-tickets, complains to Mrs Midnight that a new prize in the brothel has been promised first to Lord Bawble, adding, "You deserve never to have any but Christians in your house again:

"Midnight. Marry forbid! Don't utter such curses against me.
Zorobabel. Who is it supports you? Who is it can support you? Who have any money besides us?"

23 Colin Haydon, *Anti-Catholicism in Eighteenth-Century England, c. 1714–80: a Political and Society Study* (Manchester: Manchester University Press, 1993).
24 J. Sloane to Matthew Hutton, Archbishop of York, 11 July 1748, Bedford Estate Office, Russell Manuscripts, papers of John, 4th Duke of Bedford, volume 20.

Mrs Midnight is prevailed on to prefer Zorobabel's cash, the latter reflecting, "Soh! the money of Christian men pays for the beauty of Christian women. A good exchange!" Midnight: "'Tis he, and some more of his acquaintance, that make half the fine ladies in the town." Casual anti-Semitism was readily found in the language. In *Joseph Andrews*, pleased to meet with a kind innkeeper, Adams notes, "He was glad to find some Christians left in the kingdom, for that he almost began to suspect that he was sojourning in a country inhabited only by Jews and Turks" (II,xvi).

The strength of popular Anglicanism was fully demonstrated in 1753, when a vicious press campaign of anti-Semitic hatred, with popular backing, forced the repeal of the Jewish Naturalisation Act of that year, which had made it easier to be naturalized by private act of Parliament, dropping the phrase "on the true faith of a Christian" from the Oaths of Supremacy and Allegiance. Much of the anti-Semitism was religious as well as racial: Tories saw the Jews as honorary Dissenters who, if granted civil rights, would help Dissenters to undermine the Church. The Naturalization Act was a Whig measure and was defended in print by the Whig cleric Francis Blackburne.

The *Salisbury Journal* of 7 January 1754 recorded the celebrations in nearby Devizes following the repeal:

> "Last Friday the gentlemen and principal tradesmen of this borough, met at the Black Bear Inn to rejoice on account of the repeal of the Jew Bill; and though numbers of different persuasions were assembled on this occasion, yet party and prejudice were entirely laid aside, and all were unanimous in expressing their joy and highest approbation. The effigy of a Jew was carried through every street in town, attended with all sorts of rough music; several men had torches that the inhabitants might see the effigy, and read the paper that was stuck on his breast, containing these words
> NO JEWS!
> Reformations to the B—ps [Bishops];
> Christianity for ever.
> They made a halt two or three times in every street, drank and repeated the above, amidst the acclamations of a great number of people: a large fire was made, and they burnt the body of

the Jew, and set his head on the top of the pillory; the bells rang, and beer was given to the populace; several loyal healths were drank by the gentlemen, etc. and likewise variety of toasts, applicable to the occasion. The Thursday following (being Market Day) the head was again put on top of the pillory, which gave great delight to the farmers and other country people."

Religious issues were also an expression or aspect of other disputes, ranging from that over the succession to the crown following the Glorious Revolution of 1688–89, to the town-country tension that played a role in Anglican-Dissenter rivalries. Towns were often centers of Dissent, challenging the Anglican religious-cultural hegemony in the locality and region; just as the towns could seek to resist the attempts of the local gentry to control their parliamentary representation, and were also the foci of a changing economy. Dissent, moreover, was strongest in regions where the parochial structure was weak, particularly in the West Riding of Yorkshire where Quakers, Presbyterians and Baptists were numerous. A weak parochial structure was often one without strong landowners, and most of the latter were Anglicans.

At the same time, it is necessary not to exaggerate the divide. Some Whig bishops preached moderation in dealing with Dissenters, and Protestant unity remained a prominent theme in public polemic, and, during the Jacobite risings, Dissenters, in works such as Samuel Chandler's *Great Britain's Memorial against the Pretender and Popery* (1745), stressed their loyalty by emphasizing a broad, Protestant patriotism which could include them as well as the established faith. There was no sustained or coherent crusade against Dissent. As in the case of Catholics, Dissenters could generally live peacefully among Anglican neighbors (despite the vigorous polemics, and occasional outrages against them), and Dissenters found many ways to integrate into mainstream politics and culture. In local communities, such as Great Yarmouth, a workable accommodation was gradually worked out after the Toleration Act;[25] and the decline in church courts and ecclesiastical authority hastened by that legislation allowed a "freedom" to diverge from orthodoxy. Clerical investigations into Dissenter numbers rarely challenged

25 Perry Gauci, *Politics and Society in Great Yarmouth, 1660–1722* (Oxford: Oxford University Press, 1996).

the right of people to worship outside the church in their homes or meeting houses, and non-Anglicans devised ways—especially through Occasional Conformity and Indemnity Acts—to evade the laws against them.

The development of Methodism reflected not so much a failure of the Church of England as the contradictions inherent in a national body that had to serve all, as well as enthusiasts. Within the Church, alongside pluralism, non-residence, appointments due to patronage, and a very unequal system of payment of clerics, there was conscientiousness and the provision of regular services in most parishes. Parson Adams was not that rare.

At the same time, the paternalism that Fielding envisaged for society was one that was neglected by many of those in positions of authority, and sufficiently so to qualify and query the idea of a benign world, at least for readers, if not always for the characters. Moreover, Fielding did not necessarily suggest that progress was occurring. Indeed, his discussion of the "natural" character of phenomena led in the direction of perceiving both improvement, in terms of taming "natural" self-interest, and decline with reference to the corrupting character of civilization. Marital arrangements brought both of these aspects into contact with religion, because, as it could be all-too-difficult to recall, marriage was a sacrament and vows were exchanged. Thus, in *Tom Jones*, Allworthy:

> "by no means concurred with the opinions of those parents, who think it as immaterial to consult the inclinations of their children in the affair of marriage, as to solicit the good pleasure of their servants when they intend to take a journey; and who are, by law or decency at least, withheld often from using absolute force. On the contrary, as he esteemed the institution to be of the most sacred kind, he thought every preparatory caution necessary to preserve it holy and inviolate; and very wisely concluded, that the surest way to effect this, was by laying the foundation in previous affection." (XVI,vi)

This view was in accord with a central feature of Fielding's work, namely a practical ethics that brought the truth of Christian morality into play, rather than the hypocritical evasions of social conceit and the callousness of a mere insistence on doctrine. Worldliness was shown to rest on charity, and not on deception.

10. INTO NOVELS

Far from conforming to a common tone, form, intention or characterization, novels varied greatly in content and approach, a trend encouraged by the size and diversity of the reading public. The rise of the novel was for a long time discussed in terms of the works of Daniel Defoe (1660–1731), Samuel Richardson (1689–1761) and Fielding himself, but this approach neglected what was a far greater range of early novels, many written by women, and, in doing so, misleadingly simplified the origins, character and development of the genre.[1] Although English writers played the key role in the eighteenth-century development of novels and, indeed, the idea of the novel, there were important seventeenth-century precursors, notably Cervantes's *Don Quixote* (1605–15).[2] This greatly influenced Fielding and others, including Charlotte Lennox's *The Female Quixote* (1752), which was praised by Fielding in the *Covent-Garden Journal* of 24 March 1752, and Richard Graves in *The Spiritual Quixote, or The Summer's Ramble of Mr Geoffrey Wildgoose* (1774). Fielding's debt was brought to the fore in his play *Don Quixote in England, a Comedy* (1733), while Don Quixote is mentioned elsewhere in his work including in *Joseph Andrews* (III,ix).[3] Scenes from *Don Quixote* and Samuel Butler's mockpheroic narrative poem *Hudibras* (1663) in Littlecote House, Berkshire have recently been attributed to Hogarth in the 1720s.

More generally, the novel looked to a range of literary types, including picaresque tales, travel, books, and romances. In turn, novels took a number

---

1   J. Paul Hunter, *Before Novels: The Cultural Contexts of Eighteenth-Century English Fiction* (New York: W.W. Norton and Co., 1990); Alan Downie (ed.), *The Oxford Handbook of the Eighteenth-Century Novel* (Oxford: Oxford University Press, 2016).

2   William Egginton, *The Man Who Invented Fiction: How Cervantes Ushered in the Modern World* (London, 2016).

3   See also eg *Tom Jones* IV,viii, VIII,iv; *Voyage to Lisbon*, 27 June 1754.

of forms, including tales for children: the *Worcester Journal* of 23 March 1749 advertised *The Amusement of Little Master Tommy, and Pretty Miss Polly.* Romances were particularly important in the early eighteenth century, when a novel was often a short story of romantic love, for example Eliza Haywood's successful *Love in Excess* (1719–20). The growing popularity of novels was referred to in *Tom Jones* in the well-written inn scene in Upton where an Irish gentleman is one of the guests:

> "This gentleman was one of those whom the Irish call a cala-
> balaro, or cavalier. He was a younger brother of a good family,
> and having no fortune at home, was obliged to look abroad in
> order to get one: for which purpose he was proceeding to the
> Bath to try his luck with cards and the women.
>
> This yellow fellow lay in bed reading one of Mrs Behn's nov-
> els; for he had been instructed by a friend, that he would find
> no more effective method of recommending himself to the
> ladies than the improving his understanding, and filling his
> mind with good literature." (X,ii)

The common feature of the early novels of these decades was their claim to realism if not being factual, as can be seen in Defoe's *Robinson Crusoe* (1719), *Colonel Jack* (1721), *Moll Flanders* (1722), *A Journal of the Plague Year* (1722), and *Roxana* (1724). The subjects of these novels were very different and they looked back to varied influences—*Robinson Crusoe* to travel literature and spiritual autobiography; but *Colonel Jack, Moll Flanders* and *Roxana* to picaresque tales. Defoe could offer female protagonists ready to use their sexual attraction to help their voyage through life. However, the common theme in these alleged autobiographies was authenticity, and they had affinities with criminal biographies, a very popular and longstanding genre. The romantic tales, such as those of Haywood, also claimed to be accounts of real life and manners, while the most distinctive novelistic account, Swift's *Gulliver's Travels* (1726), was stated to be a true account.

Novels were not alone in devoting positive attention to the lowly, generally in pursuit of a morality tale. "Philo-Pater," in a piece on filial piety in the *London Journal* of 15 October 1726, ended:

"Since therefore the lower rank, and more contemptible part of mankind, are not altogether so destitute of virtue and greatness of mind, as some people may imagine; these instances of heroical virtue and magnanimity of spirit, whenever they offer themselves to our view, ought to excite and stimulate the superior class of men, effectually to maintain a real dignity of character, and an essential superiority of the vulgar (whom they hold in the lowest contempt) in the exercise of exemplary virtues, as much as they exceed them in estates and titles."

The threat was readily apparent, the *Craftsman* of 17 February 1727 discerning:

"a vicious and depraved age, when profuseness, extravagance, and a general spirit of libertinism grow predominant in every nation; especially among persons of a superior rank who are entrusted with the rights and liberties of the People; for when once luxury had fixed a deep root in their minds, it will soon get the better of their noble faculties."

This was very much an aspect of Fielding's social politics.

Gulliver's Travels' combination of traveler's tale, picaresque novella, and satire, proved inimitable, and there was only limited development in prose fiction until Richardson's first novel, *Pamela* (1740), a very popular book on the prudence of virtue and the virtue of prudence, with the title continuing *or Virtue Rewarded*. Its success encouraged the publication of more novels in the 1740s, including by Fielding, who thereby contributed to what proved an especially productive period in the context of a marked rise of publication compared to the 1700s. By 1769, booksellers were advertising nearly 100 self-proclaimed "novels,"[4] although fewer were published annually.

The appeal of *Pamela* reflected in part its ability to span sexual frisson with clear morality, to move from page-turning perils for Pamela to a happy

4   James Raven, "The Publication of Fiction in Britain and Ireland, 1750–70," *Publishing History*, 24 (1988): 32–35.

ending, and to employ the form of letters in order to provide the sympathetic insight of the heroine. Pamela, a young maidservant, resists the lascivious advances of Mr B, in part thwarting attempted rapes by fainting at
opportune moments. In the end, a realization of Pamela's virtues and an
appreciation of her virtue leads him to propose marriage, thus fulfilling the
fantasy of social aspiration: Pamela marries her employer. The importance
of writings to the structure and form of the novel was seen not only with
the letters but also because the theft of Pamela's journal leads Mr. B to this
appreciation.

Pamela's content and success invited skits and parody, especially Fielding's satirical *An Apology for the Life of Mrs Shamela Andrews* (1741)[5] in
which self-interest is to the fore, and his *Joseph Andrews* (1742), Joseph supposedly being Pamela's brother; as well as James Dance's comedy *Pamela;
or Virtue Triumphant* (1742). John Kelly offered an epistolary novel in
Pamela's Conduct in High Life (1741), which, as with Richardson's continuation and *Joseph Andrews*, presented her life as a wife, but lacked Fielding's
lightness. John Cleland's pornographic novel *Memoirs of a Woman of Pleasure* (1748–9), otherwise known as *Fanny Hill*, was in the form of two long
letters, each a volume long, rather than a series of individual letters which
was the way to exploit the opportunities of the epistolary form. Although
initially suppressed, Cleland's novel became a popular work.

The novels of the 1740s displayed considerable diversity in content
with a number of subgenres significant, notably criminal lives, spiritual autobiographies, and secret histories. With *Jonathan Wild*, Fielding produced
a major instance of the first, but not of the others.[6] In his novels, he took
the comic confusions of his plays and put them into novelistic form, and
therefore greater length; with this confusion accompanied by bawdy and
chaos.

A common theme in Richardson and Fielding was psychological authenticity. Richardson's narratives were composed of letters, which allowed

---

5   Published on 4 April.
6   Thomas Keymer and Peter Sabor (eds), *The 'Pamela' Controversy: Criticisms
     and Adaptations of Samuel Richardson's Pamela, 1740–1750* (6 volumes, Lon-
     don: Pickering and Chatto, 2001); Jerry Beasley, *Novels of the 1740s* (Athens,
     Georgia: University of Georgia Press, 1982).

him to vary the tone by using different styles for his writers; and helped give *Pamela* an impetus and an urgency matching the plot of virtue vying with seduction. In turn, Fielding insisted that his novels were "true histories" in that they revealed the truth of behavior, an approach especially suited to the ironic voice he adopted as narrator, comparable also to that he had also taken in his plays, such as *Tom Thumb* (1730). Thus, in the last chapter of *Joseph Andrews*, "This true history is brought to a happy conclusion." History indeed frequently appeared in the title of novels. The role of historian enabled Fielding to explain his chosen part as narrator, that not only of commentator, moralist and humorous reflector, but also as stage director, arranging the depiction, shaping the narrative, and encouraging the reader to appreciate more than surface meanings and unidirectional plots.

The different styles of Richardson and Fielding helped energise novel-writing as they encouraged debate as to best practice, while each had their imitators. With its emphasis on the female plight and perspective, Richardson looked forward to the sentimental novel, as did his stress on the role of the novel as instructional fiction. In *Shamela*, in contrast, Fielding presents Pamela as self-interested, rather than moral, and with her virtue very differently used as a consequence in order to obtain her advantageous marriage with Mr B.

The popularity of novels exemplified the degree to which the expansion of the middling orders ensured that élite activity was less central than hitherto to the dominant cultural world. Élite values and models remained important across society, but others were also of consequence, while considerable play was made of contrasts between these values and the actual conduct of members of the élite. This served not to deny the values or models, but to suggest a measure of hypocrisy on the part of members of the élite, as well as the extent to which appropriate values were not solely displayed by its members. In the listing of "Names of the Principal Persons" in the novel *Sir Charles Grandison* (1753–54), Richardson listed the men and women by their moral worth rather than their rank. In *Joseph Andrews* (1742), the contrast was important to the plot and explicitly mentioned by Fielding, who entered a caveat about judging groups, at the same time indicating the true quality of patronage, before continuing to deadly effect:

"As in most of our particular characters we mean not to lash individuals, but all of the like sort, so, in our general descriptions
we mean not universals, but would be understood with many
exceptions: for instance, in our description of high people we
cannot be intended to include such as, whilst they are an honour to their high rank, by a well-guided condescension make
their superiority as easy as possible to those whom fortune
chiefly hath placed below them. Of this number I could name
a peer no less elevated by nature than by fortune who, whilst
he wears the noblest ensigns of honour on his person, bears the
truest stamp of dignity on his mind, adorned with greatness,
enriched with knowledge, and embellished with genius. I have
seen this man relieve with generosity while he hath conversed
with freedom, and be to the same person a patron and a companion." (III, i)

Patronage issues brought the mismatch of rank and nobility abruptly home
to many writers. This encouraged a critique of the values of polite society,
as when Fielding wrote that the lascivious Lady Booby was "perfectly polite,
nor had any vice inconsistent with good breeding." His plots, like those of
many other works, frequently revolved around issues of inheritance, and
this was a device, appropriate for both comedy and tragedy, that struck a
resonance across society and indeed genres, playing a major role in the first
Gothic novel, Horace Walpole's *The Castle of Otranto* (1764).

The travails of a rightful inheritance, however much depicted in
landed society, also echoed at all levels. This was also seen in the leading
work of Fielding's younger sister, Sarah, her novel *The Adventures of David
Simple* (1744), in which David has been disinherited by his younger
brother's use of a forged will, while the friends he makes, Cynthia, Camilla
and Valentine, have also been harshly treated, the last two due to a dishonest stepmother. Henry wrote the preface. In Tobias Smollett's *The Adventures of Roderick Random* (1748), Roderick's father has been
disinherited.

Fielding's condemnation of false values was directed across the range
of society. In his vigorous mock-heroic novel *The History of the Life of the
Late Mr Jonathan Wild the Great* (1743), which was possibly based on

earlier writings back to the 1730s, Fielding offered a harshly ironic account of false greatness aimed not only at the criminal but, for example, also against great conquerors, Alexander the Great being among those condemned:

> "When I consider whole nations extirpated only to bring tears into the eyes of a GREAT MAN, that he hath no more nations to extirpate, then indeed I am almost inclined to wish that nature had spared us this her MASTER-PIECE, and that no GREAT MAN had ever been born into the world." (I,xiv)

The parallel of false greatness and crime had in the case of Alexander the Great and a pirate been drawn by St Augustine, in the *City of God*, which appeared in 426, Augustine commenting, "Without justice, what are kingdoms but gangs of criminals on a very large scale? What are criminal gangs but petty kingdoms" (IV,iv). Fielding in his *A Dialogue between Alexander the Great and Diogenes the Cynic* (1743) had also taken aim at the conqueror, very much one of the Ancients of note.

In *Jonathan Wild*, Fielding offered a telling piece on the subject of greatness, one that proclaimed his moral concerns and his ironic, but deeply-felt, hostility to human evil. A sense of social division was also present: "the plowman, the shepherd, the weaver, the builder, and the soldier, work not for themselves but others; they are contented with a poor pittance (the labourer's hire)." In contrast, "the GREAT" enjoyed "the fruits of their labours" (I,viii). Fielding's approach enabled him to range widely, using a very different authorial voice and method to that of Defoe's 1725 approach to Wild, which was more focused on his protagonist.

Fielding's *Jonathan Wild* includes critiques of a range of historical figures, from Alexander to Charles XII of Sweden (r.1697–1718) who was a contentious figure in Britain because he had actively intrigued with the Jacobites against George I in 1717. Wild admires Charles, whereas Fielding's approach looked to other responses to autocrats.[7] In the *Champion*, he had added for reflection Nadir Shah, the contemporary warrior-ruler of Persia,

---

7. Claude Rawson, *Henry Fielding and the Augustan Ideal under Stress* (London: Routledge and Kegan Paul, 1972).

who was very much an Alexander figure. Fielding's approach was in part a commonplace. For example, the *British Journal* of 7 September 1723 had reflected:

> "Some, not fit to govern a family, nor themselves, have governed empires ... others, with great qualities and equal vices, have overrun the world and defaced it, to signalise these qualities, and to reward them: and when they had grasped all that they could hold, and ten thousand times more than they could manage, the reward was still too narrow."

At the same time, *Jonathan Wild* was a novel as well as a morality tale, and, as a result, Wild was not only depicted as dangerously harsh but also, on the pattern of John Gay's *The Beggar's Opera* (1728), as charismatic. As such, he deserved attention rather than just castigation.

The twentieth-century films of Fielding's novels *Tom Jones* (1963) and *Joseph Andrews* (1977), each directed by Tony Richardson, present them as jolly romps, much more sexualized than in the original, and notably so in the latter,[8] with the many twists of the plots being essentially contrivances to move the stories along and to obtain comic effect. Yet, there was also, on Fielding's part, an attempt to show the follies of self-serving human searches for control. Instead, he emphasized the role of Providence; not as an excuse for an inactive contemplation of divine grace but rather as a counterpart to good human activity that itself reflects the divine plan. Parson Adams was presented in *Joseph Andrews* as an exemplary individual, not least when, oblivious to his own safety, he hastened to the aid of Fanny Adams who is resisting rape. Fanny declares that she had "put her whole trust in Providence," and Adams sees himself as the means of Providential deliverance.

This is at once humorous and deadly serious: the vehicles of divine judgement might be comic, but it alone could save the innocent from malign fate in the shape of unhappy coincidence and the wretched designs of the sinful. This indeed was a variation of the great instability of human affairs readily discerned by those who considered international and do-

---

8   Martin Battestin, "Fielding on Film," *Eighteenth-Century Life*, 11 (May 1987): 110–13.

mestic politics.[9] Furthermore, the role of Providence, alongside the explicit interventions of Fielding as author-narrator, demonstrated the need for readers to be cautious in anticipating events, passing judgement and determining the plot, thus instructing them in a humility to match that of the benign characters who are depicted. In *Tom Jones*, returning home and going to his chamber, Allworthy praying, "spent some minutes on his knees, a custom which he never broke through on any account" (I, 3). Life was far from orderly, both due to accidents but also as a result of human misperception, indeed misplacing, due to vice and foibles, notably hypocrisy.

Fanny's plight in *Joseph Andrews* can be underlined by an instance of accident from the *Cirencester Flying Post* of 12 September 1743:

> "Last Friday was se'nnight, the following melancholy affair happened near Shepton Malet in Somerset, vis John Burnton and Mary Pretton (fellow-servants) walking out together, the man used some indecent actions and expressions to the girl, which she resented then no farther than in telling him, that if he persisted in his wicked attempts, she would stick a pitch-fork in him, which she had then with her; but notwithstanding that, the fellow, when he thought they were come to a more convenient place, renewed his villainous attempts, which so exasperated the girl, that she took out a knife and stabbed him to the heart. The fellow very soon after expired; and the jury sat on his body, and brought in their verdict manslaughter."

Accident provides much of the drama for Fielding's novels, but the characterization often focused on aspects of hypocrisy. Central to *Joseph Andrews* and *Tom Jones*, Fielding turned also to his attack on hypocrisy in other works, including the introduction to his *Miscellanies* (1743). Alongside the moral critique of affectation in much of the writing of the period, and the preference for honesty as an aesthetic as well as a moral choice, and in Fielding's case as the key to redemption not least from prodigality, can be seen the sense of flux and uncertainty that led to a

---

9   Wilkes diary, September 1741, p. 118.

lack of clarity over identity and classification, or, at least, a challenge to them. In this situation of flux, "the uncertainty of human events,"[10] performance was both the condition of mankind, certainly in the intense and brittle social maelstrom of London, and a challenge to appropriate conduct and to the social categorization that it was supposed to reflect and sustain. In terms of the transgression of norms, the representation of men and women proved as troubling as that of social groups,[11] although, looked at differently, this fluidity provided plots and also satisfied public interest.

The sense of social distinction in traditional classification was captured by Fielding in his preface to *Joseph Andrew*. He showed his knowledge of Classical literature and the classification to which it had given rise when he distinguished comic from tragic romances in terms of characters, manner and language:

> "a comic romance is a comic epic poem in prose, differing from comedy as the serious epic from tragedy, its action being more extended and comprehensive, containing a much larger circle of incidents, and introducing a greater variety of characters. It differs from the serious romance in its fable and action in this, that as in the one these are grave and solemn, so in the other they are light and ridiculous; it differs in its characters by introducing persons of inferior rank and consequently of inferior manners, whereas the grave romance sets the highest before us; lastly, in its sentiments and diction by preserving the ludicrous instead of the sublime."

Homer's lost *Margites* served Fielding as an alleged model for his novels, which he claimed were "comic epics in prose." He thereby outlined the background to this novel and, more generally, to his writing. Fielding was careful to distinguish his comedy from burlesque, arguing that the latter is

10 Thomas Harris to James Harris, 13 February 1745, Winchester, Hampshire CRO, 9M73 G309/25.
11 Jill Campbell, *Natural Masques: Gender and Identity in Fielding's Plays and Novels* (Stanford, California: Stanford University Press, 1995).

unnatural; and, offering a parallel between painting and *caricatura*, placing Hogarth with the former and therefore as a comparison for him.

In social terms, the rise of the novel can best be seen as an important instance of the embourgeoisement of culture, notably in terms of patronage. Earlier, there had been an emphasis on seeking the support of individual patrons, who were presented as crucial protectors, and therefore as responsible for the cultural health of the nation. In practice, support from such patrons could make it easier for authors to deal with publishers and could provide some funds. Yet, prefiguring Dr Johnson's point about his *Dictionary* and the Earl of Chesterfield, there was also a wider social positioning, underlined by Fielding in the preface to his *Historical Register for the Year 1736*, which was dedicated to the public, whereas, he noted for his publisher:

> "What, says he, does more service to a book or raises curiosity
> in a reader equal with 'dedicated to his Grace the Duke of —',
> or 'the Right Honourable the Earl of –' in an advertisement? I
> think the patron here may properly be said to give a name to the
> book."[12]

Novels created and responded to a large readership, and were not dependent on a distinguished list of subscribers, or on political patronage. Fielding's *Joseph Andrews* sold 6,500 copies in three editions in thirteen months, and he received £183 from his energetic publisher, Andrew Millar. In the opening chapter of *Tom Jones*, Fielding compares an author to "one who keeps a public ordinary, at which all persons are welcome for their money," with, as a consequence, a need to satisfy them, and more satisfactorily so than many of the innkeepers he discussed. The patronage of the public created an additional reason to emphasize reviews, whereas, in contrast, the more rarified appeal of epics were not compatible with the commercial literary climate.

Following on from a theme in his plays, the opening chapter of *Joseph Andrews* offered a determined preference for the modern when Fielding

12   Jacque Carré, "Burlington's Literary Patronage," *British Journal for Eighteenth-Century Studies*, 5 (1982): 26–27.

referred to "those ancient writers which of late days are little read, being written in obsolete, and, as they are generally thought, unintelligible languages, such as Plutarch, Nepos, and others which I heard of in my youth." Instead, he expressed a preference for the vernacular: "our own language affords many examples of excellent use and instruction, finely calculated to sow the seeds of virtue in youth, and very easy to be comprehended by persons of moderate capacity."

Hypocrisy is the main target in the story, but it is presented not only in the affairs of the great, but also across society, not least in its consequences. Thus, Joseph's father is unable "to get him into a charity-school, because a cousin of his father's landlord did not vote on the right side for a church-warden in a borough-town" (I,iii). Trulliber, the harshly uncharitable curate, is one of the worst of the many hypocrites in the novel. Adams, who had landed up in Trulliber's parish, laments "that it was possible, in a country professing Christianity, for a wretch to starve in the midst of his fellow-creatures who abounded" (I,xv).

The nature of Fielding's narrative provided many opportunities for introducing characters who could serve as the basis for reflections. There was no necessary sequence, and the unexpectedness also incessantly visited on the protagonists was repeated for the readers, for their edification as much as their entertainment. Characters could arrive as if at random, but also could re-emerge, not least, as with Fanny in *Joseph Andrews* the novel, turning from recollection of her by others, to her personal appearance.

As in Bunyan's *Pilgrim's Progress*, characters appear both to move the story along, and also to offer a variety of role models. Thus, Joseph encounters a range of male types and characteristics, only to show that he has more integrity and purpose and is less malleable than is assumed by many. As such, Joseph is a counterpoint to some of the Lockean assumptions about humans as a *tabula rasa* for education and direction, and also for the standard way of treating lower-class women. Although a servant, he has dignity and agency.

Throughout the story, quality of character indeed bears no reference to "The Quality" or, more generally, rank. Thus, Adams is freed from a dead-end of misery by a generous and humane pedlar, a Good Samaritan, whom he meets in an ale-house: "And thus these poor people, who could not engage the compassion of riches and piety were at length delivered out of their distress by the charity of a poor pedlar" (I,15). Throughout, the point of comparison operates by means of piercing a prevalent deceit, even if that deceit is not necessarily a cause of danger.

Fielding sought to use satire in order to laugh or mock the reader away from folly or vice by enabling them to detect the gap between value and conduct, and thus provide humor but also an affirmation of this value. Thus, satire was fun and moral at the same time, with the fun part of the process of controlling the passions.[13] The satire was given greater depth by Fielding's authorial reflection, a practice that emphasized his management of both actions and characters, and thus added himself as another, but very different, character, with a separate narrative. This intervention was infrequent but ensured that the idea of the novel as reality was both interrupted and confirmed, and in an ironic fashion. Writing as a topic in itself was taken further to the fore with the frequent reflections on Classical writers. While demonstrating Fielding's cultural awareness and knowledge, this commentary also offered a deep resonance to what could be the farce of authorial comic self-reflection, one that was headlined in the prologues to the different sections of his books. Thus, book two of *Jonathan Wild* begins:

> "One reason why we chose to end our first book as we did with the last chapter, was that we are now obliged to produce two characters of a stamp entirely different from what we have hitherto dealt in. These persons are of that pitiful order of mortals, who are in contempt called good-natured."

Politics was more to the fore in the extended joke in Fielding's *Philosophical Transactions for the Year 1742–3*, an account of a new species, *Terrestrial Chrysipus*, which in fact is a guinea. The expensive role of Hanover in British foreign policy is criticized:

---

13 K.J.H. Berland, "Satire and the *Via Media*: Anglican Dialogue in *Joseph Andrews*," in J.D. Browning (ed.), *Satire in the 18th Century* (New York: Garland, 1983): 83–99.

"... it is much to be feared the species will be entirely lost among us: and indeed, in England, they are observed of late to be much rarer than formerly, especially in the country, where at present there are very few to be found; but at the same time it is remarked, that in some places of the Continent, particularly in a certain part of Germany, they are much plentier; being to be found in great numbers, where formerly there were scarce any to be met with."

With reference to electoral bribery, Fielding adds at the close: "These animals swarm in England all over the country, like the locusts, once in seven years;[14] and like them too they generally cause much mischief, and greatly ruin the country in which they have swarmed." In his *A Journey from This World to the Next* (1743), published as part of the *Miscellanies*, Fielding drew on Classical models and images to produce a series of stories in which a spirit-narrator, Julian the Apostate, Emperor from 361 to 363 and a Neoplatonic philosopher, introduced the reader to the moral reflections offered by the transmigration of souls: metempsychosis providing a satiric device that enabled Fielding to scour history in order to tilt at the universal ills of selfishness and self-regard, and their focus in the distorting impact of ambition. This is a sermon of true wit, with much narrative and flow to sustain the reiterated attacks on the conceits of power. It is difficult to engage with the spirit-narrator, but themes of the corrupting nature of dishonesty and of the nature of false greatness are handled well. The chronological perspective also helped underline Fielding's concern with posterity, including as a basis for judgement. Edward Gibbon praised the *Journey* as providing "the history of the human nature," and also favored Julian,[15] as had the Whig "martyr" William, Lord Russell.

14 Under the Septennial Act of 1717, elections had to be held at last once every seven years, and when there was the accession of a new monarch.
15 Edward Gibbon, *The History of the Decline and Fall of the Roman Empire* (7 volumes, London, 1897–1901), III, 384, footnote 13; Bertrand Goldgar, "Myth and History in Fielding's *Journey from This World to the Next*," *Modern Language Quarterly*, 47 (1986): 241–43.

The detours of *Joseph Andrews* provided Fielding, on the pattern of Cervantes (and indeed Homer, Bunyan, and other writers of narrative travelogues), with the opportunity of introducing characters whose stories could provide a moral and social compendium of England. Thus, the squire who hunted Adams and wants to seduce Fanny, is a middle-aged bachelor whose mother had spoiled him before sending him on the Grand Tour, returning:

> "well furnished with French clothes, phrases, and servants, with a hearty contempt for his own country, especially which had any savour of the plain spirit and honesty of our ancestors.... [H]e soon procured himself a seat in Parliament and was in the common opinion one of the finest gentlemen of his age; but what distinguished him chiefly was a strange delight which he took in everything which is ridiculous, odious, and absurd in his own species." (III,vii)

This matched a commonplace critique of tourists. Fielding's detours exemplify the sense of the unexpected that provides interest, excitement, suspense, variety, and a shifting judgment in which the upsets of what came next challenge the readiness of moral judgment, and both concerning specific events and about the supposed purpose of developments. Thus, Adams tells a despairing Joseph, "As we know not future events, so neither can we tell to what purpose any accident tends, and that which at first threatens us with evil may in the end produce our good" (III,xi).

Returning at the close to the Booby estate, the novel moves to a closer focus on social background, status, and dynamics. The old harshness is still there, as when Scout tells Lady Booby that the law can be used to remove whoever she dislikes:

> "We have one sure card, which is to carry him before Justice Frolick, who, upon hearing your ladyship's name, will commit him without any farther questions.... [I]t is a great blessing to the country that he is in the commission, for he hath taken several poor off our hands that the law would never lay hold on. I know some justices who make as much of committing a man to Bridewell as his lordship at 'size [assize] would of hanging

him; but it would do a man good to see his worship, our justice, commit a fellow to Bridewell, he takes so much pleasure in it; and when once we ha'um there, we seldom hear any more o'um. He's either starved or eat up by vermin in a month's time." (IV,iii)

So much for the Poor Law or for the law as far as the poor is concerned.

The arrival of Lady Booby's nephew, married to Pamela, Joseph's sister, totally alters the social dynamics, and particularly so with reference to Joseph's position, for Fanny is not suitable for the new social alignment. Fielding is able to play here with a number of themes, not least that Pamela, once a servant, has now acquired the concern with social gradation that scarcely accords with her virtuous image and thus her depiction by Richardson. From "the time of his sister's arrival in the quality of her niece," quality being a nicely ambivalent term here and elsewhere, Lady Booby sees Joseph "in the dress and character of a gentleman." In addition to her desire for Joseph, which has risen to the idea of marriage, she successfully presses her nephew to try to dissuade him from a match with Fanny who, he tells Joseph, is "so much beneath you." Joseph's opposition to discarding Fanny is treated as "wicked pride," and there is a swift clash between the two men, Booby telling Joseph: "As you civilly throw my marriage with your sister in my teeth, I must teach you the wide difference between us: my fortune enabled me to please myself." Joseph replies that his fortune allows him to do likewise.

As with so many of Fielding's characters, Pamela's intervention is exemplary only on the surface. Urging Joseph not to throw down "our family" after it has been raised by Booby, she presses him "to pray for the assistance of grace against such a passion" rather than indulging it. When Joseph tells Pamela that Fanny is her equal, she replies:

> "She was my equal, but I am no longer Pamela Andrews; I am now this gentleman's lady, and, as such, am above her. I hope I shall never behave with an unbecoming pride: but, at the same time, I shall always endeavour to know myself, and question not the assistance of grace to that purpose." (IV,vii)

Pamela also blames Fanny "for her assurance in aiming at such a match as her brother" (IV,xi). Pamela's lack of charity, and indeed hypocrisy, are matched by a reliance on grace, which is the passive approach to fate that Fielding does not support. In turn, told that Pamela and Joseph are siblings but that Pamela doubts this, Lady Booby "flew into a violent rage with her, and talked of upstarts and disowning relations" who had so lately "been on a level with her," thus angering her nephew (IV,xiii). Then, when Joseph discovers that Mr Wilson is his father, the latter expresses some reluctance at first about Fanny, but, after Joseph presses him, tells him, "If she was so good a creature as she appeared, and he described her, he thought the disadvantages of birth and fortune might be compensated" (IV,xvi). The fantasy element of the happy ending and the true Christian wedding, however, is underlined with Fielding's comment in the last chapter about atypicality:

> "The company, arriving at Mr Booby's house, were all received by him in the most courteous and entertained in the most splendid manner, after the custom of the old English hospitality, which is still preserved in some very few families in the remote parts of England." (IV,xvi)

This was very different to the confidence eventually expressed by Catherine Morland in Jane Austen's *Northanger Abbey* (II,x).

Pamela and Fanny, now sisters, are counterpointed at the close of *Joseph Andrews*. Pamela behaves with "great decency," but is rebuked with her husband for laughing in church, while Fanny relies on "the gifts of nature" for her charms (IV,xvi). The criticism of Pamela is clear. Nature is linked to Providence and good works in providing, but only at the last, a happy outcome that rests on truth, trust and activity.

11. THE MAGISTERIAL FIELDING

> "This has been one of the most entertaining weeks for the mob that has happened a great while ... yesterday (which was the top of all) Matthew Henderson was hanged, at whose execution all the world (I speak of the low-life division) were got together; and he died to the great satisfaction of the beholders, that is he was dressed all in white with black ribbons, held a prayer book in his hand and, I believe, a nosegay."

Writing to his brother, James, a friend of Fielding, Thomas Harris, a London lawyer, captured in 1746 the theatricality of justice.[1] Henderson, a servant, was hanged for the murder of his lady employer, Mary Elizabeth Dalrymple, wife of the Honourable William Dalrymple, an execution discussed by Fielding in the *True Patriot* on 13 May 1746.[2] In fact, there was no clear divide in the audiences for executions and other spectacles, attracting members of the "beau monde," such as George Selwyn, as well as the "low-life division."

The subject of Fielding's *The Life and Death of Jonathan Wild, the Great* (1743), Wild, the most famous thief-taker, exemplified the possibilities of developments in the relationships between government, capitalism and crime. Born in Wolverhampton in 1683 and originally a buckle-maker, Wild gravitated to the vortex of opportunities in London where the illegal, the makeshift, and the regular economies interacted, indeed melded. Once in the world of crime, he moved from the established techniques of extortion and protection rackets to develop the trade of receiving stolen goods.

1   Thomas to James Harris, 26 April 1746, Winchester, Hampshire CRO, 9H73 G309/31.
2   Claude Jones, "Fielding's 'True Patriot' and the Henderson Murder," *Modern Language Review*, 52 (1957): 498–503.

Sidelining the fences by paying thieves a higher price for stolen goods, Wild then used newspaper advertisements and other methods to resell them to their original owners. He also profited from the rewards for turning in criminals, including, as is shown by Fielding, members of his own gang. In the early 1720s, Wild destroyed rivals such as the Spiggott, Hawkins and Currick gangs. Fielding presents him as a ruler on the pattern of other descriptions of criminal organizations, for example that of smugglers near Grenoble in 1732.[3] Hanged in 1725 for receiving stolen goods, Wild achieved continuing fame as a character type, being the model for "Peachum" in John Gay's highly-successful *The Beggar's Opera* (1728), while his career was compared to that of Walpole.[4] Wild was also an antithesis to Fielding, both Fielding the magistrate but also Fielding the writer.

The role of London thief-takers was not ended by Wild's removal, and continued to be rife with abuse, as in 1745–54 when crimes were fabricated anew in order to collect rewards.[5] This was receiving of a particular form, but one that was different in its stance to the use of pardoning in order to win testimony against the receivers of stolen goods. The tricky nature of such a system was brought out in *Jonathan Wild* where false testimony is shown in use in order to have Mr Fierce committed. Molly Straddle "swore positively to him though she had never seen him before" (II,v). For a rural context, the issue is shown in *Tom Jones* when Black George, the dismissed gamekeeper, killed a hare while poaching:

> "The higler [trader] to whom the hare was sold, being unfortunately taken many months after with a quantity of game upon him, was obliged to make his peace with the squire, by becoming evidence against some poacher. And now Black George was pitched upon by him as being a person already obnoxious to Mr Western, and one of no good fame in the country. He was

3   *Grub Street Journal*, 10 August 1732.
4   G. Howson, *Thief-Taker General: The Rise and Fall of Jonathan Wild* (London: Hutchinson, 1970).
5   Ruth Paley, "Thief Takers in London in the Age of the McDaniel Gang, *c.*1745–1754," in Douglas Hay and Francis Snyder (eds), *Policing and Prosecution in Britain 1750–1850* (Oxford: Oxford University Press, 1989): 301–25.

besides, the best sacrifice the higler could make, as he had sup-
plied him with no game since; and by this means the witness
had an opportunity of screening his better customers: for the
squire, being charmed with the power of punishing Black
George, whom a single transgression was sufficient to ruin,
made no further enquiry." (III,x)

Here and elsewhere, Fielding shared his strong awareness of the relationship between the administration of law and both personal drives and
social patterns; with true justice shown as playing scant role in the situation.
Indeed, in his novels, Fielding captured the shifting compromises that affected the administration of the law, for example the treatment of prostitutes.[6] So also with those not involved in this administration. Thus, Tom
Jones is merciful to the highwayman who, having failed to rob him between
Barnet and London, explains: "that he had been driven to it by the distress
… of five hungry children, and a wife lying in of a sixth, in the utmost
want and misery" (XII,xiv). In this and elsewhere, Jones is shown as merciful in particulars and in his general views, and, therefore, as deserving
mercy.

The attraction of easily-gotten wealth was very much a theme of Fielding's work, notably with crime, cards and matrimony all serving as possible
means to wealth. In *The Modern Husband*, Mr Modern declares, "The whole
world is the house of the rich, and they may live in what apartment of it
they please" (IV,i). The aptly-known Lord Richly, a dishonest and manip-
ulative character, uses money without remorse to gain his ends:

"I have succeeded often by leaving money in a lady's hands: she
spends it, is unable to pay, and then I, by virtue of my mortgage,
immediately enter the premises…. My money shall always be
the humble servant of my pleasures; and it is the interest of men
of fortune to keep up the price of beauty, that they may have it
more among themselves…. Virtue, like the Ghost in Hamlet,
is here, there, everywhere, and no where at all." (II,ii)

6   Tony Henderson, *Disorderly Women in Eighteenth-Century London: Prostitution
     and Control in the Metropolis, 1730–1830* (London: Longman, 1999).

The ghost scene in *Hamlet* in turn was to serve Fielding at length in *Tom Jones* (XVI,v), providing an instance of his frequent successful rethinking and reworking of episodes.

In discussing the habit of pillaging past authors, Fielding in *Tom Jones* had presented a general lawlessness:

> "By the poor I mean, that large and venerable body which, in English, we call The Mob. Now, whoever hath had the honour to be admitted to any degree of intimacy with this mob, must well know that it is one of their established maxims, to plunder and pillage their rich neighbours without any reluctance; and that this is held to be neither sin nor shame among them. And so constantly do they abide and act by this maxim, that in every parish almost in the kingdom, there is a kind of confederacy ever carrying on against a certain person of opulence called the squire, whose property is considered as free-booty by all his poor neighbours; who, as they conclude that there is no manner of guilt in such depredations, look upon it as a point of honour and moral obligation to conceal, and to preserve each other from punishment on all such occasions." (XII,i)

In practical terms, as far as his narratives were concerned, there was crime across the country, with travelers especially likely to fall victim, as in *Joseph Andrews* and *Tom Jones*; but the vortex of greed and lack of conscience was seen by Fielding to center on London. Crime and disorder there had encouraged changes in the administration of justice in parts of the West End in 1735–36, with taxes and hiring replacing personal service in watches, and with the corresponding systematization of policing in some parishes. From there, the system of night watches spread, notably after 1748.[7] Fielding then indeed moved to take a personal role, struggling to try to control what was perceived to be the crime wave, that followed the end of the War of the Austrian Succession that year. He became a Justice

---

7   Elaine Reynolds, *Before the Bobbies: The Night Watch and Police Reform in Metropolitan London, 1720–1830* (Stanford, California: Stanford University Press, 1998).

of the Peace for Westminster in 1748, indeed principal justice at Bow Street, with crucial financial help provided by John, 4th Duke of Bedford, one of the two Secretaries of State, a key member of the Opposition Whig group that had gone into office and, accordingly, been horsewhipped by a Jacobite at the Lichfield Races in August 1747. In part, this post was a reward for Fielding's pro-government writing. These were not only journalistic, but also *A Dialogue Between a Gentleman of London, Agent for Two Court Candidates, and an Honest Alderman of the Country Party* (1747), a satirical pamphlet, designed to help the government case in the general election, in which the opposition was presented as divided and disloyal.

Fielding's role was soon after extended and, in May 1749, he was chosen Chairman of the Westminster Quarter Sessions. This was a key position as it brought responsibility for law and order in the area where the king lived and, moreover, one of the most contentious parliamentary constituencies in the country, with the "mob" there described in 1722 by a government supporter as "High Church" and "insufferably rude."[8] The election of 1741 had seen great attention devoted to the bitterly contested results for Westminster, and in 1747, at the time of the next general election, there was fresh tension there and in Middlesex. Sir Charles Hanbury-Williams, who had also been at Eton, noted:

> "The county of Middlesex has chosen two Whigs by a majority of a thousand that never sent a Whig to Parliament before since the Revolution [1688]. And the reason they gave was that the two Whigs had subscribed money in the late Rebellion [1745–46] to defend their country while Sir Roger Newdigate [Tory candidate] was heading a Grand Jury who wanted but one vote, to find and present all associations and meetings for associations for the defence of the government as riotous assemblies and contrary to law."[9]

This was very much an issue that identified Fielding on the right side. A

8   Egmont to Charles Dering, 27 March 1722, BL. Add. 47029 folio 110.
9   BL. Add. 23825 folios 276–77.

victor in the previous election, Newdigate came last in the 1747 poll in a result that summarized the electoral shift toward the government.[10]

Published as *A Charge Delivered to the Grand Jury, at the Sessions of the Peace held for the City and Liberty of Westminster*, on 29 June 1749, Fielding's first charge as Chairman of the Bench decried blasphemy, threats to pleasure, and dangerous pastimes. Indeed, in terms that clashed with a personal life that had sometimes been at the edge of acceptability, not least due to drunkenness, but terms that echoed his novels, there was a linkage between the need for security for "the enjoyment of our lives, our persons and our properties in security," and the threat posed by "masquerades, balls and assemblies of various kinds ... tending to promote idleness, extravagance, and immorality." Juries were presented as part of the liberty of Englishmen, as they meant being judged by one's peers, while there was also a clear support for the Hanoverian dynasty:

> "Notwithstanding all which the malice of the disappointed, the madness of republicans, or the folly of Jacobites may insinuate, there is but one method to maintain the liberties of this country, and that is, to maintain the crown on the heads of that family, which now happily enjoys it."

The coming of peace in 1748 had been seen as an opportunity for retrenchment, Newcastle writing to his co-Secretary of State, Bedford:

> "that His Majesty's [George II's] first thought ... was immediately upon the signing of it, to ease his people of the burdens they lie under as soon, and as effectually, as he could.... His Majesty thinks no time should be lost, in proceeding in the reductions as soon as possible."[11]

Soon after, Newcastle noted George's determination to cut the number of troops.[12] For army as well as navy, this meant officers, such as Booth in

---

10　See also Martin Battestin, "Fielding, Bedford, and the Westminster Election of 1749," *Eighteenth-Century Studies*, 11 (1977–78): 143–85.

11　Newcastle to Bedford, 23 October 1748, BL. Add. 35410 folio 29.

12　Newcastle to Cumberland, 6 November 1748, BL. Add. 35410 folios 62–63.

Amelia, put onto half-pay, while large numbers of soldiers and sailors were demobilized rapidly. In practice, men accustomed to fight were demobilized without adequate provision in a labor market in which un- and under-employment were chronic.[13] The long-serving Austrian agent Giovanni Zamboni reported in 1752 that, due to the rise in thefts and murders, it was unsafe in London, both in houses and on the streets at night, that it was dangerous to go into the provinces, and that policing was negligent.[14] Crime rates, however, are difficult to establish. Victims could be too frightened to report crimes, or not sufficiently bothered, or preferring to seek redress by direct action. There is uncertainty as to how the percentage reported varied. Thus, post-war crime peaks may in part reflect the extent to which the lack of war news led newspapers to devote more attention to crime, while more prosecutions led to more of a sense that crime was a problem.[15]

At the same time, there are significant points about the nature of crime in Fielding's lifetime. Crime was likely to run in families, was committed by the middling orders as well as the working classes, and cities provided criminals with many opportunities for recruitment, activity and concealment. Ease of access to individuals and premises encouraged crime, and, linked to this, there was also a vulnerability to dishonest servants. In *The Letter-Writers* (1731), Risque, a dishonest servant who is housebreaking, is arrested by the constable, being then told by Mr Wisdom: "Confess your accomplices this moment; you have no other way to save your life than by becoming evidence against your gang," the constable adding, "You may not only save your life, but get rewarded for your roguery."

Reporting and discussing crime and criminality was to a degree part of a wider concern about social conditions and change.[16] Many commentators

---

13 D. Hay, "War, dearth and theft in the eighteenth century: the record of the English courts," *Past and Present*, 95 (1982): 117–60.
14 Zamboni to Chancellor Kaunitz, 6 March 1752, Vienna, Haus,- Hof, und Staatsarchiv, England, Varia 10 folio 104.
15 John Beattie, *Policing and Punishment in London, 1660–1750: Urban Crime and the Limits of Terror* (Oxford: Oxford University Press, 2001).
16 Nicholas Rogers, "Confronting the Crime Wave: The Debate over Social Reform and Regulation, 1749–1753," in Lee Davison et al (eds), *Stilling the Grumbling Hive: The Response to Social and Economic Problems in England,*

blamed crime not on poverty but on social change in the shape of luxury, specifically a search for exalted status that signified a refusal to accept social position and, as a result, the spread of social disorder. This hedonistic individualism was seen to lead to attempts to acquire a social presence, reflected in clothes, watches and other goods that were believed to inspire crime. Moreover, vagrancy was treated as the mobility of the idle poor, and thus as dangerous, rather than as, more appropriately, the result of the character of the labor market and the survival strategies of the poor.[17] In his poem "London" (1738), Johnson observed: "All crimes are safe, save hated poverty."

There were other currents of crime, and contexts within which it could be perceived, as was shown in *Tom Jones* when Deborah Wilkins responded harshly to the baby found in Allworthy's bed:

> "I hope your worship will send out your warrant to take up the hussy its mother and I should be glad to see her committed to Bridewel [sic]; and whipt at the cart's tail. Indeed such wicked sluts cannot be too severely punished."

Allworthy responds with a very different response, not that of a JP concerned with social control but rather that of a benign individual, "a heart that hungers after goodness," concerned to provide for a baby (I.3).

In his speech opening the parliamentary session in November 1751, a speech written by his ministers, George II had referred to "audacious crimes of robbery and violence" in London and, linking them to irreligion and luxury, declared that the crimes "proceeded in great measure from the profligate spirit of irreligion, idleness, gaming and extravagance, which has of late extended itself, to an uncommon degree."[18] That session saw the passage

1689–1750 (Stroud: Alan Sutton, 1992): 77–120; Richard Connors, "'The Grand Inquest of the Nation': Parliamentary Committees and Social Policy in Mid-Eighteenth-Century England," *Parliamentary History*, 14 (1995): 285–313.

17 Steven King and Alannah Tomkins (eds), *The Poor in England, 1700–1850. An Economy of Makeshifts* (Manchester: Manchester University Press, 2003); Heather Shore, *London's Criminal Underworlds, c.1720–c.1930: A Social and Cultural History* (Basingstoke: Palgrave, 2003).

18 *Gentleman's Magazine*, 21 (London: 1752): 511–12.

of legislation, notably the Murder Act and the Disorderly Act, the latter providing the court provision of prosecution costs, as well as another Gin Act, while legislation against gambling followed in 1752, as did action by the Middlesex Sessions.[19] A fully-blown moral panic was in process.

Fielding and his much younger blind half-brother, John, another active JP, were at the forefront of the struggle with London crime in the early 1750s, Henry devoting much time and money to the effort and using the press to seek and provide information.[20] Thus, the headpiece of the *Public Advertiser* of 26 June 1753 declared:

> "The principal pawnbrokers within the Bills of Mortality have agreed to take in this daily paper; and if any lost or stolen goods shall be advertised in it, they will, to their utmost, endeavour to secure the property for the owner, and bring the offender to justice. NB. Advertisements of things lost or stolen, will be taken in by Mr Brogden, Clerk to Justice Fielding, at his office at the said Justice's in Bow-Street where all Persons are desired to send immediate Robbery, Burglary, or Theft committed; by which means they may often hear of their goods and the thief, without advertising at all; or if not, their advertisements will be drawn up in the most conspicuous manner, and forwarded directly to the press."

Fielding was a JP of probity, not using his position to extort fees as "trading justices" were apt to do. Indeed, the stipend of his post fell in his hands; although he was able to rely on money from his novels. In the person of Allworthy in *Tom Jones*, Fielding announces, "No private resentment should ever influence a magistrate" (I,vii). Moreover, he added later, "Such was the compassion which inhabited Mr Allworthy's mind, that nothing

---

19 Bob Harris, *Politics and the Nation: Britain in the mid-eighteenth century* (Oxford: Oxford University Press, 2010).

20 Alan Downie, "Henry Fielding, Magistrate," in Downie (ed.), *Henry Fielding In Our Time* (Cambridge: Scholars Publishing, 2008): 113–31; Francis Doherty, "Fragment of a Fielding Memorandum Book," *British Journal for Eighteenth-Century Studies*, 8 (1985): 187–89.

but the steel of justice could ever subdue it" (III,vii). As narrator, Fielding presented the administration of justice as variable, "since so many arbitrary acts are daily committed by magistrates …" and, with reference to the convicted:

> "The inferior sort of people may learn one good lesson, vis. respect and deference to their superiors: since it must show them the wide distinction Fortune intends between those persons who are to be corrected for their faults, and those who are not."

The job demanded much, not least as illness made him reliant on crutches. He saw London as a particular challenge for policing, a point brought out in his *Enquiry into the Causes of the Late Increase of Robbers*:

> "Whoever indeed considers the cities of London and Westminster, with the late vast addition of their suburbs, the great irregularity of their buildings, the immense number of lanes, alleys, courts, and bye-places; most think, that, had they been intended for the very purpose of concealment, they could scarce have been better contrived. Upon such a view the whole appears as a vast wood or forest, in which a thief may harbour with as great security, as wild beasts do in the deserts of Africa or Arabia; for, by wandering from one part to another, and often shifting his quarters, he may almost avoid the possibility of being discovered."[21]

Another section deals with Tyburn. Fielding argues that the theater of execution is a triumph for the convicted, and suggests, instead, that executions take place by the Old Bailey on the day of sentencing and with no crowd present.[22] This is seen as a way to instill terror. Prefiguring Hardwicke's argument in his speech in February 1754 to the judges before they went on circuit,[23] Fielding's theme was not that the law was at fault,

---

21 Fielding, *Enquiry*, section six.
22 *Ibid.*, section eleven.
23 BL. Add. 35870 folios 241–43.

but rather its administration by individuals who were too prone to human faults, a situation that matched the "abuse of words" he criticized in "A Modern Glossary," published in the *Covent Garden Journal* of 14 January 1752. A new proclamation against vice and immorality was issued in February 1752.

Another aspect of the moral reform of the period that was linked to an extension of control was the Marriage Act of 1753, the Act for the better preventing of clandestine marriages; which was designed to prevent clandestine marriage and bigamy and to make elopement more difficult.[24] The power of fathers which repeatedly is a theme in Fielding's works was a key part of the debate over the legislation, and one that was also directly relevant to that of husbands, as daughters became wives in a controlled situation in which the patriarch played a crucial role, one that was designed to thwart fortune-hunters. Mothers were given far less significance. Moreover, the common law rights of women in marital affairs were lessened.

Fielding's struggle with crime in London affected the content and tone of *Amelia* which repeatedly presented the judicial matrix as a dire system, one of corruption and injustice in which innocents are trapped. Beginning in Westminster, he reflects on:

> "the watchmen in our metropolis; who being to guard our streets by night from thieves and robbers, an office which at least requires strength of body, are chosen out of those poor old decrepit people, who are, from their want of bodily strength, rendered incapable of getting a livelihood by work. These men armed only with a pole, which some of them are scarce able to lift, are to secure the persons and houses of his majesty's subjects from the attacks of gangs of young, bold, stout, desperate, and well-armed villains." (I,ii)

In addition, Mr Thrasher, the JP, knew nothing about the law, and was motivated by his self-interest. He is shown being totally wrong and with disastrous consequences, and Fielding is bitter in his satire. For example:

24 David Lemmings, "Marriage and the Law in the Eighteenth Century: Hardwicke's Marriage Act of 1753," *Historical Journal*, 39 (1996): 339–60.

"The magistrate had too great an honour for Truth to suspect that she ever appeared in sordid apparel; nor did he ever sully his sublime notions of that virtue, by uniting them with the mean ideas of poverty and distress." (I,ii)

Aside from the activity of the pre-trial process and hearing cases,[25] and thus taking part in the inherent difficulties of ensuring justice,[26] the Fieldings developed what were subsequently known as the Bow Street Runners and organized police patrols in and around London. Henry made a lot of the early effort, which, after his death, John took forward, creating a successful force and being knighted in 1761. In his *Journal of a Voyage to Lisbon*, Fielding referred in 1753 to being: "almost fatigued to death with several long examinations, relating to five different murders, all committed within the space of a week, by different gangs of street-robbers." Crown witnesses offered immunity remained part of the means of justice, and problematically so, as with a major case involving John Fielding in 1775,[27] while transportation to the colonies was an important aspect of the repertoire of punishment.

When Henry Fielding was persuaded to go to Bath for his health, Newcastle, instead, pressed him to stay in order to continue acting against the gangs, which include members of the fearsome Black Boy Alley gang of Clerkenwell which had been disrupted by a mass hanging of 1744.[28] As a result of action made possible by buying information, Fielding took the credit for the fall of the London crime rate in late 1753, but soon found "a jaundice, a dropsy, and an asthma uniting their forces."[29] He stood down

---

25 Lance Bertelsen, "Committed by Justice Fielding: Judicial and Journalistic Representation in the Bow Street Magistrate's Office, January 3 – November 24, 1752," *Eighteenth Century Studies*, 30 (1997): 337–64.

26 John Beattie, *Crime and the Courts in England 1660–1800* (Oxford: Oxford University Press, 1986); Raymond Stephenson, "Fielding's 'Courts': The Legal Paradigm in *Tom Jones*," *English Studies in Canada*, 14 (1988): 152–69.

27 Donna Andrew and Randall McGowen, *The Perreaus and Mrs Rudd: Forgery and Betrayal in Eighteenth-Century London* (Berkeley, California: University of California Press, 2001).

28 Rictor Norton, *The Georgian Underworld. A Study of Criminal Subcultures in Eighteenth Century England*, http:rictorhorton.co.uk.

29 Fielding, *Journal of a Voyage to Lisbon* (London, 1755), Introduction.

in April 1754 when his ill-health became too desperate and, on 26 June, boarded a ship for his voyage to Lisbon.

This struggle against crime was but part of that against the immorality decried by Fielding in the *Covent Garden Journal* he launched in 1752 and in which he argued for "the noble interests of religion, virtue and good sense" and retracted an earlier admiration for Aristophanes and Rabelais on the grounds that they would "eradicate all sobriety, modesty, decency, virtue and religion out of the world." Indeed, this criticism of real immorality was closely linked to the themes of his fiction as well as to his *Enquiry into the Causes of the Late Increase of Robbers* (1751). Other of his relevant writings included *A True State of the Case of Bosavern Penlez* (1749), *Examples of the Interposition of Providence in the Detection and Punishment of Murder* (1752), and *A Clear State of the Case of Elizabeth Canning* (1753).[30]

The *Enquiry* stated the threat from the "vast torrent of luxury" of modern times, one linked by Fielding to immorality in a standard, but nevertheless powerful, theme. Indeed, an aspect of the resulting criminality was a desire for clothes that could not be met by production. This encouraged theft, as well as the purchase and wearing of second-hand clothes.[31] There was also the very different response of those, such as Adams, who wore their few clothes for very many years, which meant a need to mend them but also a ready measure of a lack of fashionability. Fielding's theme about luxury and immorality was related to ideas of the development of society in which, with trade bringing in luxury, there was an impact on the constitution. Indeed, in the preface, he offered an interesting corrective of the usual discussion of the latter, one that reflected his mastery of the language and ability to deliver arresting images:

30 Henry Fielding, *An Enquiry into the Causes of the Late Increase of Robbers and Related Writings*, edited by Malvin Zirker (Oxford: Clarendon Press, 1988); Alan Downie, "Authorial Contexts: Connections between Fielding's Novels and His Legal and Journalistic Writing," in Jennifer Wilson and Elizabeth Kraft (eds), *Approaches to Teaching the Novels of Henry Fielding* (New York, 2015).

31 Beverly Lemire, "The Theft of Clothes and Popular Consumerism in Early Modern England," *Journal of Social History*, 24 (1990): 255–76.

"All seem to have the conception of something uniform and permanent, as if the constitution of England partook rather of the nature of the soil than of the climate, and was as fixed and constant as the former, not as changing and variable of the latter."

As an instance of this variability, Fielding argued that "the power of the commonality hath received an immense addition" due to the increase in trade, but such that "the civil power ... is not able to govern them." Thus, as Fielding points out, the power of JPs had not really gone up. In the pamphlet, which was dedicated to Hardwicke, Fielding noted in the preface that:

"... the principal design of this whole work, is to rouse the civil power from its present lethargic state. A design, which alike opposes those wild notions of liberty that are inconsistent with all government, and those pernicious schemes of government, which are destructive of true liberty ... anarchy is almost sure to end in one kind of tyranny."

As was his practice, Fielding therefore vindicated moderation, and as part of a writing stance in which true justice was regarded as benevolent as well as firm, a theme found throughout his works,[32] and one made more necessary by the unfairness he observed in so much of his discussion of legal practice.[33] In response, he presses not only for true justice, an aspect of Patriot kingship, but also an emphasis on shame as a means to counter vice;[34] an emphasis that further ensures that hypocrisy and false values are dangerous as they counter shame.

For Fielding, as was normal in the period, concern with luxury and immorality was a Christian theme. His arguments echoed those of the contemporary Methodists, but also of other Anglicans. Aside from the spiritual

32   Robert Merrett, "The Principles of Fielding's Legal Satire and Social Reform," *Dalhousie Review*, 62 (1982): 238–53.
33   *True Patriot*, 18 March 1746; *Covent-Garden Journal*, 4 April 1752.
34   See also, *Tom Jones*, XII,ii.

wellbeing of the individual in question, care for others was part of the equa-
tion and was seen in part in terms of care for the less fortunate, as in his *A
Proposal for Making an Effectual Provision for the Poor* (1753). Fielding had
no time for code-words that often, in his view, served to present, indeed
justify, hypocrisy. Morality in practice, and morals under threat, were linked
themes of the period.

The extent of immorality, however, did not in Fielding's vision preclude
good conduct, and even so in *Jonathan Wild*, his most significant investi-
gation of perverted values. There is much wrong there, but also a JP:

> "... who did indeed no small honour to the commission he
> bore, duly considered the weighty charge committed to him,
> by which he was intrusted with decisions affecting the lives, lib-
> erties and properties of his countrymen; he therefore examined
> always with the utmost diligence and caution, into every minute
> circumstance." (IV,vi)

This was an apt description of the role Fielding was to fulfil, one that
contrasted with the splenetic attacks by Tobias Smollett in *The Adventures
of Peregrine Pickle* (1751) and *A Faithful Narrative of the Base and Inhuman
Arts that were lately practiced upon the Brain of Habbakuk Hilding, Justice,
Dealer, and Chapman, who now lies at his house in Covent Garden in a deplorable State of Lunacy ... by Drawcansir Alexander, Fencing Master and
Philomath* (1752). Yet, these very attacks were a testimony to the significance of the magistrate-writer.

12. NOVELS ANEW

Fielding's approach and style put him alongside that of contemporary historians. In the *Memoirs of the Life of ... John Lindesay, Earl of Crawford and Lindesay* (1753), partly by the prolific Richard Rolt, the distinction between historians and poets was clearly drawn:

> "But historians have always an advantage over poets; these write to the passions, those to the judgment. The language of the poets, like the finest medals in the cabinets of the curious, is only to be understood, and enjoyed, by the selected few; the language of historians, like the best current coin, is intended for the general use of mankind; and the more diffuse it grows, the more benefit it conveys. Poets can inflame; historians must instruct; in the former, morality puts on her richest garments; in the latter, she is more plainly attired, more familiar, and at ease; truth should always accompany the historian; but eloquence is the best companion for the poet."[1]

In contrast, as one contemporary, almost certainly the cleric and novelist Francis Coventry, put it in explaining "new species of writing" invented by Fielding:

> "As this sort of writing was intended as a contrast to those in which the reader was even to suppose all the characters ideal, and every circumstance quite imaginary, it was thought necessary to give it a greater air of truth, to entitle it an *History*."[2]

1 *Memoirs*: 3–4.
2 *An Essay on the New Species of Writing founded by Mr Fielding* (London, 1751): 18.

This comparison of Fielding with assumptions about history can be taken further forward with Rolt's *Impartial Representation of the Conduct of the Several Powers of Europe engaged in the late general war* (1749–50), in which Rolt argued: "It is not the true intent of history so much to load the memory of the reader with a copious collection of public records, as it is to elevate his thoughts and enrich his understanding."[3] Fielding himself praised history as opposed to poetry, and as part of his broader critique of falseness. This critique joined his views on literature with those on life; hypocrisy in his view being a moral consequence of this falseness. In the preface to his *Journal of a Voyage to Lisbon* (1755), Fielding discussed travel accounts, observing:

> "I am far from supposing, that Homer, Hesiod and the other ancient poets and mythologists had any settled design to pervert and confuse the records of antiquity; but it is certain they have effected it; and … I should have honoured and loved Homer more, had he written a true history of his own times in humble prose, than those noble poems that have so justly collected the praise of all ages; for though I read these with more admiration and astonishment, I still read Herodotus, Thucydides and Xenophon, with more astonishment and more satisfaction."

Indeed, in the preface, Fielding refers to travelling "either in books or ships," a theme that repeats one in *Joseph Andrews* where Adams praises himself on having travelled in books, and gets involved in a pointless dispute as a consequence.

Fiction had been crucial to Fielding's output in 1741–43, but, thereafter, other matters were more significant, notably his journalism. However, after the war ended in 1748, Fielding came to the fore in two respects, first as a magistrate, on which see the last chapter, and, secondly, as a renewed writer of fiction. In the magazine *The Rambler* (1750–52), Johnson claimed that novels "are written chiefly to the young, the ignorant, and the idle, to

---

3   Rolt, *Impartial Representation* (4 vols, London, 1749–50), I,x; Jeremy Black, *Charting the Past. The Historical Worlds of Eighteenth-Century England* (Bloomington, Indiana: Indiana University Press, 2019).

whom they serve as lectures of conduct, and introductions into life," and argued that they must therefore meet high moral standards. The corrective satire of the period was not always religious in language, content or tone, but the essential themes conformed to Christian social teaching. So, more explicitly, did the popular genre of criminal biographies, many of which were written by gaol chaplains.[4] While different, *Tom Jones* (1749) and *Amelia* (1751) were each more substantial than his earlier works, and both took forward Fielding's essential moral stance, while doing so in tales of great humanity. This writing put him in a good financial state, Millar giving him £700 for *Tom Jones* and a thousand guineas (£1,100) for *Amelia*, which were very good sums for a novelist.

The History of Tom Jones, A Foundling, was dedicated to Lyttleton, which was a political statement not least because this dedication included mention of "the princely benefactions of the Duke of Bedford." The book reflected the entry of the former opposition Whigs into government, with Lyttleton listed as one of the members of the Board of Treasury. Lyttleton himself was an author, and Fielding argued that this guarantees that his own work will include "nothing prejudicial to the cause of religion and virtue." Morality, therefore, was to the fore, and, in this, Fielding continued his earlier clash with Richardson. He makes his novel, a comic romance, interesting, not simply through plot and characterization, but also by means of varying the tone and language, using the immediate banal to undercut the soaring sublime. This bathos also provided a way to humanize the story, as is moreover done with Tom's moves between qualities and failings.[5]

The authorial voice was to the fore in the novel from an early stage, as with the comments on Bridget's response to her brother Allworthy's instructions:

> "As this is one of those deep observations which very few readers
> can be supposed capable of making themselves, I have thought
> proper to lend my assistance; but ... I shall seldom or never so

4   Philip Rawlings, *Drunks, Whores and Idle Apprentices: Criminal Biographies of the Eighteenth Century* (London: Routledge, 1992).
5   David Oakleaf, "Sliding Down Together: Fielding, Addison, and the Pleasures of the Imagination in *Tom Jones*," *English Studies in Canada*, 9 (1983): 402–17.

indulge him, unless in such instances as this, where nothing but the inspiration with which we writers are gifted, can possibly enable any one to make the discovery." (I,v)

Comparison with *Tom Jones* would have been available for readers of *Amelia* when it was published, but when *Tom Jones* appeared the comparison was with *Joseph Andrews*. Many of the themes in *Tom Jones* repeated or developed the latter, as with the reflections on servants which echoes Mrs Slipslop in *Joseph Andrews*:

> "As it is the nature of a kite to devour little birds, so it is the nature of such persons as Mrs Wilkins, to insult and tyrannize over little people. This being indeed the means which they use to recompense to themselves their extreme servility and condescension to their superiors; for nothing can be more reasonable, than that slaves and flatterers should exact the same taxes on all below them, which they themselves pay to all above them." (I,vi)

There is also the debate over true charity and, with it, nature and the natural, themes that were recurrent in Fielding's work, and that highlighted the moral character of his writing and his concern for a practical Christianity and citizenship. The question of natural behavior was to the fore in *Tom Jones* with the different and vigorously argued pedagogic principles of "Mr Square, the Philosopher, and of Mr Thwackum the Divine." As so often with Fielding's writing, humor and serious meanings sit alongside each other, and yet also provide strong mutual support. The two pedagogues' continual competition is not the sole instance of a debate over what is nature. So also with Jones' relationship with Molly Seagrim, which is described by Mrs Honour: "When wenches are so coming, young men are not so much to be blamed neither; for to be sure they do no more than what is natural" (IV,xii). Molly herself had presented a challenge to ideas of what was natural, or at least appropriate.

> "... though Molly was generally thought a very fine girl, and in reality she was so, yet her beauty was not of the most amiable kind. It had indeed very little of feminine in it, and would at

least have become a man as well as a woman; for, to say the truth, youth and florid health had a very considerable share in the composition.

Nor was her mind more effeminate than her person. As this was tall and robust, so was that bold and forward. So little had she of modesty, that Jones had more regard for her virtue than she herself." (IV,vi)

Soon after, the fierce and deliberately overwritten churchyard fight between Molly and the Amazonian Goody Brown leads to somewhat ambiguous reflection:

"It is lucky for the women, that the seat of fistycuff-war is not the same with them as among men; but though they may seem a little to deviate from their sex, when they go forth to battle, yet I have observed they never so far forget it, as to assail the bosoms of each other; where a few blows would be fatal to most of them. This, I know, some derive from their being of a more bloody inclination than the males. On which account they apply to the nose, as to the part whence blood may most easily be drawn; but this seems a far-fetched, as well as ill-natured supposition." (IV,viii)

At a different social level, Squire Western's sister is described as a "masculine person" who was not treated by men "in the light of a woman" (VI,ii). It is entirely appropriate that it is Allworthy's sister who has an illegitimate child and not Western's.

In line with the needs of the plot but also with contemporary assumptions about illegitimacy, Jones is presented as having "naturally violent animal spirits" (V,ix). Indeed, his naturalness in every respect is not only a key to the story, but also soon after that observation underlined by his scuffle with Blifil which follows the discussion of how life can reveal true nature:

"Nothing is more erroneous than the common observation, that men who are ill-natured and quarrelsome when they are drunk, are very worthy persons when they are sober: for drink, in reality, doth not reverse nature, or create passions in men which did not exist in them before. It takes away the guard of reason, and consequently forces us to produce those symptoms which many, when sober, have art enough to conceal. It heightens and inflames our passions." (V,ix)

The need for caution on the part of readers (as well as characters) was underlined by the frequency of abrupt plot reversals. Characteristic of Fielding's plays and novels, this was even more the case in *Joseph Andrews* than *Tom Jones*, although it was from the latter that a "little acorns, mighty oaks" warning came, one that provided Fielding with an opportunity to argue for his type of novelistic history:

"In reality, there are many little circumstances too often omitted by injudicious historians, from which events of the utmost importance arise. The world may indeed be considered as a vast machine, in which the great wheels are originally set in motion by those which are very minute, and almost imperceptible to any but the strongest eyes." (V,iv)

Hypocrisy and subterfuge could serve to keep these circumstances hidden. The situation, however, could defy human calculation, as with the unimpressive Captain Blifil's greedy determination to inherit Allworthy's fortune in order to pursue his architectural and landscaping plans. The younger Blifil anticipated:

"the death of Mr Allworthy; in calculating which he had employed much of his own algebra, besides purchasing every book extant that treats of the value of lives, reversions, etc. From all which, he satisfied himself, that as he had every day a chance of this happening, so had he more than an even chance of its happening within a few years.... [T]he utmost malice of Fortune ... he himself died of an apoplexy." (II,viii)

The theme of a machine was also brought out by Mrs Western with reference to international politics, which was a frequent comparison of the period: "the secret springs which move the great state wheels in all the political machines of Europe" (VI,ii). This image was particularly pertinent for the Balance of Power, an image used repeatedly, albeit more for the international system than for domestic politics. The item in the *York Courant* of 27 October 1741 showed how comedy could help underline the political point:

> "Whereas several crafty, designing people have given out, and many among the credulous and half-witted have believed, that the famous political machine called the Balance of Europe has been, for above twenty years past, in the custody of a certain extraordinary personage [Walpole], now living in Downing Street, this is to assure the public, that the said machine is at present in the hands of one of the most exquisite artists in the universe, living on the other side of the water; who has added several new springs and wheels to it, and quite reversed the system by which it was governed before; as will be easily conceived by the adepts, when they are informed that France is now become the first mover."

Although publishing in peacetime, *Tom Jones*, like those of Jane Austen, is a book written during a bitter and difficult conflict. On the one hand, for both writers there is the apparent peacefulness of a society focused on the turmoil of hearts, but the background also comes through. Unsurprisingly, this is more true of Fielding, who was politically active as a journalist, than of Austen. The turmoil comes forth with specific comments, as when Squire Western approves of lechery as a means toward "recruiting those numbers which we are every day losing in the war" (V,xii), but also with regard to the very uncertainties and swift turns of the plot which match those both of Britain's war effort and of her politics. The challenge by the advancing French in the Low Countries is readily presented, not least as part of a sense of unfairness and one akin to disease:

> "Thus the doctor and the disease meet in fair and equal conflict; whereas, by giving time to the latter, we often suffer him to fortify and entrench himself, like a French army; so that the learned

. gentleman finds it very difficult, and sometimes impossible to
come at the enemy. Nay sometimes by gaining time, the disease
applies to the French military politics, and corrupts nature over
to his side, and then all the powers of physick must arrive too
late…. The advantage they [French] have over other nations, in
the superiority of their engineers." (V,vii,xii)

Western mocks her Tory brother as stupid: "Indeed, brother, you would
make a fine plenipo [plenipotentiary] to negotiate with French. They would
soon persuade you, that they take towns out of mere defensive principles,"
only for the squire to turn this back on his Whig sister: "Let your friends
at court answer for the towns" (VI,ii),[6] a reference to the failure of the Allied
coalition to block the French. Tom Jones' less-than-robust response to seduction by Mrs Waters is described in terms of a siege by the latter: "I am
afraid Mr Jones maintained a kind of Dutch defence, and treacherously delivered up the garrison, without duly weighing his allegiance to the fair
Sophia" (IX,v).

Possibly partly as a consequence of the bleakness Fielding encountered
as a magistrate, *Amelia,* published on 18 December 1751, is a far more bitter work than *Tom Jones,* in large part because it is an angry social criticism
that does not rely on satire to indict corruption, but rather sees the latter
as insistent and damaging.[7] Although Fielding's concern matched that of
other writers about moral crisis,[8] for example Arthur Murphy in the *Gray's
Inn Journal* of 29 December 1753, this bitterness may help explain why
the novel did not sell very well, which helped ensure that Andrew Millar
thought it unwise to attempt a second edition. The anger of the work, indeed, broke with contemporary ideas of good taste. Separately, alongside

6   For other references to the French, VI,v, VII,iii.
7   The notes in the edition by Martin Battestin (Middletown, Connecticut: Wes-
     leyan, 1983) provide much of value. Mona Scheuermann, "Man no Provi-
     dence: Fielding's *Amelia* as a Novel of Social Criticism," *Forum MLS,* 20
     (1984): 106–23.
8   Kathleen Wilson, "The good, the bad and the impotent. Imperialism and the
     politics of identity in Georgian England," in Ann Bermingham and John
     Brewer (eds), *The Consumption of Culture 1600–1800: Image, Object, Text*
     (London: Routledge, 1995): 237–62.

the need for social reform as an obvious consequence for what is discussed came the sentimentalism that makes Amelia cry often. This combined to offer a didacticism different to that of the more facetious *Tom Jones*.[9] *Amelia* has been seen to parallel the *Aeneid*, but, looking ahead, it had Dickensian characteristics, and notably in its sharp scrutiny of London.

With *Amelia*, which was set in 1733, there are parallels with the repeated hardships encountered by the Heartfrees in *Jonathan Wild*. These include the vividly described scenes in Newgate in *Amelia*, but also the travails outside, including repeated attempts on the virtue of the female protagonists. In Mrs Heartfree's case, her journey includes a storm-driven visit to an Africa of animals far more different than those who really lived there, notably an extraordinarily large elephant. Near the close of the adventure, there is a return to "civilisation," and, in that, a reference to the slave trade: "A number of slaves, who had been taken captives in war, were to be guarded to the sea-side, where they were to be sold to the merchants, who traded in them to America" (IV,xii). This provides an opportunity for Mrs Heartfree to leave Africa, and, at sea, she transfers to a warship en route back to Britain. There was no discussion of the slave trade. Instead, the depiction of human cruelty focused on Britain. Thus, in *Amelia*, the travails of those exposed to the law are depicted at length, with the bailiff, Bondum, who detains Booth, compared to a butcher in a passage that rapidly mounts to the horror of a devouring callousness:

> "The bailiff was reckoned an honest and good sort of man in
> his way, and had no more malice against the bodies in his cus-
> tody than a butcher hath to those in his: and as the latter, when
> he takes his knife in hand, hath no idea but of the joints into
> which he is to cut the carcase; so the former when he handles
> his writ, hath no other design but to cut out the body into as
> many bail-bonds as possible. As to the life of the animal, or the
> liberty of the man, they are thoughts which never obtrude
> themselves on either." (VIII,i)

9   J. Paul Hunter, "Fielding and the Modern Reader: The Problem of Temporal Translation," in Andrew Wright (ed.), *Henry Fielding in His Time and Ours* (Los Angeles: Clark Library, 1987): 1–28.

In a situation described in *Amelia*, creditors could have debtors jailed for a debt of forty shillings or more, a sum that it was easy to reach given the extensive reliance on credit. The conditions in prisons were grim as wardens charged prisoners extortionate fees for lodging, food, and other "favors," thus recouping the cost of purchasing their posts, but also indulging spite and sadism. In 1729, a parliamentary committee chaired by James Oglethorpe, later founder in Georgia, investigated the issue and produced very grim accounts of treatment, including murderous cruelty; but the committee restricted itself to criticizing corrupt individuals, notably Thomas Bambridge, the Warden of Fleet Prison from 1728, and William Acton who lived in the Marshalsea; and the fee system was not replaced.[10] The scale and longevity of the problem ensured that another committee followed in 1754. A less gripping but still resonant echo of imprisonment in debt is provided in the Museum of London with the cell from the Wellclose debtors' prison.

Fielding had personal experience of the problems of being a debtor including from his time as a novelist. This was an aspect of the realism of personal experience repeatedly seen in *Amelia*, not least in terms of both his parents' and his own first marriage which is echoed in that of Booth and Amelia. Imprisoned in the Fleet for debt in November 1740, his father died in the Rules of the prison the following June.

At the same time as the harsh realism in the novel, Fielding is careful in *Amelia* to offer consolation to the good, notably contrasting Amelia with the procuress Mrs Ellison accordingly, before turning to his audience, closing a chapter with a moral message:
"Hence, my worthy reader, console thyself, that however few of the other good things of life are thy lot, the best of all things, which is innocence, is always within thy own power; and though Fortune may make thee often unhappy, she can never make thee completely and irreparably miserable without thy own consent" (VIII,iii).

---

10 Alex Pitofsky, "The Warden's Court Martial: James Oglethorpe and the Politics of Eighteenth-Century Prison Reform," *Eighteenth-Century Life*, 24 (2000): 88–102. For a diary of imprisonment in 1728–29, John Ginger (ed.), *Handel's Trumpeter: The Diary of John Grano* (Pendragon Press, 1998); Jerry White, "Pain and Degradation in Georgian London: Life in the Marshalsea Prison," *History Workshop Journal*, 68 (2009): 69–98.

13. CONCLUSIONS

"Whoever thou art
That lookest with disdain on
the virtue of Modern Times
while thou commendest the
manners of the Ancients,
    know
that a man more adorned with learning
and with simplicity of manners
Antiquity never produced.

Sincerity, Justice, Piety,
If ever they belonged to man
belonged to him
He exerted the utmost Charity to his own
but his own were all Mankind."

Fielding's translation of Henry Heaton's Latin inscription for Edmund Castle (1698–1750), a theologian and cleric who ended his career as both Master of Corpus Christi, Cambridge from 1745 and Dean of Hereford from 1749,[1] provided a contribution not only to the longstanding Ancients versus Moderns debate, but also to a sense of Fielding's values. They were both of his time and timeless.

Fielding himself died as Britain moved into war with France: the Seven Years' War is dated 1756–63, but hostilities began in North America in 1754, and it is worth considering what the war would have meant for his creativity had he remained alive. Conflict for example offered Tobias Smollett fresh topics. The

1   Robert Masters, *The History of the College of Corpus Christi* (2 volumes, Cambridge: Cambridge University Press, 1753–55): II, 239.

previous period of national emergency in 1745–46 had seen Fielding turn to journalism, which was the only rapid response possible to the Jacobite rising. There were comparable emergencies in 1756–59, from concern over the risk of a French invasion in 1756 to the French plan for an invasion in 1759. These might well have moved Fielding anew to journalism. Indeed, it would have been interesting to see his comments on the anger that led to Admiral Byng's execution in 1757.

His novels had not dealt with war, and it is unclear whether that would have seemed an evasion, during the Seven Years' War. The different approaches of Smollett and Sterne indicated the extent to which there was room for a variety of comic voices and humorous approaches, and there was no need for him to take his characters into conflict. Indeed, although Tom Jones is ready to serve and joins up accordingly, he is not exposed to war. At the same time, Fielding's discussion of the mechanics of military units is more searching in terms of human tensions than contemporary journalism, as for example in the account of the *Leeds Mercury* of 22 April 1740 about troops en route for Portsmouth.

As well as war being largely neglected by Fielding, with the exception of naval action and privateering in the English Channel, the interaction with the outer world that briefly and fantastically occurs in Africa, during *Jonathan Wild*, is not pursued. Thus, while engaging with the historical imagination, Fielding does not do comparably with the geographical one. A very different public world emerges in the advertisement in the *Leeds Mercury* on 1 April 1740: "Lectures upon the use of globes and maps (each subscriber to pay five shillings) ... performed by George Gargrave, writing-master at his school ... in Leeds."

The possibility of Fielding covering other topics does not detract from the extent to which he managed in his short lifetime to deliver a range of achievement and acquire an international reputation, *Tom Jones* being translated into French in 1750. Fielding could work within conventions as his homage to existing authors makes clear, but also, as his extensive discussion of them makes readily apparent, was capable of his own reflections and developments. Indeed, his rapid dramatic output shows him using a variety of approaches. As with his friend Hogarth,[2]

---

2   Ronald Paulson, *Hogarth* (3 volumes, Cambridge: Lutterworth Press, 1992–93); Jacqueline Riding, *Hogarth: Life in Progress* (London: Profile, 2021).

the possibility of establishing or suggesting a multiplicity of meanings, references and assessments, underlines the variety of judgment of his work. The satire, however, is essentially at the disposal of a humane representation of the world.

This representation places a great emphasis on reason, and the latter is seen not only as a challenge to hypocrisy but also as a barrier against the fear that is repeatedly an issue, as with the episode of The Man of the Hill. Partridge, "whose head was full of nothing but ghosts, devils, witches, and such like," first thinks the man's house frightening, to which Jones sensibly replies, "The people are either fast asleep, or probably as this is a lonely place, are afraid to open their door." Then Partridge thinks the old woman who lets them in a witch, which provides Fielding with a Whiggish opportunity to indicate progress: "Indeed, if this woman had lived in the reign of James the First [1603–25], her appearance alone would have hanged her, almost without any evidence" (VIII,x).

This, however, is not the sole affirmation of reason. Having rescued the Man of the Hill from two attacking ruffians, Jones explains that Providence has taken effect because, "I have only discharged the common duties of humanity, and what I would have done for any fellow creature in your sentence" (VIII,x). Including the Man of the Hill as a fellow creature brings into society a figure that has been living as a recluse. His description is reminiscent of those who have been shipwrecked and forced, like Robinson Crusoe, to live as if with nature:

> "A long beard as white as snow. His body was cloathed with the skin of an ass, made something into the form of a coat. He wore likewise boots on his legs, and a cap on his head, both composed of the skin of some other animals." (VIII,x)

Fielding's ability to draw parallels across society was perhaps one of the most arresting features of his insight, as well as serving the narrative purpose of anchoring his story, in providing the opportunities both for linkage and reflection. Thus, with Squire Western detaining Sophia in London, there is a particularly harsh passage, one that looks toward *Amelia* in the extent to which the metropolis provides a starker account of human actions and of reflections thereon:

"Western beheld the deplorable condition of his daughter with no more contrition or remorse, than the turnkey of Newgate feels at viewing the agonies of a tender wife, when taking her last farewell of her condemned husband; or rather he looked down on her with the same emotions which arise in an honest fair tradesman, who sees his debtor dragged to prison for £10 which, though a just debt, the wretch is wickedly unable to pay. Or, to hit the case still more nearly, he felt the same conjunction with a bawd when some poor innocent whom she hath ensnared into her hands, falls into fits at the first proposal of what is called seeing company. Indeed this resemblance would be exact, was it not that the bawd hath an interest in what she doth, and the father, though perhaps he may blindly think otherwise, can in reality have none in urging his daughter to almost an equal prostitution." (XVI,ii)

Soon after, Fielding refers to Mrs Western as treating marriage as "legal prostitution for hire" (XVI,viii).

The London section in *Tom Jones* includes references to Greenland and Hottentots, both of whom are taken as uncivilized (XV,vi, XVI,viii), but, in practice, that serves to direct attention to the truly uncivilized nature of the city. So also with his frequent references to animals. Fielding opposes cruelty toward them, Tom Jones not agreeing "with the opinions of those who consider animals as mere machines, and when they bury their spurs in the belly of their horse, imagine the spur and the horse to have an equal capacity of feeling pain" (XII,ix). He also presents vulnerable humans as like animals who are hunted, comparing a young woman of fortune to a doe designed for "the jaws of some devourer or other" (XVII,iv). A similar image is offered in *Jonathan Wild* as Wild seeks to seduce Mrs Heartfree: "He had projected a design of conveying her to one of those eating-houses in Covent-Garden, where female flesh is deliciously dressed, and served up to the greedy appetites of young gentlemen" (II,ix). This is very much Fielding, like John Webster in T.S. Eliot's *Whispers of Immortality*, seeing "the skull beneath the skin," and that element is present as a qualification of the humor.

This threat to Mrs Heartfree accords with the attacks on disorder in London, notably the Disorderly Houses Act. Grand Juries in the early

1750s complained that insufficient was done to suppress these houses and there were calls for speeded-up action,[3] the sort of action that would make manipulation by criminals and the corrupt, as shown by Fielding, more difficult. Such manipulation included the movement of cases between courts, thus increasing legal delays and costs. John Fielding later noted that his brother Henry tried to encourage prosecutions by the use of anonymous informers, thus cutting through pretense and protection rackets.[4]

There is the irony of a moralist with Henry Fielding, but the morality comes first, as also with the narratives offered by Hogarth's print sequences, which were praised by Fielding.[5] Scornful of the idea of a Devil, Jonathan Wild argues that "death brings an end," (II,xi), but Fielding ended the story not only with just deserts for the criminals, but also with juxtaposing the praise which the majority offer the powerful with, on the other hand:

> "Some in cells and cottages, who view their GREATNESS with a malignant eye; and dare affirm, that these GREAT MEN, who are always the most pernicious, are generally the most wretched and truly contemptible of all the Works of the Creation." (IV,xvi)

More positively in *Amelia*, there is a human nature that is far from evil, but that is led in that direction by bad individuals and practices, and their creation and use of mischance. Many victims would have benefited from their assailants heeding the Act to Amend and Strengthen an Act against Perjury and Subornation of Perjury of 1750, for Fielding shows perjury as as endemic as self-interest. One solution to the situation is "the Family of Love," that of the Heartfrees at the close of *Jonathan Wild* (IV,xvi). In *Amelia*, Booth reflects on the happiness of "the poorest wretch who, without control, could repair to his homely habitation and to his family" (VIII,i). Another solution is that of the individual hermit, as in The Man of the Hill

---

3 *Whitehall Evening Post*, 23 October 1751.

4 John Fielding, *An Account of the Origin and Effects of a Police set on Foot by his Grace the Duke of Newcastle in the Year, upon a Plan Presented to his Grace by the late Henry Fielding, Esq* (London, 1758): 30.

5 Jakub Lipski, *Painting the Novel: Pictorial Discourse in Eighteenth-Century English Fiction* (Abingdon: Routledge, 2018).

in *Tom Jones* (XVIII,x–xv). In *Dialogue between Alexander and Diogenes*, Fielding has Diogenes emphasize "true" honor: "It results from the secret satisfaction of our own minds, and is decreed us by wise men and the Gods." What is adopted as an almost throwaway sentiment by Voltaire at the end of *Candide* (1759), "Il faut cultiver notre Jardin" ("we must cultivate our garden"), an acceptance of human nature, alongside a depiction and defiance of human vice, is given substance across the breadth of Fielding's writing, but with an active Christian citizenship to the fore. Philosophy in practice encompassed his stance as a man of action as well as a reflective writer of genius.

SELECTED FURTHER READING

The Wesleyan Edition of the Works of Henry Fielding, edited by William Coley and others (Oxford Clarendon Press, 1967).

Battestin, Martin, with Ruthe Battestin, *Henry Fielding: A Life* (London: Routledge, 1989).

Battestin, Martin and Clive Probyn, *The Correspondence of Henry and Sarah Fielding* (Oxford: Clarendon Press, 1993).

Campbell, Jill, *Natural Masques: Gender and Identity in Fielding's Plays and Novels* (Stanford: Stanford University Press, 1995).

Cleary, Thomas, *Henry Fielding: Political Writer* (Waterloo, Ontario: Wilfrid Laurier University Press, 1995).

Defoe, Daniel, *A Tour Through the Whole Island of Great Britain*, ed. P.N. Furbank, W.R. Owens and A.J. Coulson (New Haven, Connecticut, Yale University Press, 1991).

Downie, Alan, *A Political Biography of Henry Fielding* (London: Pickering and Chatto, 2009).

Downie, Alan, *To Settle the Succession of the State: Literature and Politics, 1678–1750* (Basingstoke: Palgrave, 1994).

Downie, Alan (ed.), *Henry Fielding In Our Time* (Cambridge: Scholars Publishing, 2008).

Harris, Bob, *Politics and the Nation: Britain in the mid-eighteenth century* (Oxford: Oxford University Press, 2010).

Hitchcock, Tim, *Down and Out in Eighteenth-Century London* (London: Hambledon Continuum, 2007).

Hume, Robert, *Henry Fielding and the London Theatre, 1728–1737* (Oxford: Oxford University Press, 1988).

Hunter, J. Paul, *Occasional Form: Henry Fielding and the Chains of Circumstance* (Baltimore, Maryland: Johns Hopkins University Press, 1975).

McCrea, Brian, *Henry Fielding and the Politics of Mid-Eighteenth-Century England* (Athens, Georgia: University of Georgia Press, 1981).

Shoemaker, Robert, *The London Mob: Violence and Disorder in Eighteenth-Century England* (London: Hambledon Continuum, 2007).

Stevenson, John, *The Real History of Tom Jones* (Basingstoke: Palgrave, 2005).

Stoler, John A. and Richard Fulton, *Henry Fielding: An Annotated Bibliography of Twentieth-Century Criticism, 1900–1977* (New York: Garland, 1980).

Thomas, Donald, *Henry Fielding* (London: Weidenfeld and Nicolson, 1990).

Uglow, Jenny, *Hogarth: A Life and a World* (London: Faber, 1997).

Varey, Simon, *Henry Fielding* (Cambridge: Cambridge University Press, 1986).

White, Jerry, *London in the Eighteenth Century. 'A Great and Monstrous Thing'* (London: Bodley Head, 2012).

Wilson, Jennifer and Elizabeth Kraft (eds), *Approaches to Teaching the Novels of Henry Fielding* (New York: The Modern Language Associatoin of America, 2015).

Among internet sources, there is the printed evidence for trials at the Old Bailey from 1674 to 1913, together with the Ordinary (Chaplain's) account of the lives of criminals sentenced to death from 1679 to 1772: www.oldbaileyonline.org.

INDEX

Citizen, 148
City Elections Act of 1725, 73
The City Jilt (Haywood), 108
City of God (Augustine), 189
clandestine marriages, 130, 210
Clarke, J., 70
class distinctions, 117, 137, 143–54, 165, 206
classical teaching, 136
A Clear State of the Case of Elizabeth Canning (Fielding), 212
Cleland, John, 186
clergy/clerical life, 58, 99, 132, 134, 136, 163–64, 166–68, 170–75
Clerkenwell, 64, 69, 211
Clive, Kitty, 15–16
clubs, 58–59, 75, 154
coastal trade, 91
Collier, John, 123
comedy, 6, 12–18, 27, 112–13, 192–93, 221. *See also* satire
Commission for Building Fifty New Churches in London and Westminster, 71
Common Council, 73
conduct, 131–32, 136, 187, 192, 195. *See also* politeness
The Conduct of the Allies (Swift), 129
confessional warfare, 158
Considerations on Several Proposals lately made (Gray), 151
consumers, 97, 111, 119
Convention of the Pardo, 36
conversion, 45, 174
Convocation, 161
Cook, James, 92
Copyright Act for the Encouragement of Learning, 10–11
Coram, Thomas, 111
corporations for the poor, 151
corruption, 14, 20–21, 31, 39, 66–67, 82, 142, 210–11, 222, 224

Count of Broglie, 69–70
Covent Garden, 62, 67–68
Covent-Garden Journal, 4, 51–53, 183, 210, 212
Covent Garden theater, 25
The Covent-Garden Tragedy (Fielding), 12–13
Coventry, Francis, 215
Craddock, Charlotte, 2–3
Craftsman, 12, 20, 31–32, 185
credit and debt, 132–33
crime, 68, 164, 176, 189, 200–212
criminal biographies, 184, 217
cultural relativism, 93

D
Daily Advertiser, 51
Daily Courant, 102
Daily Gazetteer, 31–32, 34
Daily Post, 128
Dalrymple, Mary Elizabeth, 200
dame schools, 133, 136
Dance, James, 186
Daniel, Mary, 4
Dawkins, James, 130
debtors, 132–33, 140, 224
Declaration of Indulgence, 58
The Decline and Fall of the Roman Empire (Gibbon), 8
Defoe, Daniel, 144, 183–84, 189
degrees, 136
deism, 167–68
Devonshire House, 62
devotional literature, 169
A Dialogue Between a Gentleman of London, 204
A Dialogue between Alexander the Great and Diogenes the Cynic (Fielding), 189, 230
A Dialogue between the Devil, the Pope, and the Pretender, 41
Diogenes, 230

direct action, 155, 206
The Directory (Keat), 70
discontent, 155
disease, 64, 68, 72–73, 115–16, 120, 125, 133, 149, 221–22
Disorderly Act, 208
Disorderly Houses Act, 228
Dissent, 58, 138, 160–65, 167, 174, 176–77, 180–82
divorce, 121
domestic manufacturing, 107
domestic service, 105–7
Don Quixote in England (Fielding), 2, 14–15, 35–36, 63, 88, 95, 105, 112, 183
Dorset, England, 1, 102, 135
Downing, George, 140
dramas/plays, 6–28, 37, 42, 57, 66, 82, 94–95, 101, 104, 114, 117, 119–20, 126–27, 143, 147, 186–87, 220
drinking water, 72–73
Drury Lane, 2, 12–13, 15–16, 25–26, 68
Drury Lane Journal, 51
Dunton, John, 33
Dunwich, England, 140

E
Earl of Shelburne, 96
economy of the poor, 105, 107–8
education, 123, 133–36, 143, 153, 167, 171–72. *See also* literacy rates
elections, 20–21, 73, 196n14
electoral bribery, 20, 196
Elibank Plot of 1751–53, 45, 57
élite, 58–59, 93–97, 111, 130, 132, 136, 138–43, 145–48, 156, 163, 175, 177, 179, 187
Elizabethan Poor Law Acts, 150–51
Ellison, Henry, 94
employment, 105–7, 124, 132, 149–52

Enclosure Acts, 140
Enfield, 69
Enlightenment, 158, 174
Enquiry into the Causes of the late Increase of Robbers (Fielding), 153, 209, 212
The Enraged Musician (Hogarth), 65
Enthusiasm of Methodists and Papists Compared (Lavington), 174
equality between men and women, 118
An Essay on the Life and Genius of Henry Fielding Esq (Harris), 2
established churches, 165, 173
Eton, 1, 136, 204
Eurydice (Fielding), 22, 156
Eurydice Hiss'd (Fielding), 25
Evelyn, John, 79
Examples of the Interposition of Providence in the Detection and Punishment of Murder (Fielding), 212
excise powers, 74–75
Exeter, England, 87, 151, 160–61, 176
The Expedition of Humphry Clinker (Smollett), 66
expulsion of paupers, 150–51

F
A Faithful Narrative of the Base and Inhuman Arts (Smollett), 214
The Fall of Mortimer (Fielding), 12
false values, 120, 188–89, 213
family life, 105–7, 120, 122–25, 130–31, 139
fashions, 4, 111, 147, 212
Fatal Curiosity (Lillo), 6–7
fathers, 106, 113, 210
ferries, 69, 86, 89
Fetter Lane Society, 58
fiction. *See* novels
Fielding, Edmund, 1

Great Awakening, 174
Great Britain's Memorial against the Pretender and Popery (Chandler), 181
Griffier, Jan, 70
Griffier, Robert, 70
Grub Street, 11, 29
Grub Street Journal, 25
The Grub-Street Opera (Fielding), 11–12
Gulliver's Travels (Swift), 184–85
Gunpowder Plot, 177–78
Guy, Lydia, 104

H
Hamlet (Shakespeare), 22, 160, 202–3
Hanbury-Williams, Charles, 1, 204
Handel, 59, 71
Hanoverian dynasty, 40–41, 48, 165, 205
Hanover Square, 62, 71–72
Harbin, George, 10, 38
Hardwicke, 130, 209, 213
Harris, Henry, 65
Harris, James, 2
Harris, Thomas, 42, 200
Haymarket, 27–28, 62
Haymarket Theatre, 62
Haywood, Eliza, 108, 184
Heaton, Henry, 225
Hell Upon Earth, 65
Henry, 3rd Duke of Beaufort, 37
Herring, Thomas, 170
Hewitt, William, 56
hierarchy, 20–21, 94, 105, 129–30, 136–37, 138–39, 143–44, 147, 154, 164, 170
High Churchmen, 46, 164
High Court of Chancery, 87
Hildrop, John, 168
Hill, John, 51–52
Hilton, George, 115

The Historical Register for the Year 1736 (Fielding), 17, 21, 31, 193
The History of Our Own Times, 34, 40, 96
The History of the Life of the Late Mr Jonathan Wild the Great. See *Jonathan Wild* (Fielding)
The History of the Present Rebellion in Scotland, 41
The History of Tom Jones, A Foundling. See *Tom Jones* (Fielding)
Hogarth, 65, 66, 74, 98, 170, 183, 193, 226–27, 229
Homer, 192, 197, 216
homosexuality, 65, 121–22, 128
honor, 22, 32, 120, 156, 230
horsedrawn wagon services, 80
houses and squares, 71–72
Hudibras (Butler), 183
human nature, 229–30
"Humphry Gubbins" letter, 47
hunting, 93–94
Huntingdonshire, England, 135
Hyde Park, 56
Hyp-Doctor, 10
hypocrisy, 3–4, 11–12, 22, 24, 27–28, 50, 115–16, 171, 176–77, 187, 191, 194, 199, 213–14, 216, 220, 227

I
Idler, 132
illegitimacy, 106, 111, 117, 219–20
illiteracy, 135
imaginative literature, 109
immigrants, 105, 149
immorality, 210, 212–14
Impartial Representation of the Conduct of the Several Powers of Europe (Rolt), 216
Indemnity Acts, 164, 182
The Independent Patriot, 46